NO WALLS *and the*

RECURRING DREAM

ani difranco

NO WALLS *and the*

RECURRING DREAM

A Memoir

VIKING

VIKING
An imprint of Penguin Random House LLC
penguinrandomhouse.com

Insert credits: pages 1, 2, 3, and 4: author's collection; page 5: Scot Fisher; page 6, top: Scot
Fisher; page 6, bottom: author's collection; page 7, top: Karen Robinson; page 7, bottom left:
Scot Fisher; page 7, bottom right: author's collection; page 8, top: author's collection; page 8,
bottom: Andy Stochansky; page 9, top: josephcultice; page 9, bottom left and right: Scot Fisher;
page 10, top: Robert Yahn; page 10, bottom: author's collection; page 11, top: Toni Armstrong Jr.;
page 11, bottom: © Susan Alzner / www.susanalzner.com; page 12: author's collection; page 13,
top: Steven Stone; page 13, bottom: author's collection; page 14: author's collection; page 15, top:
Heidi Kunkel; page 15, middle: author's collection; page 15, bottom: © Susan Alzner /
www.susanalzner.com; page 16: © Danny Clinch 2019.

Library of Congress Cataloging-in-Publication Data

Names: DiFranco, Ani, author.
Title: No walls and the recurring dream : a memoir / Ani DiFranco.
Description: New York, New York : Viking, 2019. |
Identifiers: LCCN 2019003676 (print) | LCCN 2019005388 (ebook) |
  ISBN 9780735225183 (ebook) | ISBN 9780735225176 (hardback)
Subjects: LCSH: DiFranco, Ani. | Women singers--United States--Biography. |
  Women social reformers--United States .--Biography | Singers--United
  States--Biography. | Social reformers--United States--Biography | BISAC:
  BIOGRAPHY & AUTOBIOGRAPHY / Personal Memoirs. | BIOGRAPHY &
  AUTOBIOGRAPHY / Women. | BIOGRAPHY & AUTOBIOGRAPHY /
  Composers & Musicians.
Classification: LCC ML420.D555 (ebook) | LCC ML420.D555 A3 2019 (print) |
  DDC 782.42164092 [B] --dc23
LC record available at https://lccn.loc.gov/2019003676

Printed in the United States of America
10   9   8   7   6   5   4   3   2   1

DESIGNED BY MEIGHAN CAVANAUGH

Penguin is committed to publishing works of quality and integrity.
In that spirit, we are proud to offer this book to our readers;
however, the story, the experiences, and the words are the author's alone.

for peter, without whom ...

contents

introducing . . .

I remember being on stage once in a tight little dress, the bottom of which kept riding up my thighs . . . all the way to my crotch as I moved around and sang (why was it doing this?!!) . . . my face growing hotter and hotter as I tried to hide behind my guitar.

I remember once walking out in New York City to get some kind of queer award and getting booed . . . for not being queer enough . . . before I even reached the podium.

I remember seeing something warpy and reflective from stage, it was in Amsterdam, and saying on mic, "What the fuck is that?!" only to walk over and see it was a young woman in the audience living with such severe palsy that she had to lie back in a special wheelchair with an elaborate series of mirrors in which to see the world beyond her knees.

In other words, I've had many experiences of being on stage and wanting to die or disappear. I've had many experiences of being trapped in spotlights and time suddenly slowing way down, the sound of my own blood pounding in my ears taking over from some distant sonic background in which angry words are being flung at me from a deep darkness.

Somehow this was worse.

It was not just crying but sobbing. It was Carnegie Hall, spring of 2002, and the sobbing from the third balcony was getting louder and louder until it began echoing around the room. Plus, she was not even the only one crying. A moment of paralyzing trepidation came over me and I heard my voice falter and begin to move into a distant slow motion. It was the culmination of so many recent moments of paralyzing trepidation. Having been in Manhattan on 9/11 (months earlier) and having breathed in the acrid blue smoke of the towers. Having hit the road mere weeks afterward when everyone else was canceling their tours and staying home behind closed shutters. I traveled around a country in a state of emergency. I played to half-empty houses that took months to slowly fill up again. I felt, all the while, a great pressure to lift up the small audiences that were brave enough to come out. A pressure to make sense of it all. To make hope happen.

I was confronted nightly with an impossible task: *How am I supposed to make a whole show filled with all kinds of songs about all kinds of things when there is just one big thing pressing down on all of us?* How could I possibly sing or talk about anything other than the all-encompassing panic in the air or the ominous march to war? And even if I could magically, suddenly make a whole show around this one looming thing, what the hell would I say? It was a challenging time to be a folksinger, at least, if you take your job seriously. The message that it was unpatriotic to criticize the president and his "just go shopping while we bomb the shit out of 'em" rhetoric was everywhere. Even from people and sources where you wouldn't expect it. It was weird, watching what fear did to people. Unnerving numbers fell into lockstep.

I tried to make myself into a lightning rod for critical thinking and accountability. I studied and I made notes and I got my facts straight. I stayed up debating and discussing late into the night with the most politically astute of my friends. I consulted trusted sources like Noam Chomsky and *The Nation* for guidance in sorting through the mainstream media quagmire. I traveled around the country and I talked to people everywhere I went.

I wrote and I wrote and I wrote and I wrote. On each stage, I unfolded a different permutation of a poem that came to be called *"Self Evident."* I attempted to engage people directly with this poem in real time. But now here I was, laying a poem about 9/11 down on the very people who had shouldered the brunt of the violence, the brunt of the loss. It was Carnegie Hall, it was only seven months later, and I was alone on stage when the question of "How can I possibly talk about anything but this right now?" suddenly wheeled around and became "How dare you talk about this right now?"

It was too late. I was trapped again. The spotlight was on me and there was no time to rethink my decision. I heard my distant voice finish reciting the poem. I think it may have even sung a few more songs. Then I was back in a dressing room full of smelly lilies and roses and there were pats on the back and congratulations-you-just-played-Carnegie-Hall hugs. Time inexplicably kept going.

I will never know what is the right balance in art between painful truths and painful silences. There is no right balance to be known. It is a question to be asked of every moment and its answer pertains only to that moment and no other. It's the spontaneous deal we strike with others, the conversation or lack thereof. Having played my part every which way, I'm not even sure what I'd recommend. I just know that we need to be willing to make mistakes. I know that we need to allow for our differences. I know we need to forgive each other.

I've managed to transcend my own trepidation many times and I've lifted whole groups of people up with me and, of course, I've also failed miserably. I have caught glimpses along the way of something very powerful and I'm not sure that I can tell you what it is but if you give me a chance maybe whatever it is will show itself.

Which brings me back to that night in the mid-nineties (I was quite young at the time) when that gawdawful dress kept riding up my ass. It took me about four songs before I decided that the only thing to do was to take the dress off. There was no fixing of the problem, only the conquering of fear.

Get ready: The truth is too valuable to put safety first.

Get set: No amount of exposure is unbearable unless you let it be.

Go: If you get caught with your pants down, take 'em off.

SELF EVIDENT

yes,
us people are just poems
we're ninety percent metaphor
with a leanness of meaning
approaching hyper-distillation
and once upon a time
we were moonshine
rushing down the throat of a giraffe
yes, rushing down the long hallway
despite what the p.a. announcement says
yes, rushing down the long hall
down the long stairs
in a building so tall
that it will always be there
yes, it's part of a pair
there on the bow of Noah's ark
the most prestigious couple
just kickin back parked
against a perfectly blue sky
on a morning beatific
in its indian summer breeze
on the day that america

fell to its knees
after strutting around for a century
without saying thank you
or please

the shock was subsonic
and the smoke was deafening
between the setup and the punch line
cuz we were all on time for work that day
we all boarded that plane for to fly
and then while the fires were raging
we all climbed up on the window sill
and then we all held hands
and jumped into the sky

and every borough looked up when it heard the first blast
and then every dumb action movie was summarily surpassed
and the exodus uptown by foot and motorcar
looked more like war than anything i've seen so far

so far . . .

so far . . .

so fierce and ingenious
a poetic specter so far gone
that every jackass newscaster was struck dumb and stumbling
over "oh my god!" and "this is unbelievable" and on and on
and i'll tell you what, while we're at it,
you can keep the pentagon
keep the propaganda
keep each and every tv
that's been trying to convince me

to participate
in some prep school punk's plan to perpetuate retribution

perpetuate retribution

even as the blue toxic smoke of our lesson in retribution
is still hanging in the air
and there's ash on our shoes
and there's ash in our hair
and there's a fine silt on every mantle
from hell's kitchen to brooklyn
and the streets are full of stories
sudden twists and near misses
and soon every open bar is crammed to the rafters
with tales of narrowly averted disasters
and the whiskey is flowin
like never before
as all over the country
folks just shake their heads
and pour

so here's a toast to all the folks that live in palestine
afghanistan
iraq
el salvador
here's a toast to the folks living on the pine ridge reservation
under the stone cold gaze of mt. rushmore
here's a toast to all those nurses and doctors
who daily provide women with a choice
who stand down a threat the size of oklahoma city
just to listen to a young woman's voice
here's a toast to all the folks on death row right now
awaiting the executioner's guillotine

who are shackled there with dread
and can only escape into their heads
to find peace in the form of a dream
peace
in the form
of a dream

cuz take away our playstations
and we are a third world nation
under the thumb of some blue blood royal son
(who stole the oval office and that phony election)
i mean,
it don't take a weatherman
to look around and see the weather
jeb said he'd deliver florida, folks
and boy did he ever!
and we hold these truths to be self evident:

number one, george w. bush is not president
number two, america is not a true democracy
number three
the media is not fooling me

cuz i am a poem heeding hyper-distillation
and i've got no room for a lie so verbose
i'm looking out over my whole human family
and i'm raising my glass in a toast

here's to our last drink of fossil fuels
may we vow to get off of this sauce!
shoo away the swarms of commuter planes
and find that train ticket we lost
cuz once upon a time the line followed the river

and peeked into all the backyards
and the laundry was waving
the graffiti was teasing us
from brick walls and bridges
we were rolling over ridges
through valleys
under stars
i dream of touring like duke ellington
in my own railroad car
i dream of waiting on the tall blond wooden benches
in a grand station, aglow with grace
and then standing out on the platform
and feeling the air on my face

give back the night its distant whistle
give the darkness back its soul
give the big oil companies the finger finally
and relearn how to rock-n-roll!
yes, the lessons are all around us
and a truth is waiting there
so it's time to pick through the rubble
clean the streets
and clear the air
get our government to pull its big dick out of the sand
of someone else's desert
put it back in its pants
quit the hypocritical chants of
freedom forever!
cuz when one lone phone rang
in two thousand and one
at ten after nine
on nine one one
which is the number we all called
when that lone phone rang right off the wall

right off our desk and down the long hall
down the long stairs
in a building so tall

that the whole world turned

just to watch it fall

and while we're at it
remember the first time around?
the bomb?
the ryder truck?
the parking garage?
the princess that didn't even feel the pea?
remember joking around in our apartment on avenue d?
"can you imagine how many paper coffee cups would have to change
    their design
following a fantastical reversal of the new york skyline?!"
it was a joke
at the time

and that was just a few years ago
so, let the record show
that the FBI was all over that case
that the plot was obvious and in everybody's face
and scoping that scene
religiously
the CIA
(or is it KGB?)
committing countless crimes against humanity
with this kind of eventuality
as its excuse
for abuse
after expensive abuse

and it didn't have a clue!
look, another window to see through
way up here
on the hundred and fourth floor
look
another key
another door
ten percent literal
ninety percent metaphor
three thousand some poems disguised as people
on an almost too
perfect
day
must be more than pawns
in some assholes' passion play
so now it's your job
and it's my job
to make it that way
to make sure they didn't die in vain
shhh. . . .
baby listen
hear the train?

one

NO WALLS

The house I grew up in had no walls except, of course, around the outside. And around the boiler in the middle of the first floor and the little bathroom in the middle of the second floor. My mother, whose idea the whole donut-house thing was, wanted to create a log cabin feel in a carriage house in North Buffalo. She was fresh out of MIT School of Architecture (a woman pioneering in an all-male world) and freshly married to my father whom she had met at school. He was a returning student, the first in his immigrant family to go to college. He'd come back to school to upgrade from builder to engineer. He was ten years older and a foot shorter than she and, as a couple, they were at least memorable and likely irresistible. They were like an intellectual's *I Love Lucy* show, the wide-eyed redhead in her life-of-the-party dress, and her dark and exasperated sidekick with a steady love behind each shrug. They had Lucy and Desi's charm and their secret unhappiness, too.

I knew families who would've done great in a log cabin. Families who slapped each other with towels when they were naked and laughed and sought each other's company. But my family was not one of those. My parents' bed was visible from my bed and so was my brother's but we were not close. At least, if we were, it is before my memory. My memories are of all the things that were not said openly. My brother and I crouched down low behind our twin beds to change into and out of our pajamas. We formed allegiances with neighborhood kids but never with each other. We would wake in the dark Buffalo winter, eat breakfast, and then pile on hats and boots to go stand by a snowbank and wait for the school bus.

The bus took us on a forty-five-minute, meandering drive downtown to the shore of Lake Erie, picking up every kind of kid along the way. I was the wildly expressive girl with the rainbow socks pulled up over my overalls and pigtails in my hair. A bright smiling clown. I was my wildly expressive mother's understudy and I earned the label "weird" from the other kids. My friends were immigrants. Kids who had no other friends. Tanala was from Africa somewhere and Li was from Vietnam. We could often be seen chatting away under a desk instead of doing our schoolwork but my teachers, in their love of misfits, rarely gave us the business.

This was the mid-seventies and Waterfront School was a visionary new concept called a magnet school. It drew kids from every neighborhood in the city. It also had no walls. There were large open pits, like land formations, where classes were given to students sitting around on wide, carpeted, coliseum steps. At the bottom of each classroom pit stood a blackboard with a pull-down screen and on the plateaus between the pits were small divider walls where study centers were hung. Other than that, it was all open. There were sight lines to other groups of monkeys doing other things over there.

One whole side of the classroom vector was a big bank of windows looking out onto the largely undeveloped waterfront of Lake Erie. Just garbage-strewn fields underneath a tangle of raised highways and some abandoned grain elevators in the distance. The Bethlehem Steel Plant was spewing slag into the water somewhere just beyond that, mercifully out of view.

Buffalo emanates like a spoked wheel from the ass-end of Lake Erie where it funnels into the Niagara and down the escarpment to the falls. Weather systems sweep down the great east-west expanse of the lake, gathering momentum, and our whole school would thrill to the drama of towering storms rolling in. One day a huge twister spun drunkenly down the lake towards us and everyone pressed to the windows, eyes wide. The twister died when it hit land just before reaching the school, a waterspout I guess, and good thing, too, since lining up in front of a bank of windows is probably not what is suggested in anyone's tornado preparedness manual.

On the other side of the classroom vector was another bank of windows, this one looking onto an interior skylit hallway and the cafeteria and gym beyond that. Unlike the incessant fluorescent of the classrooms, the dark tiled hallway was lit only in dim, muted daylight like the entrance to a cave. It was cool and reverberant there compared to the blinding buttes and depressions of the carpeted desert just the other side of the glass. I loved the hallways and I worked hard to make myself known to all the teachers as the best candidate for any kind of errand they might need run.

The teachers came in clusters as did the kids. Two or three teachers worked with two or three grades at once. Grades 1–3, 4–6, and 7 and 8 were grouped together and were given lessons collectively. Groups of people from places like Japan were always walking through with clipboards and cameras to study the way we were learning. Sometimes I was asked to take these people on tours. I told them I liked my school. I told them no, it was not difficult to learn this way, it was cool.

In between our classes were periods of independent study in which children roamed from one study center to another, completing that week's "work contract." I was always either hiding somewhere reading a book or in conference with the misfit crew so I almost never managed to finish a contract. I began to get failing grades. Mrs. Summers bought a big picture book of horses (she knew I loved horses) and told me it was mine if I finished my work contract that week. She figured I just needed a little motivation. She called me over to her desk and pulled out the big bottom drawer, just so. There it was. Two palominos frolicking on the cover. She was right about the motivation and I loved that horse book but as soon as it was in my possession I was right back to not completing my work.

I lived for the "artists in residence" that my magnet school drew in from the city around it. Each one of them made an impression on me, the long-haired white lady who called herself a poet especially. Her name was Joan Murray. Poetry found an instant and resounding yes in my body and she was my favorite. I was immediately captivated by the idea of making language communicate beyond its borders. I was shown diverse forms, from iambic pentameter to haiku, and asked to reproduce them. I began writing a lot of poems and the adult world seemed to notice and approve. One time I wrote a book in verse called *Utopia* and the principal of Waterfront School asked if she could borrow it to use in her presentations. I never did get that book back.

The long journeys on the school bus from my experimental house to my experimental school and back again were filled with mayhem. It was every kid against every other kid and me against the bus aide. I cringe now when I think of the battles that I picked with those minimum wage–earning bus attendants. I can picture my pigtails leaning into the aisle and my lips moving as though I was speaking to another kid after everyone on the bus had already been punished with a moratorium on talking. "Ani, I see you talking!" the bus lady would shout. "You don't see people talk, you hear them," I would shout back in some pre-planned, dazzling display of logic. I think some part of me felt I was already better educated than those women and that part of me was compelled to challenge their authority. When I look back now, I am the bus lady and I see the scene through her eyes. I look at the smug kid trying to assert her intellectual superiority with her pig-logic and I feel the deep weariness of a world of hierarchy perpetuating itself.

PEDIGREE

I knew how to use my dad's record player and I am grateful for the deep passion he had for music because his records were to become my musical subconscious. His collection celebrated all things American. There was the composer Aaron Copland and the guitarist John Fahey. There were Alan Lomax recordings and Blue Note records. Both my parents had an immigrant mentality, which is to say, they loved America as only immigrants can. Elizabeth Compton Ross, a Canadian who grew up in Montreal, and Dante Americo Di Franco, the first American-born son of an Italian family, took being American very seriously. My father's middle name expressed the pride his parents felt just to have gotten here. My parents were patriotic about paying taxes and taught me all of what you get for it in America. They not only voted, but my mother volunteered her time to local candidates she believed in. I sat with her stuffing envelopes and licking stamps in circles of laughing women and I went canvassing door to door holding onto her hand.

My mom also helped organize a food co-op in our neighborhood. Every weekend in the summer, farmers would come lay out their bounty on the floor of the church up the block and everyone from the neighborhood would bring bags or boxes over and buy their food right off the floor. She helped to form an organization of architects and urban planners called Women for Downtown. Their mission was to try to attract investment in, and achieve revitalization of, Buffalo's inner city. She could wax poetic about the very concept of the city and the great value cities held for humanity as centers of culture and ideas.

For the entirety of my childhood my mother worked for Robert Coles Architects in downtown Buffalo. Bob was another pioneer in the field of architecture, a black man who started a firm in the seventies that attempted to compete with the big boys in The City for major state bids. They never seemed to get the sexy jobs though, the ones with budgets big enough to afford the architects artistic license. My mother dreamed of designing atriums into buildings but they were not called for in the prisons and gymnasiums that were the firm's usual fare. I remember smartly dressed black men and white women working together with determination and hope in their eyes. They believed they were every bit as talented as the powerful firms and if they just worked hard enough eventually the world would take notice. I'm not sure if that ever did happen but work fucking hard they did.

My father meanwhile had gotten a job at Bell Aerospace and, impressively, had broken into the burgeoning field of aeronautical engineering with no pedigree or connections shepherding him. He worked at a research lab that famously produced planes like the X-1, the first airplane to break the sound barrier. The application of aeronautical advances towards making war did not seem to bother my father, the military was a necessary evil, but years later when the lab got sold out to what he considered to be commercial interests, he fought the move and lost his job because of it. My mother said he quit his job on principle but, whatever the case, a feeling of shame seemed to fall over him. His ritual one-martini-a-night turned into two and three and strain began to show in them both.

Losing that job haunted him to the end of his days and many years later, sitting with him in the nursing home, I would have to talk him down when the orderlies would suddenly become the bad guys coming into the lab to strip his life of self-respect and the grace of pure science. He yelled at those poor orderlies.

My dad was really the gentlest of souls. He stood five foot two at his tallest but so do I and by the end of his life I towered over him. Because of his stature, he was condescended to in many ways in this world. Ways that I witnessed and, I'm sure, ways that I didn't. He never did seem to get ruffled by a world that called him "Danny" and patted him on the head, though. Notably and endearingly, he hadn't a whiff of Napoleon complex in him. He was the bearer of unconditional love in our family and supremely lenient as a parent. His stance was: Let them eat a box of donuts! They will get sick and throw up and they will learn! To which my mother would scoff. She was the rule maker and the rule enforcer. He was Santa.

PLANS

Our carriage house originally belonged to a larger mansion that was torn down. I never knew why the big house was torn down but the rectangle ghost of its foundation was still visible in our front lawn. That was the lawn where I sold off all my childhood toys, my purple tricycle, my pogo stick, even my first guitar, after hanging signs around the neighborhood that said "Yard Sale." I did this on my own, the way I did things, and somewhere in the background my parents shook their heads and gave permission by default. The silences in my house had begun to start yelling and throwing things and my parents had become preoccupied. As I lay there in my bed, with only the armor of my eyelids shut tight, I learned to completely leave my body. I learned to develop my escape fantasies into plans.

I discovered in the back of my parents' Sunday *New York Times* there were ads for things like summer camps. A camp was a place a kid could go for a long period of time, away from her family. I just needed my parents' consent. I began to do research every weekend after they discarded their paper. Finally, I set my sights on a horse camp in East Aurora, not far outside of Buffalo. I waited for the right moment and I took a deep breath. I asked my parents if I could go for two months to camp Long-acres and I showed them the ad. They consulted and said it was too expensive. "How expensive would be not too expensive?" I asked. They consulted again and came back with, "Two weeks would be not too expensive." I stood there and weighed my odds, then I said, "Can I go for a month if I promise to pay for half?" I remember my father was sitting in their prized Herman Miller chair. I remember he looked down behind his paper and stifled a smile. They agreed to my terms. I imagine because they didn't think I could do it.

I can't remember exactly how much money I needed to earn but it was a lot for a kid. I bought blank greeting cards and pressed flowers and leaves under contact paper on their faces, up-selling them to any adult I could charm. I went with my mother every Saturday to the Broadway Market and sang songs with my guitar case open while she did the week's shopping. I babysat. I offered my landscaping expertise to the whole neighborhood. I sold everything that was "mine." Eventually some kindly cousins got wind of my crusade and offered me a matching grant for every dollar I earned. By summer, I had succeeded in my mission and could hardly stand the excitement as my parents drove me to East Aurora. My mother told me later that she cried when I took off running from the car and never looked back.

There was a path between the cabin that I shared with six other girls and the barn, and a path from the barn to the mess hall. There was a feisty little pony named Pepper that I fell in love with and there was a girl named Alexine from Brooklyn who would become my pen pal for years. There were frogs and crayfish in the creek and fireflies in the meadows in the evenings. I had experiences of riding horses down creek beds and even into deeper water. I rode horses while they were swimming, while they were running, and while they were lying down to roll. We learned equestrianship in the corrals and we learned joy and freedom riding bareback through the woods. I was in heaven.

When I returned to Buffalo I wanted to continue my association with horses so I got a friend to go with me to the stables I'd seen in Delaware Park. We walked into the barn and offered to help sweep or muck stalls or groom or feed horses, whatever they needed. We told them we had experience, because we did. I returned to those stables a few times and they always found work for me when I showed up, but I never made friends there. I just went to be around the horses because it made me happy.

MARTIN LUTHER

The front door of the donut house was five feet wide. It was one half of the two big barn doors that used to open up the whole face of the carriage house. My parents had had the middles cut out of each door and glass put in. A lot of glass. The wall-less house was mostly glass on one side because of those doors. Luckily, that side faced sideways into the yard, not out to the street, or we would have had the first reality TV show. The hinges on the doors were gothic iron monstrosities about the size of my torso and probably heavier. The glass ended at about waist level and the hinges began. A third hinge was up top. One day I came home from school to see two big stickers, printed with typeset words, stuck in the middle of the glass. "These premises are no longer under the supervision of the housewife system," I read while turning my key. I stopped. It was my mother's resignation.

My mom had become the main breadwinner in our house after my father lost his job, but she was also (still and always) the cook and the housekeeper. Plus, to her own detriment, she seemed to be driven to excel at everything. On the kitchen counter were incubator tubs where she made yogurt. In the oven were trays of burning granola. On the table, full place settings with cloth napkins that would soon need washing. She cleaned the windows with Windex and the brass with Brasso. She scrubbed the toilet with Ajax and the floors with Pine-Sol. She even washed all our clothes by hand though it would seem we could've afforded a washing machine. I remember my father did none of these things. My mother's response, after working insanely long hours at the office, was to come home and quietly scrub and seethe.

She was part of another lost generation of feminists who slipped through the cracks of history and became victims of their own liberation. She was free to over-perform her way into the professional workplace but she still had to shoulder the bulk of the parenting and housekeeping duties because no one could conceive of anything different. She martyred herself, my mother, and then one day, in a rage, she quit. She would eventually quit us all and leave her dream house behind but those stickers were stuck there on the front door for many years, after the words had completely faded away in the weather . . . and she was long gone.

In the meantime, it became my job to make dinner. I heated up jars of tomato sauce and boiled spaghetti. I cubed a loaf of bread and melted a package of fondue. Sometimes, I tried to get fancy and make a stir-fry. I remember making pizza dough. I especially remember the first time because I used two cups of oil instead of two tablespoons, having misread the recipe. That is the kind of drop-out in perspective you can have when you are a child imitating a grown person. It is a bizarre and puzzling experience to try to stir two cups of oil into pizza dough. You only do that once.

I fed whoever in my family sat down to dinner on any given night but that was becoming less and less predictable. The cooking job got really easy when my whole family started dropping out like a weak radio signal. My older brother was freaking out (embodying the atmospheric freakout) and there was a suicide attempt and other cries for help. His main thing was to lock himself in the bathroom and wash and wash himself raw. My parents, unable to make him come out, went in. Together they spiraled into an endless tournament of muffled yelling behind the bathroom door and, in contrast, I ventured further and further afield.

Their triangulation became complete when my brother was checked into a series of psychiatric hospitals culminating with Boston Children's Hospital. That institution required both parents to be present for bi-weekly family meetings so my parents went to Boston to live in a Ronald McDonald House. I stayed behind in Buffalo. I was placed with this friend or that and caught various buses with various routes to Waterfront School.

My friend Ingeri, who lived a few blocks away, seemed to have a happy family. I lived at her house as much as anywhere and my clothes mixed with their laundry. Her house was a Victorian beauty and she and I used to take turns being the bride and wedding each other on the stairs. Ingeri's father, Fred, was a professor who played guitar and sometimes there were guitar pickin' parties. There were mint julep, Kentucky Derby parties and cigar-smoking, card-playing parties. There were popcorn-making movie parties and there was laughter in that house. Ingeri's mother was a union organizer and she was cool, too. My actual family could enter or leave the picture at any time depending on treatments and hospitals. It was all beyond my knowing. My brother had sucked my parents into his far-out orbit and in so doing was keeping them together, fighting for their son.

My parents were so relieved at my relative happiness and self-sufficiency that they leaned on it heavily. I remember beholding early on, in their sheepish praise, the message that I could do anything I wanted as long as I continued to require nothing of them. It was the freedom I needed, the freedom I became accustomed to, and eventually I'd spin it into a reason to be out of the house every waking moment. They didn't seem to blame me. I'd barely made double digits when I became something of a self-governing body in the donut house. Like everything else in our family, it was unspoken but obvious.

EXPOSURE

I'm not sure if this is typical but I, personally, had seen a lot of penises by the time I was ten. I have strong, fear-based sense memories of the men who pulled up next to me in their cars as I played on the sidewalk or drove alongside me slowly as I pedaled my bike. I could take you to Buffalo right now and point to the exact few feet of curb where this happened and that. Fear is inky. Fear stains the white sheet of consciousness that one comes swaddled in and no amount of earthly scrubbing can make it completely clean again. Is that a chocolate ice cream cone that dark-skinned man is offering me? Does that pale, veiny old man need help? Oh, no.

Ingeri and I shared a few of these experiences but we didn't talk about them. It seemed like the kind of thing that just happens, like thunder, to make you suddenly jump out of your skin. I certainly never considered telling an adult. You just develop a sense of the matter. Eventually, you know better than to even approach the car. You don't move, you just pause your game like fauns and prepare to run.

Us kids had a neighborhood that was much bigger than the adults' version. We knew all the secret routes and the weak spots in fences. We knew where the treasure was buried. Freedom's only parameters seemed to be the following of one global rule: go home when the streetlights come on. In summer, that is gloriously late and can allow for an eternity to be spanned inside a day. But we didn't fuck around, we got to know the bend in the dusk that triggered the lights. When they flickered on, we'd disperse.

NAMES

M y grandfather Giovanni came on a boat to Ellis Island and then worked for seven years to establish himself before sending for his wife and son back in Campobasso. When the couple was finally reunited, my father, Dante, was the result. Giovanni's wife, Angela Maria, is the grandmother I am named after. Angela Maria had had all of her teeth extracted as a teenager by a medical establishment in Italy that believed total tooth extraction to be a good cure for menstrual-related gum issues. This fact of my namesake's existence was told to me casually, as if horrific medical abuses were a part of life to be expected. She had no dentures in Italy, either, and by the time she got to America she apparently didn't need them. My grandmother's gums had become so toughened over her lifetime that, in the end, they were hard as any teeth. They said she ate raw apples and carrots as an old woman. And said very little.

Angela is pronounced with the first syllable "Ahn" if you're my father, so when he introduced me as a newborn to my two-year-old brother, my brother blinked and said, ". . . Ani?" "No, Angela," said dad. ". . . Ani?" They started calling me Ani and that was that. The spelling was my mother's flourish. Every time I filled out a form, or one was filled out on my behalf, we always just wrote Ani as my name. By the time I was a young adult, all bureaucratic channels (save for my birth certificate) concurred: My name was simply Ani. Looking down at my passport today, I smirk with the knowledge that the truth is anything with a paper trail.

It's either a testament to how quietly accepting my father was, or how far Erie, Pennsylvania, is from Italy, that I was ever given that name, with that spelling, to begin with. It wasn't until three decades later, after I had toured Italy many times over as a professional musician, that I found out what Ani actually means in Italian: Assholes. Plural. I couldn't understand why these people in Italy, interviewing me on TV and radio, were working so hard to draw their lips back in a toothy grin and pinch the "A" in my name to mimic the American "Annie" the name that I had spent my whole life correcting . . . or not. Here I was in the home of the long "A" (the motherland!) and people were bending over backwards to pronounce my name in a way that was almost impossible for them to do. When I finally found out why, I wanted to run around Rome ripping every last one of my gig posters down. Life is nothing if not humbling. It is comforting to me that my favorite uncle back in Erie, the kindly Polish man who married my aunt Gene (Luis Gina), is my Uncle Dick.

My mom's extended family was paler and more Protestant. They straddled the Canadian border and set up shop on both sides. Their surnames were Compton and Mott and Ross and they had lots of scratchy wool blankets in family tartans to drape over their knees when they went for evening paddles in canoes. They were woods people but also clergymen and judges, writers and architects. There was a Nobel Prize–winning physicist and a Nobel Peace Prize–winning missionary in the mix. My mother's aunt Leila was secretary to the bigwig missionary and traveled with him to places like India and the Middle East in the early part of the twentieth century. Goddess knows what he was putting down. I know the physicist worked on the A-bomb.

Leila lived to be ninety-eight years old (back when that was still a rarity) and she would retell the same handful of stories to me each time my mother and I would visit her in the nursing home. There was the story of riding out a sandstorm in a tent in Saudi Arabia and the one about driving the Model T across China and Iran in the twenties. There were not even roads for half the journey, they just carried on with their compass across the terrain.

Leila, the world traveler, never married, nor did her sister Marybelle. Instead they remained together their whole lives in the house they were both born into. A creaky two-story farmhouse with a barn now situated right in the middle of Wooster, Ohio. They were my grandmother Martha's two sisters and they were the closest thing to grandparents I ever had, since Martha and all of my actual grandparents died before I could know them. They were forced into a nursing home together in their nineties when Leila, who was still driving, blew their cover by running the old Chrysler through the barn door.

That house was a portal into another time where exotic foreign relics from Egypt and China mingled with the spartan wood furniture and creepy tock-tocking clocks of their pious Protestant forebears. The overgrown gardens out back, where herbs had once been harvested to make every kind of tincture, were equally mysterious and creepy. Before the nursing home years, I watched Leila and Marybelle feel their way through the brambles outside the kitchen door and the dusty stacks of cookbooks and Bibles inside. They were blind old witches (not a derogatory term if you're me) reading their darkening world in braille. Shafts of light shone between thick curtains in the windows and moved slowly around the cluttered rooms as time kept going along outside. I could hardly begin to fathom their world. The black and white sweeping movie epic of Leila's worldly adventures and the Great American Novel of Longing that was Marybelle's life of waiting for everything and everyone back home.

One time in their house, digging through a drawer in the study, my friend found a .22 caliber gun disguised as a pen. Total James Bond shit. I saw him over by the desk studying something for a while and then he exclaimed, "Oh my god! This is a gun!" He then pointed it at me as a joke and pulled the trigger. A very loud pop! shocked us both and time stopped. I started crying spontaneously from shock and happiness at being alive. It was loaded with blanks.

THE LAKE

My mother's family assembled itself every summer around a lake in the Laurentian Mountains north of Montreal. It was land that had once been stewarded by the Algonquins but now every town and mountaintop sported the name of a French Catholic saint. Half the land around this lake had been purchased by my Scottish great-grandfather for a song in 1890. He logged all the old trees, sold off the lumber, and then parceled the land out to his four sons and his two best friends. The land was divided up and passed down many times over and a big extended family tree that I hang off of grew into the peat and pine needles of that parcel of Quebec soil.

Connected by paths were rustic houses that had been inhabited for at least three generations, some with very little change. Our particular abode was on an island about an acre in size, accessible only by canoe or rowboat. It was a log house with no electricity or running water, just an outhouse nearby and some kerosene lamps to read or play cards by at night. It was the very cabin that had been the template for the donut house, the cabin where my mother's happiest memories resided.

I was also very happy there, running free in the woods as a child. I am grateful to have had the repeated experience of living like a nineteenth-century person each summer, with only a wood stove on which to cook and water that one ladled from buckets that had to be carried up from the lake. My mother and I tended the fire in the wood stove and made meals. We even baked in the stove's little oven compartment. The side next to the fire was way hotter than the other side of the oven and all baking things had to be turned often. Boiling water required a clean, ash-free chamber and a big stoked fire. Producing and tending to big, cozy coals was necessary for cooking a long, slow dish. We brought the ash out to the outhouse to cover up the poop that piled up in the hole. We washed our bodies in the cold lake.

So remote was this lake of my childhood that the Milky Way was clear as can be on moonless nights and the Northern Lights would often make appearances, too. I would go out to the middle of the water in the canoe at night with a flashlight and my copy of H. A. Rey's *The Stars* and study the constellations. When I tired of studying, I would just lie down in the bottom of the canoe and float out there, listening to the loons calling . . . stars slowly drifting by my view.

Because of this alpine homestead, I have an impressive number of people in this world that I call cousin. Some of the coolest people I know. There's Gail and Peter, who are activists, hosting refugees in their church one minute and organizing food drives the next. Thanksgiving at their house was always like a meeting of the United Nations and my family was fortunate enough to have been invited for many years. It was Gail and Peter who gave me the "matching grant" so I could go to horse camp that first year. Their generosities were endless. Between horse camp and the lake, I spent that entire glorious summer outside. My other favorite cousin was Haj, the joke-telling, guitar-playing professor of linguistics. Haj, also a poet and weedist (his term), and I are related in two ways (there was a lot of intermarrying at the lake) but I feel like we are related in even more ways than that.

My father, who had to go on this ride every summer into the nineteenth century with his crazy wife and her huge family, dealt with it in typical good humor. No martinis, no record player, just a series of "lake projects" like jerry-rigging broken stuff or splitting more wood. Every morning, we were awoken by choking smoke as my mother tried to rekindle the fire in the stove which never drew well due to a long horizontal run in the chimney pipe. Then, finally, when fire was achieved, the smoke would slowly dissipate and be replaced by the smell of perking coffee. Then my father would step outside to shave his face in the foggy little mirror that hung outside the cabin in the sunlight.

There was freedom for me in the woods, and solitude, and a great deal of satisfaction in being able to paddle a canoe deftly, even silently, like an Indian hunter, without lifting my paddle from the water. Memories of my childhood at the lake are especially valuable to me now because they stand as proof that happiness is not contingent on any of these things that are right now all around me. A fact that I might otherwise surely doubt. It is liberating to have felt the absence of conveniences and distractions and know that life goes on.

Because my mother's impressive family and personality dominated our lives, I think I may have assumed as a child that all of the intellectualism and engagement that swirled around us were brought on by her. It wasn't until many years later that I would understand how much more there was to the story of my parents than just my experience of my mother in the driver's seat. As a girl who'd spent more time in the woods of Quebec than anywhere else, my mother had started out kind of provincial in her own way. My father, the older, more worldly one at the time, became her ticket to American citizenship and to all the glamour and culture that came with it. Many years later, a few overheard words became my window into this arc of my parents' relationship. They came right after my father's death.

There I was, working on a high-pressure record in L.A. when I got the call, "Dad is not doing well." I didn't know what to do but to the credit of my assembled recording team, they looked at me squarely and said, "Go." I flew to Buffalo and drove straight to the nursing home. I sat by your side for an hour or so and then I said fuck it and crawled into bed with you . . . throwing my arm and my leg across your body . . . kissing your cheek . . . whispering into your ear. A few times the drugs wore thin enough for you to surface and you uttered a quiet sound, "Guuuuuh." I understood you: good. We lay this way for two days. Your body quaked periodically. With what? Pain? Cold? Your internal systems shuddering down?

The second night, after visiting hours were over, I was sent back home to pace, cry, and plan for the next day. Which guitar to bring? Which snacks to pack to get me through the day? Tears spilling from my eyes onto Ziploc bags. At three in the morning I realized it had become cold outside. Dammit . . . dammit.

Why did I leave the window open in your room?
Dammit! That was so stupid!
That gross nursing home. I hate that nursing home.

What if you are cold right now? In that gross place. Without me.

Dammit . . . dammit . . .

What would happen if I went there right now?

Maybe I should just go there right now . . .

and then

WHOOOOOOOOOOOOOOOOOOSH

A sensation of deep, abiding peace hit me. I was suddenly standing in a place of calmness in the proximity of joy. The feeling stopped me in my tracks and I inhaled it. Every thought spinning around in my brain, every worry, in a wave, was silenced. I realized then: It's all perfect. Everything is perfect. I don't need to do anything. There is nothing to do. I stopped crying and I went and lay down. I slept soundly as is rare for me. I was awakened in the morning by a ringing phone, "Dad died last night. At about three in the morning."

You came to say goodbye.

You came to make sure I knew you were okay. That everything is always okay.

You came to show me that death is beautiful.

You showed me to not be afraid.

I drove in a daze back to that nursing home one last time.

I stepped back from your body and allowed your wife to step in.

Standing there next to my brother, I heard her whisper to you,

"You gave me art, you gave me politics, you gave me these two kids, thank you."

DANCING

A round the time of my brother's implosion, my interests shifted wholly from horses to music and dancing. I asked my parents if I could take a dance class and they obliged and enrolled me in "modern" dance. After the classes were over, I didn't want to leave the studio so I just started hanging around. Janice Blum allowed me to begin sitting in on other classes and I slowly became a fixture at her little dance school. Eventually she just kindly muttered something about a scholarship and let me take every class. I took ballet and modern and "jazz" dance. I took kids' classes and classes with married ladies where we did a lot of sit-ups. It got so Janice would just pick me up at my house every afternoon on her way to work and then drive me home with her at the end of the night. Her sponsorship was the blessing my life was looking for.

Expressing music with my body was freeing to me and I put my whole little soul into dancing. We danced to everything from Stevie Wonder's *Songs in the Key of Life* to Rimsky-Korsakov's *Scheherazade*. Janice was married to a radio DJ at a soft rock and R&B station and together they exposed me to artists like Michael McDonald, James Ingram, and Donald Fagan, whose melodies still toss around in my head. My favorite times were the periods of free dance at the end of the children's classes where Miss Janice would just put on music and let us go. I remember seeing the adults huddle and whisper about me. I didn't know what they were saying but I imagined they were admiring my dancing. To become a dancer replaced jockey as my dream of a career.

About the age of twelve was the height of my dancing and it took me away from everything, including my guitar, for a time. I received a scholarship to the Buffalo Ballet Theatre and started riding my bike to their studio every day after school. After ballet classes and on weekends there were endless rehearsals. My life, for a while, mimicked that of a serious ballerina. So thorough was the mimicry that the ballet's director told me I had to lose weight and put me on a diet. Balanchine and the New York City Ballet's emaciated dancers had ushered in a new conception of ballerina that fit with the new conception of female beauty being put forward by fashion magazines: skin and bones. Apparently even twelve-year-olds in Buffalo were not immune to the standard they set.

I was by no means overweight, I was simply not skinny enough for the head of the Buffalo Ballet Theatre, so I was taught to count calories. I was told to keep a close eye on the food calorie charts that he printed out for me. Nuts have more fat than seeds, stay away from nuts. Avocados have lots of fat, stay away from avocados. I found myself hungry all the time and started taking diet pills. My jaw responded by locking up and staying locked up. I remember trying to make myself vomit after eating. Bulimia seemed easier than the rest. I came to loathe the thickness of my thighs. Then one day I woke up with a feeling of weightlessness like I'd been released from jail. It was as if in my dreams the night before, my heart had become resolute and now I simply had to go through the motions in my waking life to follow through. In a haze, I called and quit the ballet company. In a haze, I hung up.

Still, I would return to dance over the next few years. True to my father's love of Americana, the high drama of the Martha Graham technique would become my favorite. I danced with several troupes in my teens but with each performance, I felt a little less inspired. The dance community seemed to be performing for one another. Dance, at the level I was experiencing it, was a thing set away from other things.

My experience with music couldn't have been more different and the contrast only grew more stark with time. I became deeply interested in music and dance around the same age and I pursued them both for years but it seems obvious to me now why music won out. Unlike dancing, music brought me deeper and deeper into the world. Music was an entry point, like a passport or a key that allows you through an invisible portal into the beating heart of the world. The collective heart that unites us . . . (in a unified field of consciousness, in the bodily experience of being animals in time) and also into the hearts of individuals . . . (into that person and that person). Music showed itself to me as a fractal way in.

Through music I met my lifelong friend, Michael Meldrum, and I came to know the streets of Buffalo and all the crazy characters that were about. Michael was a songwriter and by his side I beheld the world through the eyes of a troubadour. In the professors, poets, barflies, bums,

and hippies that populated Michael's Buffalo, I found kinship in my oth-
erness and access to the adult world. Michael's guitar case often stood in
for his wallet and he showed me that a song has currency and can be
exchanged for a smile or a drink or an ally.

But I am getting ahead of myself. I should tell you how I got my guitar
in the first place.

two

HELLO FRIEND

My father had a colleague at the aeronautical lab with a stern manner and a long grey beard, his name was George Fejer. He was a German Jew, ten years my father's senior, who was the sole survivor in his family of the Nazis. His wife, Nelli, was the Swiss girl who had harbored him during the war and then emigrated with him to America. George and Dante hit it off at work and then their wives, Nelli and Elizabeth, one-upped them by becoming best best friends. My brother and I called the Fejers Aunt Nelli and Uncle George.

At the Fejers' house was an upright piano that I would quietly amuse myself with on nights when the adults would take to talking and talking around the table. The two couples shared the experience of having had to prove themselves good enough for America (all but my father, who was ironically the most by-the-bootstraps immigrant type among them). They had each studied American history and government, been questioned and tested, and then they had each stood and pledged allegiance with their right hands in the air. They had all suffered a degree of contempt at the hands of the gatekeepers and had to display the appropriate humility at the appropriate times. They shared stories of humiliation.

Half listening and half not, I absorbed an understanding that their gratitude towards America was not dampened by any unfriendliness of the entry process. Their humility was genuine. My Italian grandparents had merely fled poverty and toil; George and Nelli had fled genocide. When you are fleeing like George and Nelli, I imagine bowing down before your savior is immaculately easy. In retrospect, I am amazed that even educated, professional would-be Americans undergo such initiations and it makes me shudder to think of the typical experience of the uneducated and unskilled. Or maybe there is a special hazing process for the oh-so-you-think-you-know-so-much set? I don't know.

My mother had taught me a Chopin nocturne and while the adults deepened in their bond of friendship, I played that song quietly over and over again in the next room, with more dramatic flourish each time. After the Fejers' two sons moved out to go to college, they offered their piano to my parents. In retrospect, I think they were giving it to me.

As soon as it was at our house, you could often find me sitting at that piano, messing around, making up songs. Before long, my parents asked me if I wanted to take piano lessons. For as much as I was into exploring the piano and making stuff up, I said no to lessons. I don't know if it was because of its volume and conspicuousness in my wall-less house or maybe just because it was their suggestion, but regrettably, I declined. I have wished many times since that I had learned to play piano when given the opportunity. Instead I told them I wanted to play guitar. I don't remember where I got the idea. They were skeptical and bought me a small, fifty-dollar guitar. It was a little Yamaha with a big cracked bubble on its wooden face. Damaged and dinky, I still loved it.

I started taking lessons at Carlone's Music on Allen Street from a fellow named Rich Fustino. He taught me how to read music and play simple melodies note for note. Later I would learn how to pick out more sophisticated pieces like Scott Joplin's "The Entertainer" and only after that did he teach me how to chord. My hands were small and the tips of my fingers protested mightily against this new endeavor but a guitar was a tool with which one could make music in secret so I was utterly committed. My teacher praised my patience and my progress. When I learned a new chord, I would put it next to every other chord I knew, just to hear what happens. I would go round and round with these melodies and scales and chords, juxtaposing.

There was a spiral staircase up to an attic loft in the donut house (the old hayloft in the carriage house) and my brother had claimed it. As a teenager, back in the donut house and on medication, he had finally achieved his own room. Then he got an after-school job and earned enough money to buy a stereo. Rock and roll thumped through the floor and wailed down the stairs. The attic was still an open hole in the ceiling and had no door per se, but to him it was Shangri-La. While I was getting to know my acoustic guitar, my brother had a passing fancy to play, too, but he wanted an electric guitar. He got his hands on one for a while but never really played it much. We were in very different worlds with our guitars, my brother and I. He had a goal and then he abandoned it for the next goal. I had no goal and just kept on with my juxtapositions.

Mr. Carlone of Carlone's Music was no fool and he made my parents regret their decision to buy me the cheapest guitar possible. He convinced them that my dedication to my instrument warranted getting me a better one. My mother and father dutifully bought me another Yamaha that cost a hundred dollars more. I was thrilled with my new full-size guitar and fell asleep playing it underneath the Christmas tree. It was magic, smelling the tree and squinting up though its branches and the hazy colored lights that spoke of everything merry and bright. I lay there on my back and played softly after everyone went to sleep.

That Christmas was particularly fraught and my father and I had gone to get the tree the night before, on Christmas Eve, as a form of escape and a last-ditch attempt at normalcy. I remember thinking, *Look at the people out here buying trees on Christmas Eve . . . we are a sorry bunch.* The silences were so thick that year in the donut house, they could choke you. My father and I set up the tree and decorated it while bad vibes rained down upon us.

This was an era in Buffalo when fire engine sirens were a very common thing to hear. I don't know if it was true, but we often joked that we had the highest instance of arson of any city in the United States. Basically, Buffalo had become nothing but one empty, dilapidated building after another, suddenly worth less than their insurance policies and the lots they stood on. It was a sorry running joke, the constant sirens. By the time I had eyes enough to see such things, my city looked like bombs had been dropped on it. Even Frank Lloyd Wright's majestic office building downtown was razed.

That particular Christmas night, the sirens came more numerous than usual. It sounded like a really big fire this time and close. I bundled up and went out in the dark to find it. The Trico windshield wiper factory burned that night and was never recovered. As I stood back from the assembled crowd and watched the huge factory burn, the melodrama was so perfect I think I may have fallen in love with it. Christmas night . . . destruction and inferno silhouetting my sadness and longing. Self-pity is a trap but when you already feel trapped, it can be a comfort.

AND HELLO FRIEND

My first guitar was a turning point for me and Michael was the centrifugal force that did the turning. He walked into my life through the front door of Carlone's shop and though he was to become both teacher and mentor to me, he presented himself as a pal. Happenstance brought us together once a week for a few minutes, sometimes longer, and our first conversations involved looking sideways at each other while sitting in two adjacent vinyl chairs along the side wall of Carlone's shop, behind a row of cheap guitars. Michael taught "folk" guitar at Carlone's and he and I always seemed to be waiting in the shop together for our respective lessons to begin.

Michael was a dapper man with an expansive wardrobe of secondhand fedoras and vests. He combed Buffalo's thrift stores for ascots and cufflinks, suit jackets and scarves. He smelled of cigarettes and beneath that a combination of cedar, patchouli, and mothballs, and beneath that a sweet/minty scent that I would later come to understand as whiskey disguised in mouthwash. He was Irish from Buffalo's South Side and one of eleventy-seven hundred siblings. I was nine and he was thirtysomething but no amount of unlikeliness could stop our friendship.

One day, while Michael and I were waiting in the shop together, he stepped across to the counter and bought me *The Beatles Complete Song Book* that was enshrined in the glass case next to the microphones and stomp boxes. He was working with a musician's income but he insisted on laying down the forty bucks or whatever outlandish sum the book cost and then he insisted I take it. That book became my bible for many years and Michael and I would sit around whatever kitchen table he had parked his ashtray on, in whatever girlfriend's house he was not yet kicked out of, and pore through its pages.

Michael could not read music or pick out complicated classical pieces like the other dudes at the shop. He just played like he was sawing wood and sang like his life depended on it. To him it was all about the song. Soon he would be bringing me with him as he made the rounds of Buffalo public schools as an artist-in-residence himself. He would spring me from my own school and off we would head on foot to City Honors or somewhere else to talk to kids, sometimes older than myself, about songwriting.

Enlisting me as his sidekick was his way of drawing kids in and making songwriting seem accessible to them. He was also a bit of a rough character so a sidekick that bestowed a glow of harmlessness to his one-man operation served him well. He took me everywhere. We hung out in bars and coffeehouses, busked on the street, foraged in thrift stores. We dug the same kinds of ties. He single-handedly made songwriting accessible to me and always treated me like an equal in music and in conversation, implausible though that must have been.

MAKING SONGS 1

People have often asked about my songwriting process and all I can say is this: It takes many forms. Intentionally so. I don't ever want to write the same song twice so I try taking different routes to the finish line. Experimentation leads to unpredictable results and is not the path to surefire success but it is a path to discovery and discovery is way more fun. I've always felt the predictable perfections of pop music to be numbing. They feel more like anti-art than art to me, those songs that cashiers sing along with the radio. Am I a snob? Anyway, I think my songs tend to connect with other people who also enjoy encounters with the unexpected.

Songs can come through in something like a moment of alignment and, at those times, there is very little need for a lot of earthly intentions steering the process. Mostly my songs seem to come through while I'm in an altered state and the very best part is waking up from the trance to a feeling of profound satisfaction. I wake up to the fact that I have transformed my pain into something more beautiful and useful than it was in its original state. I wake up to a vindicating calm because I've allowed something to leave my body and be reborn in the world as something better. And not only that, now I have something to offer the world: a contribution.

Songs like that, that come of their own volition, often have a vitality that serves to carry them along through the world. They are born with their purpose, like some people are. But not all songs are like that. No . . . not even close. Other songs can be more elusive in their purposes or flat-out refuse to sign up for a purpose at all. Or they may veer off from my best intentions and invent some tragic purpose all their own. Some take a lot of wrestling to even find a place where they can exist. Some are epic and require sustained dedication and concentration. Those ones will challenge your stamina and leave you equally drained as satisfied. It's true what the songwriters say: Songs really are like children.

GIGGING

I started performing with Michael at his nighttime gigs and not long after that, I could be found at almost every one. The charm factor of his act must have gone up considerably with Pippi Longstocking standing next to him, backing him up on Beatles songs like "Blackbird" and "Yesterday," her little squinched-up face crooning, "I am not the man I used to beeeeeeee!"

With Michael, I learned the basic human fact that singing together with others is just plain old-fashioned good times. Through his example, I learned to sing with abandon and with no other aim than the freeing of my own soul. My parents' laissez-faire approach to my upbringing already firmly established, I was free to discover the magic of music and this new association with Michael. If anyone wondered where I was, I was either at Janice's dance studio or I was with him.

Michael organized a benefit concert at the University of Buffalo to save whales and dolphins (from harmful fishing industry practices). He enlisted me to play it along with some actual professional folk musicians, including the nationally known Rosalie Sorrels. I was thrilled to see that

I even made the poster, and also the show, thrillingly, was to happen on my eleventh birthday. At the end of the show, Michael brought a cake out on stage and Rosalie and everybody came out to sing "Happy Birthday" to me in front of the whole room. My heart burst open that night and a goodly sum of money was raised for the cause.

We were an odd pair, Michael and I, and we attracted our share of curious eyes but my parents never questioned our friendship. Before my mother moved out, Michael would often eat dinner at our house and sometimes end up sleeping on the sofa. In the morning, my parents would discover their liquor cabinet quite depleted. Those were the funnest nights around our table. Michael had a knack for getting everyone to sing along while he played human jukebox. He was not polished or "naturally talented" in his music-making but he sang from his spleen and the force of his personality attracted people.

Sometimes he would bring other songwriters to join us at our table. Sometimes they, too, would stay the night. He had begun promoting folksingers in coffeehouses and bars around town. Many of them came up from New York City in an ongoing series he called the Greenwich Village Song Project. I met some of them as they enjoyed the hospitality of my parents and I saw them all play. Songwriters like Rod MacDonald, Cliff Eberhardt, John Gorka, Christine Lavin, and Suzanne Vega came through repeatedly. Suzanne slept in my brother's vacated bed on at least one trip. She signed her picture that she left for me, "To my Buffalo little sister."

Trouble with having Michael as your promoter was that everyone who showed up to the concerts was someone to whom he felt personally indebted in some way (such as my parents) so he would never want to charge anyone. Those folksingers would come and go having earned very little money and I can picture my conscientious mother arguing with Michael at the door of these shows, insisting that he take her money.

EMANCIPATION

When my mom moved out, she did so wordlessly. First, she started walking to work and back, I imagine because it gave her time to be alone and exhaust her spinning mind with her moving body. She walked clear across town and it took her an hour and a half each way. Then she graduated to sleeping at the office and not coming home at all. Then she just quietly got an apartment in Allentown and quietly moved into it. My father and brother were both back in the donut house but living with them felt more alienating than ever. The morning I woke up, thighs and sheets covered in menstrual blood and not quite sure how to deal with it, I called my mother. Though her apartment was small, I asked her if I could come live with her. She gave me the bedroom and slept on the couch.

We lived that way for several years until the summer she decided to take a job in an architectural firm out of state and moved to Connecticut. I think she just wanted to start over as someone else. I drove with her to Connecticut to be her wingman and we slept in her car in a state park until she found an apartment. I remember her changing into her linen suit in the park and then driving to her new job. I whiled away the hours reading and drawing in my journal as she worked. I sat outside on a picnic table and played guitar. Then evening came and it was back to the car. By the time she found an apartment, I was confident that living in small-town Connecticut was not for me so I returned home to Buffalo to strike out on my own.

The first place I rented was a spare bedroom in Amy's house. Amy was the Lebanese lady who owned the diner next door to Top Shelf Music. Top Shelf was the guitar store that I frequented after Carlone's closed. Amy was always taking in strays and I was destined to become one of them. I'd gotten to know all the dudes at Top Shelf and through them I'd gotten to know her. Scotty, the proprietor of Top Shelf, was a bass player and he knew me to be a writer and a singer of songs. He had seen me play around town with Michael and had even seen my first humble attempts at playing my own sets of music. He offered to play bass with me and said maybe he could help us get gigs. That all sounded great to me so I started coming by the shop after hours so we could rehearse.

Scotty had an employee who played acoustic guitar, too, and he started to hang around after work to jam with us. Before I knew it, we were a trio and I had my first boyfriend. After rehearsal, the three of us would pass through the back way to Amy's place and sit with her while she held court in the back booth of her diner. Amy would be smoking like the Bethlehem Steel plant, fielding requests from all the neighborhood ne'er-do-wells, and handing out loans like the Godfather. The First Boyfriend and I would make eyes at each other while Scotty fidgeted and twisted his thick mustache and Amy made us all laugh with her steady stream of bawdy opinions.

The First Boyfriend had a mustache, too, arching down to a studiously sculpted pencil-line beard. Everything about him was precise and German. Everything in his world had to be a certain way. He was in his thirties, an ex-hippie grown back into his true nature: control freak. For a girl immersed in a life of chaos and uncertainty, his sternness and in-chargeness was a blanket. I also found him very handsome.

Coffee and French fries having just been set down steaming in my face, I told my crew at Amy's Place of the plight of my mother moving to Connecticut. Amy looked up and said I could rent the extra bedroom in her house if I wanted and that was that. I was fifteen and my father had just turned sixty-five so he had started collecting Social Security money. Three hundred dollars a month for each underage dependent. It was my godsend. I just started going to him and collecting the three hundred bucks and turning it over to Amy. The rent that I paid her included "room and board," which meant that I could eat at her diner after school. Between the ages of fifteen and eighteen, my father's Social Security check was key to my survival, or at least the key to my continuing education. If it wasn't for that money, I would have dropped out of school.

What foiled this new best-of-all-worlds situation was that Amy decided she was in love with The First Boyfriend herself (a man much closer to her age than mine) but he had his sights set on me so Amy got sad. No sooner had I hunkered down in my new digs, she asked me to leave. In my pride, I moved out very quickly and slept in the bus station downtown for a few days while I figured out my next move. I wasn't about to move in with The First Boyfriend (nor was I invited) and it didn't feel like an option to go back to the donut house with my father and brother. I just couldn't go back there.

I remember those few days in the bus station well because they spanned my sixteenth birthday. I made note of the humorous fuckitude of my sweet sixteenth. I used the bus station McDonald's as my study and sat nursing a Styrofoam cup of coffee there for hours. Beyond that, I roamed, searching for newspapers. I looked through the apartment listings and made notes. I stood at the pay phone with fistfuls of coins and made calls. If memory serves me, calls were a dime. I had just about enough money for a one-month deposit on a place. I was also looking for a job.

There are no benches in the bus station. Everyone knows that would encourage people to sleep on them. No, the bus station was not designed to be a harbor for in-transit folks like me. Instead it was festooned with a fuck-off-sized collection of hard orange plastic chairs, all bolted to the floor in evenly spaced rows. Sleeping on the concrete floor was the only option. Under the blinding fluorescent lights, sleep was hard to achieve for every reason there is and sleep deprivation accumulated in my brain over the course of a few days. I practiced my force field of *stay back* and grabbed an hour or two at a time. The fluorescent lights and all the crazies and the noise felt safer than any alternatives, though, so I stayed put.

My friend Christian from high school came at dawn on my birthday and bought me breakfast at McDonald's (arranged the day before at school) and then we walked together across the condom and needle-strewn field between the bus station and the building where we were spending our days: The Buffalo Academy for Visual and Performing Arts.

Performing Arts (as we called it) was housed in a gargantuan grey stone building with the words "girls" and "boys" chiseled above the two big front doors. As high schools go, it meant well but the Buffalo public schools had been fighting a losing battle ever since the white flight to suburbia of the sixties and seventies had slowly robbed the city of its resources. Now it was the mid-eighties and my school, like most of the city schools, was in hard decline. I was thirteen when I arrived as a freshman, and I immediately knew the whole thing was not going to be worth the time it was going to take.

I worked out a plan where I could acquire all the necessary credits to graduate in three years and I went to the school principal with my proposal. I told him if he didn't allow me to execute my three-year plan, I would quit and get a GED. "If I let you do this, everyone's gonna wanna do this," he told me. "No . . . they're not," I said. He didn't want to see me drop out of school so he consented with the caveat that I keep the whole thing as discreet as possible. It was a theme that was just starting to appear in my life: Okay, I will let you be the exception . . . just don't tell anyone. I didn't know it at the time, but this theme was to carry all the way through to my eventual relationship with the music industry and its gatekeepers. I set my own rules and seeing that I was ready to walk out the door, people would secretly comply.

I managed to move right from the bus station into my first apartment. I convinced this cool Rastafarian superintendent on Main Street between the Record Theatre and Freddie's Doughnuts to rent me a one bedroom. I promised him the rent would always be on time and I wouldn't tell anyone my age. I also got an after-school job waitressing at a Greek diner. I just lied about my age on the job application.

For the music gigs I was starting to get in places that served alcohol, I used my mantra: I won't drink, I won't tell anyone my age, I won't be any trouble and of course, I always had fake ID on hand. Somebody had tipped me off that a medical emergency card looked pretty official and you could get one real easy. I went down to the DMV, filled out the form, paid the fee, and took the picture. Next thing you knew, I was using that card all over town. The fact that it worked so well is especially funny because I'd spelled diabetes wrong.

THE BIG APPLE

I fell in love with New York City as a teenager and one trip in particular felt like the beginning of the end of being a Buffalonian. I rode there in the back of a van with Michael and a couple of his friends who had made a business of absconding with the spoils of the Buffalo thrift stores and then driving the shit to The City to resell it for five times as much. We stayed at Rod MacDonald's apartment on MacDougal Street in what was once the heart of the sixties folk revival scene. Eight hours on the I-90 and suddenly I was Michael's shadow in the most fascinating city on earth. It was the late eighties and the conservative revolution that had driven so many into homelessness and drug use was preparing its "tough on crime" backlash. I was terrified and devastated and thrilled by the vastness of human experience that was suddenly all around me.

There were punk bands playing in the bandshell in Tompkins Square Park and illegal squats in all the abandoned brownstones. (The driver of our van was staying at one of them.) There were elaborate shantytowns popping up on the Lower East Side and even a faint bohemian aroma still wafting through the West Village. CBGB's was still CBGB's and Times Square was still nasty old Times Square. The City seemed to be in the hands of immigrants and artists, punks and queers, and I felt drawn to it like iron to the center of the earth.

Michael and I put in time singing folk songs in Washington Square Park like Woody and Ramblin' Jack and then we went out on the street to busk our way to a dinner at Mamoun's Falafel. Michael insisted we leave the park before we put out a guitar case for money. He muttered something about ordinances, but I think he was just honoring the sacred space of that park and its role in the expression of people's songs. He was teaching me my folksinger history in the self-adapted, half-made-up way that all history is taught.

One morning we awoke to the old homeless man who haunted Mac-Dougal Street sleeping on the couch next to us. Rod would sometimes take him in and let him shower and sleep in his tiny apartment. Rod and his Italian girlfriend were in the loft, me and Michael on the floor, and the homeless man on the couch. That equaled five in this tiny studio apartment. And this was just one of the apartments in this one brownstone! I couldn't get over the scale of it all. Like studying Astronomy 101, I turned New York over and over in my mind and I felt dizzy and thrilled.

The day that we decided to go down to the Financial District to busk, instead of working the Village, floats like a Zen koan in my memory. We never encountered more hostility or made less money. The Wall Street gamblers and money shifters resented stepping over us on their way to remaking America and we were an inconvenience at best. After the better part of a day, we had barely made enough money for a single sandwich and eventually we gave up and went off looking for a sandwich to share. By this time, the lunch hour was well over and most of the places in lower Manhattan had pulled down their gates. We were winding our way back to the Village on foot with our guitars on our backs when we came upon a luncheonette with its gate only halfway down. Badly in need of sustenance, we peeked our heads under the gate and made a nuisance of ourselves.

There were a bunch of men dealing out cards and lighting up cigars around a back table. The posters on the walls were the same pictures of Lebanon that hung at Amy's Place back in Buffalo. One of the men saw our guitars and called out in a thick accent, "Play us a song!" We immediately obliged and before we knew it, an aluminum pie tray was being passed around and three times as much money as we'd made all day was being dropped into it. Then one of the men excused himself from the game and made us food in his already cleaned-up kitchen. Their money was recycled from the tray into the cash register till and we left with hot gyro sandwiches and baklava in our hands. Years later, when I heard the adage, "The people who have the least give the most," my mind flashed to the morning I watched Rod handing a cup of coffee to the ghost of MacDougal Street and then went off with Michael to busk on Wall Street. My head must have been nodding.

That trip to The City could not have lasted more than a few days, but because my universe exploded and was expanding at such a rapid speed, time stood still. Each experience imprinted itself on me like it would a newborn child. When I came home I think I called my mother and told her I was moving to New York and I think she said something to the effect of, "I trust your judgment." It took me a few years, but eventually, that's exactly what I did.

THE UNREAD NOTE

They never let me read my father's suicide note. I'm not even sure who "they" were. I have always resented "them" for it and all other acts of arbitrary control and intrusion. I can witness my father's pain, day in and day out since the dawning of my consciousness, I can carry it in my own body and slowly exorcize it through the movements of my own blood and electrical synapses, but I cannot read the few words that he wrote to me and my brother upon his attempted exit from the world. That, according to some assumed authority, would have been too much.

His suicide was unsuccessful (he survived after a good stomach pumping, just like my brother), but seeing him locked inside a mental ward, humiliated and powerless in his open-in-the-back hospital gown, was sad like death. It was also a foreshadowing of the nursing home years that would come later down the road, once again stripping him of his dignity and leaving him naked before me.

My father's sadness was profound and, to my mind, somewhat justified. I didn't get, right along with him, why we couldn't all just get along. My father sat quietly for decades waiting for the unconditional love and support that he put out to come back to him but his life did not seem to be able to make good on the karmic deal. He met his sadness with acceptance and discretion and he showed the world a smile, but to me it was heavy and I can feel its weight still.

I took pleasure in being his ally and my only regret is that I never had much time for him. I always seemed to be on a mission and he always seemed to understand. He told me he was proud of me. He met me with open arms and open heart no matter how long I'd been away. He taught me the art of unconditional love and between us we formed a trusty circuit, unbroken by time and space. "Eat when you're hungry, sleep when you're tired," he would say with a smile every time I bid him farewell.

When he let me carry him onto the toilet and then wipe his butt for him, I actually felt my respect for him deepen. I know it should have been he who was humbled by those moments of weakness and incapacitation, but it was I. He showed me even more deeply then, by saying nothing but an unapologetic "Thank you," how unconditional love looks and acts. He gifted me with a confidence in how truly strong and unashamed it is. However you appear in a moment, in weakness or in strength, real love endures.

Endurance was another hallmark of my father's life. His family was denied him, his wife would never return, and his children would continue to struggle in realms beyond his control. "Surviving," he would always say, in answer to the question, "How are you doing?" He always said it like it was a joke and save for the exception of that one suicidal moment, he seemed to get the joke. He took his glimmers of joy where he could. Mostly when I was walking up to him, arms outstretched.

SUZI

The First Boyfriend's house was a study in dysfunction. It was heavily curtained and dark with the main living room/dining area being used only for storage of things that nobody cared about in big draped piles. It had been his grandmother's house in what was then the German ghetto on Buffalo's East Side. The Germans had long since assimilated and it was now an African-American neighborhood. His family's lives, like most working-class Buffalonians, had belonged to Bethlehem Steel and their happiness had lived and died with the plant. They all made one exit or another when the place closed down.

Surrounding piles of what I assume were the remnants of his grandmother's life were a kitchen, a bathroom, and a small bedroom which he was renting out to another can't-quite-get-his-shit-together bachelor. His own bedroom was upstairs in the tiny attic under a steeply sloped roof that allowed just enough headroom to stand in the center of the shaggy carpet. There was a mattress on a box spring against one four-foot-high wall and stacks of milk crates filled with record albums against the other. There was a record player stationed under a little window, the size of a chess board, which looked out onto the front sidewalk and the overgrown railroad tracks across the street.

In his bedroom, I got hip to Santana, Crosby, Stills, Nash & Young, Joni Mitchell, and a host of other heroes of the hippie cosmos. The ones that I took deepest into my heart were Joan Armatrading and John Martyn. I pulled his copies of Joan's early albums *Back to the Night* and *Joan Armatrading* out of their places in the crates and made cassette copies that went from my boom box to my Walkman and back again. I wore those tapes out. But it must have been John Martyn's *Solid Air*, more than any other record, which became the soundtrack of my teenage life. I knew nothing about John as an artist, I still don't really, but I believe his guitar playing resides deep inside mine and his circular, jazz-inflected grooves wove their way slowly into my DNA.

I had to make sure I put The First Boyfriend's records back in exact alphabetical order, not just by artist but by album title, too. I had to learn his way of doing everything. Downstairs, in the dim kitchen he taught me how to make what he called "fettuccine Alfredo" according to his precise specifications. He would come in and check to see if I was cutting the peppers and onions to an exact quarter-inch dimension. The only bathroom in the house was adjacent to the rented bedroom and he and I were only to use the toilet and sink there. The bathtub was designated as the renter's bathing facility. The First Boyfriend had rigged up a shower in the basement for himself.

It was cold and creepy in the basement, with just one bare bulb hanging by the base of the stairs and a wooden pallet covered by a rubber mat separating wet feet from wet concrete floor. The hot water would periodically get shut off due to nonpayment of bills, much to the renter's chagrin. Eventually, the renter moved out and I watched in amazement one Buffalo winter as The First Boyfriend took an icy, military-style shower in his freezing cold basement every morning for weeks. Unbelievable. It was apparently not an option for him to just not shower and he was not into going across town to my apartment on Main Street to do so. I think the cold showers made him feel tough, whereas showering at his sixteen-year-old girlfriend's apartment would have made him feel ashamed. Needless to say, I showered at my place.

On the nights that I stayed with him, I would walk from his house to catch the yellow school bus to Performing Arts which stopped a few blocks away. It was not my bus, I was not supposed to be on it, but the bus driver looked away and said nothing whenever I boarded with all the usual kids. For a few months there, girls were being abducted in The First Boyfriend's neighborhood and raped and killed. Two or three went missing, always early in the morning, and were found later. For about a week after the second news report came out, The First Boyfriend walked me to the bus and waited with me, but that fell off pretty quick. He didn't have the discipline for seeing me on the bus in the morning that he did for the cold showers.

High school was a place where I inadvertently nodded off at my desk when I was there at all. I was a frequent recipient of "detention" due to my attendance record. The detention room is where Suzi and I met. She was a foot taller than me and would have been blonde and pretty if she weren't so good at making herself un-pretty with her greasy green faux-hawk and unkempt clothes. She had the habit of shuffling down the school halls in those knee-high woven alpaca slippers that you buy in stores where they sell incense and pot pipes. Everything about her countenance echoed my same feeling of: I'd be better off sleeping right now. We hit it off immediately.

We laughed quietly together as we went through the exercise of writing a hundred times, "I will not skip school" or whatever the hell our respective punishments were. She was part hippie, part punk, and underneath that was a troubled rich girl gone wrong . . . underneath that was a sweet and giving person. She had been kicked out of every private school in town and dropped in to Performing Arts for her senior year to slum it with the ruffians and wannabes.

Because of my three-year course plan, I was taking both junior and senior-level classes that year and sliding sideways into the class of '87. There were lots of cool kids in that class and I had some sweet friends, including Jesse Martin, who later went on to TV fame in the show *Law and Order*, but Suzi was to become my closest pal and our friendship exceeded the bounds of the building. Between my apartment and her pickup truck (on permanent loan to her from her folks), we were unstoppable. My mobility and her truancy were fortified by our friendship.

Suzi and I had a relationship based on escape and together we escaped many things. First it was the confines of high school. After sitting in our respective "homerooms" in the morning, long enough to say "Present!" when our names were called, we would sneak out the unlocked maintenance door on the side of the building and take off in her truck, not to be seen again until homeroom the next morning. We were gaming the system of attendance to a fine degree and, luckily for me, I had a knack for getting good grades despite rarely attending classes. We moved on to escaping her parents and my boyfriend. I couldn't bring myself to exit his control entirely but, running from his house and jumping into the cab of her pickup, I would laugh as she would shake her head and mumble under her breath, "fuckin' sick," while peeling away.

We escaped Buffalo entirely as much as we could, holing up at her parents' empty farm or beach house just across the border. We escaped the hypocrisies of the whole adult world and we made each other feel one degree less crazy as we played our respective left-field positions. She had a dyke sister in New York who was living with Michelle Shocked (back before Michelle went all Adam and Eve on our asses) and one of our grander escapes was all the way to The City to visit her. The sister seemed to be a citizen of the gutter punk nation that had invaded the East Village with its found-object sculptures and communal gardens. There were still roosters strutting around the Lower East Side in those days, and the caustic aroma of crack pipes on the breeze. The only white people who were daring to inhabit the crumbling brownstones east of Avenue A were a rarified breed of trustifarians (trust-fund babies gone AWOL), junkies, punks, street urchins, and dykes. We fit right in.

Later still, Suzi would become the second-ever employee of my company, Righteous Babe Records, and work there for years when RBR was in its larval stage, helping to construct systems where there were none. In this way, she helped me escape the clutches of the music industry. She would also end up coming on the road with me for a spell as I began to tour in earnest, helping me to escape the grasping hands of this new population of people called "fans." Even in deepest obscurity, I was blessed with listeners who supported and affirmed my existence in the way that I so craved, but also, right from the beginning, I was challenged by their high demands. The intensity in me, naturally, was finding its likeness in the world.

At its inception, Righteous Babe Records was simply Righteous Records but after a couple years of scribbling that moniker onto my homespun cassettes, I tried to trademark the name and discovered that there was already a Righteous Records in Oklahoma. They put out gospel music. The Oklahoma Righteous Records did not take kindly to sharing their name so it became incumbent on me to change my name. "Babe" was what Suzi and I called each other as one of our many running jokes. It was our way of taking the piss out of the world of lecherous men and their constant taunts. "Hey babe, wanna ride with me?" "Hey babe, what's your name?" "Hey babe! Come and talk to me, baby!" That is like the sound of the breeze when you're a young woman, always in the background of your waking, walking life. Inserting "babe" into the name of my DBA was just the most ironic way I could think of to keep from getting sued.

In retrospect, it was a great gift that gospel music label in Oklahoma gave to me. After that, RBR's true identity spoke loud and clear to anyone with ears to hear it.

PRECIPICE

There were hurdles to being an emancipated minor, but I had been training for it my whole life so I became pretty adept at passing in the adult world. I was still sixteen when my three-year course plan was faithfully executed and my high school diploma was handed to me. Then I was really free.

I immediately got a couple student loans and enrolled myself in classes at Buffalo State College. I signed up for what interested me, which at the time was drawing and painting, philosophy, and art history. I found a little dance crew at that college, too. We called ourselves Floorplay. Meanwhile, I was playing music with my bass man Scotty and we had weekly gigs on the books, sometimes two. Michael had bequeathed to me the job of hosting the Monday open mics at Nietzsche's and I was playing Saturday nights at the Essex Street Pub. He also helped me get gigs like opening up for Shakespeare in the Park in the summer or for touring songwriters like Shawn Phillips, who dared come through in the dead of winter. Michael was forever putting together a poet's night at People's Coffeehouse or a songwriter's showcase at the old Casablanca Club and it went without saying that I was always invited. Though we weren't really hanging out much or playing music together anymore, Michael was always there, in the background, pushing me along.

My journey through puberty disturbed the ecosystem of Michael and me. Our friendship was true and deep but when one of us changed from a little girl to a woman, it became confused. . . . *The whole thing imploded in slow motion one day as you leaned down gently to kiss me. You, having been abducted by the notion that our story was some kinda timeless folk ballad, or smoky French film or something. "Our love has come full circle," you said and for a few days you seemed giddy with this full-circle thing. Then I watched as that fantasy crumbled inside your eyes and an immense guilt descended into your heart. You, who had been swept away by your artist's spirit and by the tide of my budding sexuality. You, who was then visibly crushed under the weight of regret.*

For my part, I was not as nauseated by the whole roller coaster ride because I knew you loved me and because never for an instant was I scared of you. A young woman becomes familiar with the sight of men struggling with the opposing forces of attraction and propriety and, mostly, what I felt in that moment was a deep sympathy for you. Because I loved you back. It would be many years before we would come together again as we had been. Water under the bridge, my friend.

REPRODUCTIVE SYSTEM

I never met a boy my own age who could return my gaze so it was somewhat inevitable that I would end up with a man. When The First Boyfriend and I became attracted to each other, it was all aboveboard and, to my undiscerning eye it looked consensual and balanced. We courted much like people the same age would court. We stammered while sparks flew between us and we circled closer and closer in. His biggest fear was that what he wanted to do was illegal and an accusation of statutory rape could end his life as he knew it. My biggest fear was getting pregnant. Together we decided that I would go on the pill and we would wait for a month until it was safely in effect to act on our desire. That was a sexy-ass month.

I must have been the only teenage virgin to ever walk into the Buffalo Planned Parenthood to properly plan for having her first run-in with a penis because I was an instant celebrity. The nurse practitioner took me around the whole office and introduced me to everyone. They all acted proud of me and it felt like I was giving them hope. Maybe some of the educational efforts they had been putting forth were having an effect on society. Maybe the world was changing for young women.

This made it all the harder to walk into that same Planned Parenthood a few years later, pregnant and crying my eyes out. Their steeled looks of disappointment compounding the disappointment I felt in myself. I had been on the pill but in those days the pill was like a hormonal sledgehammer on a tiny one-hundred-pound girl like me. After a few years of feeling like I was gonna pass out with dizziness every time I stood up, I just couldn't take it anymore. I went off the pill and instantly I was pregnant. "Why, why would you stop taking it?" the nurse asked me as I cried in her office. "I don't know," I whimpered, "I just made a mistake."

I didn't know I was pregnant for quite a while. Denial is powerful stuff. But when your body has been doing nothing but transforming itself before your eyes for years, the fact that your tits might one day grow to twice their former size does not seem unheard of. Nor does the menstrual period being screwy, since it's always been screwy and you have not learned to pay attention to it anyway, so actually you have no idea. Instead I just thought I'd taken my familial turn towards the suicidal. I wanted to lie in bed all day, I had no energy, I was severely depressed for the first time. I felt suddenly hopeless. I languished in this state until it was almost too late to have an abortion. Then, finally, the period not being around as much as I'd vaguely remembered made my denial bubble burst. When I was finally walking up to WomenServices on Elmwood Avenue to terminate my pregnancy, I could not have been more sure of what I was doing. The news that I was pregnant hit me like a rock and then transformed itself into the greatest relief I'd ever felt. This was a solvable problem, not the end of my life.

Writing poems and songs, playing guitar, painting, dancing, those were my joys and my first intuitive steps towards finding peace within myself. I had gigs around town to look forward to. I walked up and down Elmwood Avenue, hanging up my flyers. You just can't imagine (unless maybe you once were an eighteen-year-old girl yourself) how much the thought of becoming a "mom" was unthinkable to me on every level. Not to mention, the idea of being permanently soldered to The First Boyfriend. That felt like the greatest of all curses.

I had to steel myself against the forces of shaming that came rushing at me from all sides. I walked past those anti-choice protesters yelling at me with their gory placards and I tried to exhale their rage and my guilt as I pushed open the WomenServices door. The guilt in me came not from wondering if I was committing murder, but from worrying that I was supposed to be feeling *more* remorse than I did. My body's strong sense that those protesters were deeply full of shit (not to mention totally wrong about what was right and merciful for everyone involved) was in conflict with my mind, which lurked in dark, self-defeating places and waited for opportunities to turn on me.

The First Boyfriend said he would help me by paying for the abortion but he never did. He said I should have the baby and marry him but that was the opposite of what I was thinking. I had spent three years with him, but after the abortion I told him I wanted to break up. He resisted mightily. There was the wrenching of phones from walls and the kicking-in of doors. There were holes in the plasterboard right next to where my head had been. Then there was quiet and a new era for me began.

SILENCES

I never was a strummer. The beauty of an acoustic guitar, to my mind, is that it's not only a melodic but a percussive instrument. In fact, I might even say it's a percussion instrument first. A hollow box with strings running across it is like a drum with a supernatural ability to feed tone and color into rhythm. Though many people seem to catch all the fun they desire in its melodic waters, I believe an acoustic guitar's ability to make sound and silence sit right next to each other is at the core of its power. As with any rhythm instrument, the spaces are essential. Strumming an acoustic guitar erases the beginnings and the ends of its sounds and eliminates the spaces. It ignores the instrument's potential to produce intense dynamic contrast. To put it opinionatedly, strumming an acoustic guitar is akin to scratching on the surface of a drum: antithetical to its nature.

This was not some sort of idea that came to me but more a feeling in my torso that came alive when the instrument that I had been holding against it really began to speak. For one thing, Michael showed me a fingerpicking pattern wherein you hold a chord with your left hand and use the individual fingers on your right hand to pluck a single string at a time in a repeating pattern. I was captivated. I practiced that fingerpicking pattern over and over until I could make the rhythm of the pattern flow seamlessly from my right hand and then I practiced it some more until I could manipulate the feel of the syncopations at will. The spaces between the notes gave a shape to each sound. Feeling the instrument breathe against my body made me turn subconsciously away from the world of strumming and never look back.

Michael's style was more sloppy and strummy and he showed me the fingerpicking pattern more as a useful exercise (like a boxer working a speed bag) than something meant to be an actual part of the game of music. But I also had my father's John Fahey records playing through my dreams and, thanks to Michael, I had Suzanne Vega coming in and out of my waking life. They weren't strummers. Suzanne was something of a new breed when she appeared on the Greenwich Village folk scene in the late seventies. Her songs were female and urban (not urban like Black, urban like some folk shit that ain't "Jimmy Crack Corn" or "I've Been Working on the Railroad"). Her style of playing was different from the boys and something about her presence provided me with subliminal proof of my own difference. Her playing told me I could find my own way with the acoustic guitar.

I have been asked steadily since the early days about my musical influences and I have never been good at answering, which has always made me feel like a jerk. Like I'm shirking, instead of availing myself of, opportunities to pay my respects. But the truth is, I've always been somewhat sincerely stumped by the question. For one thing, who stops and examines themselves in the middle of a journey? What made me take that step?! Hmmmm. And that one? Plus, when growing up is a difficult time, forgetting becomes an important ingredient to moving forward. It is a survival mechanism. I was not able to compartmentalize my forgetting, I guess. It was an all or nothing deal. There is a lot that only seems clear to me now, after months of sitting here, staring off into space, stepping gingerly back across the threshold of memory.

This is the answer I was never able to give: I began my musical journey at the intersection of Suzanne Vega and John Martyn with the drunken ghost of John Fahey flyin' around overhead. Joan Armatrading was somewhere up ahead of me and Michael was walking by my side carrying the *Beatles Complete Song Book* and holding my hand. My next evolutionary leap would come a good decade later when my ears suddenly stretched wider and I heard jazz music, I mean really heard it, for the first time. Also, coincidentally, around that time I started smoking pot. Thelonious Monk and Miles Davis were the melodic and harmonic masters (not to mention arresting players) that shifted my whole sense of things. Betty Carter, the singer, changed the way I sing.

All through my twenties and thirties, I was also on a steady diet of groove music. From groovy African guitar and kora players like Ali Farka Touré, Baaba Maal, and Mansour Seck (all of whom I even got to see live) to American groove masters like James Brown and the Meters (who I didn't). Maceo Parker (Brown's left-hand man for three decades) became a musical comrade and teacher to me towards the end of my formative years. And then, of course, there was Sekou and Utah . . . but I will tell you about all of them later.

As a teenager, having drifted from Michael's side and embarked on playing my own gigs, I was faced with the task of holding my own in bars full of drunk people who had no intrinsic interest in listening to the girl in the corner with the acoustic. They had no reason to stop trying to seduce or argue with the person next to them. It was my job to give them a reason. My dive into dynamics became more extreme then. I started grabbing and spanking the strings of my guitar harder and I expanded the silences in between the sounds. I learned that extreme dynamics (a loud sound, a pencil line, silence) could leave an oblivious person's talk suddenly hanging out there, naked in the air. At that moment, they would simultaneously become aware of themselves and of me and they would turn. In that moment lay an opportunity. I would look them in the eyes then and sing directly into them. In that way, I believe my biggest influence may have been just playing solo in bars. By introducing silences, I called attention to the music. By manipulating the silences, I created my sound.

760 ASHLAND AVENUE

LAYLAH ALI
ANI DIFRANCO
TANYA ZABINSKI

That's what the label on the upstairs mailbox at 760 Ashland Avenue read. We used to joke that our mailbox looked like the United Colors of Buffalo, with a quintessential cross-section of Buffalo's cultural bedrock, African, Italian, and Polish-American represented. The three of us met at Buffalo State College, in the art department, and decided to move in together in an apartment a few blocks away. It was 1987, Tanya and Laylah were twentysomething, and I was seventeen.

It was a two-bedroom apartment so we hung a curtain across one half of the front room and that was my lair. My lack of a wall was easily made up for by the fact that I had access to the porch door. I could go out on the front porch at any time and play my guitar amongst the potted herbs, disturbing no one. It was a classic, spacious Buffalo apartment, the wide-open second story of a house, with wood floors and generous windows. We covered the windows in sheets of plastic in the winter, to keep the frigid air from pouring in.

With Tanya and Laylah came whole new communities of young people more "my age" than anyone I'd been hanging out with. I thrilled to the political radicals, artists, and students that invaded my world in the form of new friends. Tanya was far and away the gentlest spirit I'd ever encountered except for maybe my father. She had a light chortle of a laugh and black, twinkling eyes. She had a thin body without a mean bone in it. She was an enlightened cook at a very young age and an all-around artist who made silkscreens and paintings and puppets. She was the first truly spiritual person I ever met, with deep and spooky theories about the way the world works that have all since been proven right. I learned so much from her about how to focus on and draw out the positivity in the world. The lesson of her example would take a while to germinate in me, but it worked its magic eventually. I saw it work its magic on her future husband, Joe, too.

Laylah was a painter with a sardonic sense of humor that was edgier than Tanya's or mine. With an unkempt, majestic fro and a bemused deadpan, she was my energetic opposite. She would squint at me often with that expression of: And why exactly are you so jolly? Because I was intimidated, I loved her company. I was taking in the silences. In both Laylah and Tanya, I encountered the silences and pauses of people who take their time. I marveled at those pauses. To make it through them, the wheels of my mind would rev wildly and spin and spin in their own mud. I saw my own social frills and grinning for the first time from a slight distance.

Laylah had this job at some huge camp every summer baking bread so her bread-making skills bestowed upon our household amazing accompaniments to Tanya's delicious food. My life basically improved one hundred percent when I moved into that apartment on Ashland Avenue. A strong feminine energy suddenly, for the first time, held me. Tanya, Laylah, and I made a peaceful, artful abode, the tenor of which I would encounter many times over in my future travels. Feminist households would forever be met in me with deep recognition and comfort.

Twenty years later, Laylah, having taken the art world by storm, came back to Buffalo to do a one-woman show at the Albright Knox Art Gallery only a few blocks from our old digs. The Albright is an internationally renowned gallery of modern art and her show there cemented her local-girl-makes-good status in a way that I could relate to. She is known for her deceptively simple paintings that speak volumes about power dynamics between people within the folds of empire. Tanya's art is an expression of the simplicity of kindness and awareness, like if Pete Seeger was a painter. From the beginning, the three of us were kindred and, in a way, our art forms a kind of circle.

In the meantime, Laylah was the first to move out, following a scholarship, and in her place, Scot moved in. He was one of the carpenters who worked with Tanya's boyfriend, Joe. They had recently started their own construction outfit called Wildcat Builders. I had met Scot a few times, once when we all went to the Albright Knox to see a movie about Frida Kahlo and once when we went to a Billy Bragg concert in Toronto. I got really into Billy Bragg for a while. I had *Talking to the Taxman About Poetry* and *Worker's Playtime* in heavy rotation. They married well with *My Aim Is True* and *This Year's Model*, those early Elvis Costello records that I also loved. So here, Laylah was moving out and Scot was moving in. The feminine vibe in the apartment, with the smell of baking bread wafting past the Georgia O'Keeffe paintings, shifted somewhat when the construction dudes landed, Scot into his room and Joe into Tanya's.

SCOT FISHER

Scot was the height, dimension, and color of a redwood tree with a formerly majestic mane of hair that was quickly receding. What a thing it must be to have your very identity center on flaming red, Robert Plant–style hair and then one day to have the gods tap you on the shoulder and say, "Welcome to manhood, son, hand over your hair." When I met Scot, he was twenty-seven and transforming. He had just spent the past six years out in Angola (the town, not the prison . . . or was it?) fixing his grandmother's old plank-construction farmhouse. He had embarked on the quest to save it from falling down around her when she was still alive and then, after she died, he vowed to finish what he started.

He rebuilt that house top to bottom while living in it, including the plumbing and electrical work. He learned much of what he needed to know as he went. He survived cold and bleak winters working alone with only a hotplate on which to cook. He dug a basement under the house by hand and then he dug a six-foot trench out to the street to lay pipe. In the end, he made a sunburst pattern in the front porch railing and painted it lavender. He was gaunt as a man who had been on a pilgrimage when he finally moved back in to Buffalo.

First thing he did at 760 Ashland was to clomp up the stairs, carrying huge armfuls of 2x4s, and build a loft in his bedroom. The room was small and he said he wanted to maximize floor space. Underneath the bed, he built a desk but, as he had to stoop down very low to sit at it, he ended up using it mainly for book storage. He might have done better with a futon on the floor and a bookshelf, like the rest of us, but my tendency was not to question but to simply marvel at human beings' different approaches to life. I credit my mother for teaching me to value the unfamiliar—in fact, to seek it out.

The first time Scot came to see me play, he came by himself. I can picture him in his Carolina boots and flannel shirt, leaning awkwardly on the bar, plaster dust and paint splatters on his pants and a rough hand wrapped around a pint of beer. We were in the tiny Essex Street Pub and he was sitting on a bar stool about six feet from where I was singing. There were only a handful of people in the room but I had eyeballed them all into paying attention. I was not shy about eye contact in those days and I was already not a mincer-of-words so it must have been intense to be there listening to me sing my songs. Afterwards, Scot and I sat at the bar and really talked for the first time. A nervousness entered the room and sat between us and I started to get the feeling that we were going to be more than housemates.

I woke up to a blizzard. The snow was furiously gusting and ballroom dancing in flowing dresses around the house. The winds were so strong that the plastic coverings over my windows were slapping in and out like sails. I rolled over and turned on the clock radio to listen to the news. Sure enough, all schools were closed, government buildings, too. I lay there for a while listening to the howling of the wind and the radio announcer enumerating road closures, then I swung my legs out from under the warmth of the covers and I pulled aside the curtain that was at once the wall and the door of my room. I padded quickly through the cold apartment and gently pushed open the door of your room. I climbed the ladder up into your sleeping loft for the first time. "It's a snow day," I said, "No one's going anywhere."

TALENT CONTEST

My bass man, Scotty, saw an ad in the paper one day for a talent contest at a hotel in Niagara Falls. "You should enter it!" he tells me, "The first prize is free studio time!" Then he says, "I'll drive you up there!" So off we went, to Niagara Falls, to the Marriott Hotel or some shit, Scotty, me, and my guitar.

It would be hard to overstate the degree of contrast between myself and the other contestants. It was like an *American Idol* contest only in the middle of the pageantry, something beams in from another planet. At least that's how I felt walking up on the risers and approaching the mic. I felt like an alien landing. I played one of my original songs and I didn't imagine for a minute that I'd "win" but for some reason the people of their planet deemed me the winner. One of the judges of the contest was the rock critic for the *Buffalo News*, a man by the name of Dale Anderson. He approached me afterwards and gave me his card. He said he had connections in the music industry and he could help me get a record deal. He said I should call him. This was quite an amazement to my ears. I said, okay, wow, amazing, I will call you! Scotty and I drove home feeling all victorious. Free studio time and a guy who says he wants to help me get a record deal! What could be better than that?

I called the number on the card and the first thing Dale did was set up a meeting with a lawyer friend of his. He wanted me to sign a contract with him that says if he gets me a record deal I'll give him x percentage of something-or-other blah blah blah. He said the contract would be for one year and if I didn't have a record deal within a year, the thing was up. I thought: *What the hell? Why not? It's only a year.* It's not like I had any big plans.

There was this yellow lined sheet of legal paper that I carried in my guitar case, on which I had written the names of all of my songs. By the time of my first recording session, there were eighty-some titles written on that paper. I remember, top of the list was "Winter Mist," the first song I'd written, when I was fourteen. Of course, I didn't write down the chords to these songs and my journal might or might not even contain a cohesive version of the lyrics, so the songs came and went with my memory. My teacher was Michael Meldrum, human jukebox and archive of popular song, so it's no surprise my ethic was: If a song couldn't be remembered, it wasn't worth remembering.

A few years later I had to soften my theories about the folk process and buy a handheld cassette recorder. I was losing too much. Of course, then I developed the problem of filling cassette after cassette with song sketches and grooves and these cassettes would pile up, the idea of mining through them too daunting. Years after that, I would realize that writing down chord charts and lyrics in an organized fashion in my journal-of-the-moment was the only way to really keep a song alive across time. Still, sometimes I manage to do so and sometimes I don't. I have waves of organization.

That first twelve-song recording was spun by Dale as a demo which he would then "shop to labels" but to me it was just the first document I ever had of my songs.

WILDCAT BUILDERS

I started working for Scot and Joe's contruction company, Wildcat Builders, as a grunt laborer and, being small and female, I had something to prove, so I was a terrific worker. The men would tease me as my body shook around a Sawzall or as I heaved heavy garbage cans full of debris up into dumpsters with just my sheer force of will. Each evening, Scot and I came home, stumbled into the shower, and blew out huge globs of black dirt, plaster, and wood dust from our noses, cleaning out the day's cuts and wounds.

This was pre-nail-gun construction so there was a lot of hammering over the course of a day which was a bitch even for the more practiced among us. Of all the valuable experiences that I've had in my life which have bestowed upon me the blessing of deeper empathy for others, the experience of coming home physically exhausted and in pain from manual labor, day after day, month after month, is right up there. I just wanted a wife to set a hot meal in front of me and get me a beer . . . and if I could've yelled at her, I would've.

The first time I ever helped Scot on a construction site was before I was officially in the employ of Wildcat Builders. He was behind schedule on a job and I went with him on a weekend to help him get some shit done. We were on the third floor of a house that had been taken down to the joists so you had to step carefully, beam to beam, trying not to look down through the spaces in between to the second floor below you.

The task at hand was to sister new joists to the old ones, which had had to be cut in the course of the renovation. He showed me how to measure down some inches, make a mark, measure again, check the mark, drill a hole through both joists, and then fasten a bolt through the hole. I went through the process on the next beam while he observed. Then, satisfied that I was competent, he went off to do something else. I went through the process on one more beam before it became apparent to me that I could make my work more efficient by measuring each beam first, then drilling each beam and then bolting each beam in a flow. I saw Scot look over and smile at my efficiency. Our partnership had only just begun.

We were opposites in many ways but Scot was the smartest, most informed person I'd ever met and we connected in the arena of our political idealism and on the mountain of our shared work ethic. His formative years were in the honorable Jimmy Carter's America and then the whole Iran-Contra deal came to kick off his adulthood of outrage and disillusionment. He was an activist who had been protesting the Reagan Revolution and the havoc it was wreaking in places like the Middle East and Central America . . . and in Rust Belt cities like Buffalo. He had graduated with a degree in history from the University of Buffalo and introduced me to books like Dee Brown's *Bury My Heart at Wounded Knee* and Howard Zinn's *A People's History of the United States*. He introduced me to Lenny Bruce, Mark Twain, and Noam Chomsky. He had exactly ten years on me and he was a veritable fountain of information. I was nothing if not an eager student.

Scot, a builder-of-things, was an excellent friend to have as I happened to be preparing to set out on a journey that would require an arc. I would eventually present Scot with his greatest building challenge (Righteous Babe Records) and he would meet it and help me rock some old ideas about the music business from their foundations. The record company will take years to develop though, and by that time, the tables will have turned and he will be working for me.

THE ROAD NOT TAKEN

Ingeri got impregnated by a questionable dude when we were both sixteen. Not only did she have the baby, she married the dude. Our paths, already divergent, would diverge sharply then and in her life path

I could see the road not taken for me. I went to her wedding as a guest, I rode my bike there, and was saddened to see how sad she was that day. Two of her bridesmaids didn't show, an indication that the group she'd fallen in with was not really supportive of her, did not really care about her, would soon leave her a lonely single mom. She stood there at the altar next to the mean dude, pregnant, with tear-stained eyes and nobody to back her up.

We got together a few times in the remaining years that I spent in Buffalo, me, her, and her baby, but we had less and less in common. She would tell me about her job at American Brass and I would tell her about my adventures. We struggled to relate to each other. My world began to feel impossibly free and unfettered compared to hers. Just as I was hitting my stride and moving into my own skin, she was being deflated, her shoulders bending under some invisible weight. She was growing bitter and sarcastic. I looked up with a sigh and counted my lucky stars every time I left her apartment. I felt sad for her and then I felt guilty for feeling pity. I felt lucky and then I felt childish for feeling lucky.

We would eventually fall out of contact altogether until almost twenty years later when my dad died. I was standing by my father's open casket, his body strangely bloated from the work of the undertaker, looking more like Mussolini than my dad, when in she walked. I couldn't believe how good it was to see her face. She who really knew me at my core. She who really knew my father, too, back when he was still fully himself. It was suddenly like no time had passed and the old friendship that we'd shared as girls returned.

I was grateful that she showed up that day and I have been grateful for her friendship ever since. She has worked factory jobs most of her life and I have traipsed around the world playing my guitar. Around the time I became a mother, she became a grandmother. But it no longer seems hard to relate to each other. We speak directly to each other's hearts, bypassing the skin of circumstance. We have a lot in common.

three

MAKING SONGS 2

For me, they mostly start with a single stance, almost like a mood or an as yet unnamed hue. I favor hues that are hard to name. *Is that a brownish gold? Or a greenish tan?* Plus, I like it when the color changes depending on how you look at it. Maybe it's a line or two with some sort of energy humming inside it. Maybe it's a whole first verse and a sketch of a chorus, all thought up while walking along or lying in bed. A song's seed can be thin and frail or fat and strong. If the seed manages to blow into my journal, it looks around for allies or some earth in which to stake a claim. A song might start wordlessly, while I'm just hanging out with my guitar. Just a chord progression and a groove. But always inside is a feeling, too. Some energy, some exact color, trying to make itself known.

You want to know something weird? I have noticed (now with literally hundreds of songs behind me) that I will repeat a certain sound a lot during a certain period of my life. I mean, like a letter sound. As in: oh yeah, that was my "r" period. (Recently, I moved through an "i" phase.) I have noticed, too, that certain musical keys and harmonic relationships will dominate depending on my state of being and that seems to make sense but . . . *letter sounds*? Do certain basic uttered sounds have emotional or psychological, *energetic* corollaries? Could all these complicated narratives that I've been weaving be just an excuse to make the "s" sound a lot? I mean, maybe these sound clusters are coincidental but . . . maybe not. "The medium is the message" indeed.

The initial spark of inspiration, that's the easy part for me. There are so many haunting, interesting, and beautiful hues to bear witness to in this world. If anything, I consider the elusive step of 0 to 1 (the part that presents the challenge for so many) to be the easy part. The challenge for me is taking all those fleeting hues and painstakingly executing whole paintings with them. It's the elaboration process that's the killer. An emotional color is something to focus on while moving through the exhausting realm of words but "fleeting hues" (sarcastically now, I am teasing myself) usually resist allowing words to come and nail their asses down. It can become an excruciating struggle. Between the opening lines and the final notes of a song, there are bushes to be whacked and ditches to be dug in the realm of words. There is the brain-breaking work of laying a road through wilderness. And of course, once there is the semblance of a road, there are many optional turns to take. There are cliffs to avoid.

MY OTHER OTHER VOICE

Singing was always a very different matter from playing. I discovered the voice in my guitar when I was still a kid but I would be a grown woman before I would really start to find the voice in my own body. In the meantime, I followed my spleen and my subliminal influences into singing. Standing back from myself and hearing the sounds I was uttering, making adjustments accordingly . . . that would come years in the future.

Before even Michael, my first singing teacher was my mother. She was the one who sang me to sleep at night as a child and it was her voice that floated above all the rest in church. My parents rejected organized religion in favor of a more modern context for morality known as civic engagement, but up at the lake every summer we made a particular exception and attended regular Sunday services. Around the lake, "church" was held at a different house every week (except for ours because we lacked space and basic amenities) and was a matter of family and community more than religion.

Each Sunday, we would paddle over to some cousin's house and listen to a service conducted by that person, the content of which was their choice. The piano players would play at the houses that were graced with pianos and otherwise we would just stand and sing from the Protestant hymnals that had factored so hugely into our extended family history. My mother sang only and always in a trilling falsetto and her tone was quiet but piercingly clear. She had a dead-ringer pitch that she graciously gifted me with, but her style was reserved and never once did I hear her open her mouth and really use her full voice.

My mother's influence on my singing included peripheral elements like sitting up or standing very straight and enunciating clearly. Both of those instructions were given to me constantly as a child, whether I was singing or not, and were considered aspects of being a respectable person. I was also instructed to look people in the eye when speaking to them and to use proper grammar. "Ingeri and *I*, not Ingeri and *me*," my mom would say each time I misspoke and I would have to repeat back to her the correct grammar before I could finish my sentence. To mumble or look down or slouch was disrespectful and it was drilled deeply into me by the time I was a teenager to do none of those things.

If I look back at how I approached the world as a young adult, including performing and singing, my mother's influence is everywhere. I was aggressive with eye contact and diction and posture. I echoed my mother's energy and wit and even her trilling songbird tone. Deeper inside I carried her feminist outrage and eventually I would express that, too. My father's gentle gaze, his relaxed and accepting approach to life and to all manner of human character would have to lie in wait inside me for a safer, more relaxed time. The time that was stretching out before me was to be no less stressful or more safe. I was about to leave Buffalo behind.

IF YOU CAN MAKE IT THERE . . .

My two-month summer sublet on Hudson Street just below Fourteenth was in the Meatpacking District of Manhattan. The smell of meat and piss and diesel was enough to gag a pedestrian on a hot afternoon. At night, the queer sex clubs turned on their red lightbulbs and led people down into the basements of our building and others in the vicinity. I could lean out my wide-open warehouse window at night and watch the transvestite prostitutes work the cobblestone street below me, getting into fancy cars and driving off briefly, then coming back. It was like living in some dank forgotten corner of the city where all the messiest stuff was allowed to spill and then be washed away with the rain. There was an edginess to the neighborhood that made my adrenaline turn on its pump every time I left the building.

My room was in a loft on the top floor of a triangular-shaped brick warehouse positioned like a runaway ship that had come unmoored down at the Holland Tunnel and plowed into Fourteenth Street. The building was full of raw communal lofts in developing states of habitability and legality. The homesteaders on the fourth floor had just made a killing hosting some filming of the popular movie *Fatal Attraction*. Glenn Close's character (the bunny-boiling she-devil) was a fictional resident of the fourth floor but unfortunately, the freight elevator only worked long enough for Close and Michael Douglas to make out in it. Once the movie company had gone, the elevator was off limits again and it was a real-life walk-up.

The fifth floor was a gay S&M bar before it became the dwelling of six or seven rock-n-rollers that I moved into. There were two toilet stalls and two sinks in the bathroom and a raised stage right in front of you when you walked in the door. AIDS had swept through the landscape like a dark cloud and shut down many of the sex clubs overnight. A collection of items had been left behind in our apartment, including a big two-ended dildo, some Mexican wrestling masks, and a ten-foot bullwhip. My particular room was equipped with a floor-to-ceiling cage that had shackles still hanging from the top crossbar. It made for good book storage.

The summer of 1989 was a hot one. I walked from my hot room down into the hot subway every day and took the L train across the East River to a hot kitchen situated underneath the base of the Brooklyn Bridge. I had gotten a minimum-wage job at a high-end catering company which was hired to do events such as Rupert Murdoch's birthday party on a Concorde flight from New York to Paris. It was a great job for a starving kid because not only did I get to eat from the lunch that the chefs whipped up on the side every day, I frequently went home with the ends of tomatoes or potatoes, whatever was left over from the day's prepping. The day I came home with a big bag of veal scraps, I suddenly became my housemates' favorite new person.

My duties in that kitchen were: Clean what they tell you to clean, chop what they tell you to chop. One day, what needed chopping was a big sack of jalapeño peppers and first, all the seeds removed. Nobody bothered to give me gloves to work with so I learned that the oils from those peppers will eventually soak into your skin and cannot be washed out. I was up all night crying with my hands on fire.

I also took the subway uptown to an art school and picked up work as a nude model for some drawing classes. Having taken my share of figure-drawing classes back at Buffalo State when I was sixteen and seventeen and being a dancer from way back, I had more than what it took to be a good artist's model. I noticed on the employment form that "draped" models made a higher wage than "undraped" ones. *How terrific!* I thought, *more money and I don't have to get naked!* I told the lady behind the desk that I wanted to be a draped model. She looked at me drolly over her glasses and told me they were not looking for draped models.

The continuing education classes at that art school were the best because they seemed to be populated by kindly older Jewish men who would insist and insist until I let them buy me a cup of coffee or a sandwich and tell me about how I reminded them of their daughters. No harm in a sandwich. My pride usually forbade a handout of any kind but these men seemed to need me even more than I needed a sandwich so I accepted their kindness to be kind.

There were so many moments when I should've milked men for goods and services in my young life but each time, my pride forbade it. I was often left wondering: If someone in these stupid scenarios has to be the sucker then why the hell am I always electing myself? Like that time I got a call from that lawyer friend of Dale's in Buffalo, the one who had made the contract between us. He called to say he was in New York and did I want to get together? I was surprised. I took the train up to the Theater District to meet him at some restaurant with celebrity 8x10s hanging all over the walls. We had burgers and fries and spoke of Buffalo and of our mutual acquaintances. I had gotten my nose pierced on the street that day by some random dude with an ear-piercing gun (why not?) and lawyerman couldn't get over this punk rock move.

He suggested we go for a walk in the park but said he needed to pick up something from his room first. When we got up to his hotel room he put the moves on me in some gross blurry way and I found myself dematerializing and rematerializing by the door. When he realized I was slipping through his fingers, he tried to hand me a twenty for "a cab home" but I said no thanks and spun away. *You could've at least gotten the twenty bucks!* my mind shouted at me all the way home on the train. *What the hell is wrong with you?!* Leaning back, shimmying in the seat, face serene, eyes closed . . . all the while, my mind pacing and gesticulating . . . *Twenty bucks coulda made your fuckin' week, stupid!*

At some point, traversing the East River to make a pittance on the Brooklyn side started to seem less than ideal so I quit the kitchen job and followed a classified ad to the UPS factory on the West Side Highway north of my neighborhood, in Hell's Kitchen. I endured the week-long training course and then was handed my shift, 3:00 a.m.–11:00 a.m., and told to report to work the next day. Stepping out of my building on Hudson Street in the middle of the night, I walked across Fourteenth Street and waited for the bus to take me to Port Authority.

Port Authority was in fine form at that time of night and I was quick to get out of there, though the scariest part of my journey was still ahead of me. I had to make the terrifying walk to the UPS central packing facility entrance all along the dim, deserted side of the block-long building. Every ten feet or so, there was another indentation in the building big and deep enough for several men to stand in. You could not see into these recesses until you were upon them and my stomach was so tight by the time I reached the front door that I leaned on the wall after getting safely inside, to recapture my breathing.

I was shocked at what went down that first morning at UPS. My foreman, a Puerto Rican man named Jesus, showed me which truck was mine to fill and pointed up at the chart hanging above the conveyor belt as though it was supposed to explain everything to me. (Shit, did I miss this part of the class?) I had no idea which packages to pick up and put on what shelves of the truck when the belt suddenly started running and boxes started hurling down. I looked around, is this really happening? Jesus was gone. I started picking up all the boxes that were not too big or too heavy and loading my truck by putting the lightest boxes up the highest. I can't begin to imagine what happened to the driver of that truck that day or any of the days that I worked for UPS.

Lucky for UPS, I soon realized that getting to that job every morning was gonna get me hurt or killed so I succumbed to the irrefutable math and quit. One of the men I worked with told me I should hang on because the company was trying to reach affirmative action quotas by hiring more females and I could probably get promoted to driver before any of them. "Drive a UPS truck around the crowded streets of New York?! Oh, geez no," I said, "That would not be good. I don't care how much it pays."

EPONYMOUS DEBUT

I was in New York for all of about five minutes when I had written a whole new batch of songs that rendered all the songs I'd written in Buffalo obsolete. I returned to Buffalo on the Lake Shore Limited train to commit these songs directly to DAT (this newfangled thing known as digital audio tape) in front of two microphones in a humble little recording studio. Dale helped me get two hundred and fifty tapes run off (we were being ambitious) and a black and white jacket printed up. It is the record now known as my eponymous debut. When I first started seeing reviews of my tape in local entertainment rags, the word "eponymous" came up each time. Why does everybody think my record is so eponymous, I wondered? What the hell does eponymous even mean? (Oh.)

Scot was still living at 760 Ashland and I would periodically come back and visit from New York, wearing more combat armor each time from doing battle in The Big Shitty. The other inhabitants of the apartment had shifted, as Tanya and Joe had moved out and Suzi moved in. Suzi was sharing her room with Steve, the man she would later marry. Scot offered to take a photo of me with his old Nikon camera for my album cover. He turned on all the lamps in his bedroom and snapped a few pictures. I had shaved off all my hair and it was a shorn me staring back into the camera.

The shaved head was an instinctual move on my part to exit the world of male come-ons and exact credibility and respect as a card-carrying member of the American Radical Left. I had heard and read all about the sexism of the antiwar and civil rights movements, just to name a few. (Question: What was the position of women in the [fill in the blank] movement? Answer: prone.) My decision as a young woman to shave off all my hair and wear army boots as footwear was an insistence that the objectification of women in the people's revolution shall stop with me. "Look upon me as you would Che Guevara or Huey P. Newton!" my uniform said. "Run me down, lock me up! Just whatever you do, don't treat me like something to fuck or not fuck." The shaved head was a re/action that engendered fear and suspicion from the general public but was instantly recognized and understood by other young women for what it was.

It is especially funny to me that I started getting followed around stores by security guards and even asked to leave certain places once I had a shaved head because all of my shoplifting had been done years earlier when I was sixteen and had long, flowing hair. As an emancipated teenager, I experienced some lean years and shoplifting (in corporate chain stores, never in Ma and Pa operations) got me through. Bulk food was just starting to catch on in big supermarkets in Buffalo in the mid-eighties and I would go into them and graze my way to a full belly while shopping for a few meager supplies. I would open a drink and consume it while I wandered around the store. I got caught more than once and was given a slap on the wrist and told not come back to this store and then to that one.

One time I got caught shoplifting a shirt at the Main Place Mall downtown and got myself arrested. I guess I never really was all that good at shoplifting. I was brought to the Buffalo Holding Center and put in a cell with a skinny, twitchy old black lady. I say "old" but she was probably not much older than I am now . . . or much skinnier really. At one point, she pulled a joint out of her underwear and asked me if I had a light. "Are you crazy?" I whispered. I suggested she flush it down the lidless toilet that was the only object in the room other than a bench. She didn't. Instead she put it back in her underwear. "Man, lady," I said, "you'd better watch it with these people."

Finally, I was let out of the cell to make a phone call and I called Ingeri's dad, Fred. He came down and posted my bail and drove me home to my apartment. I had to pay Fred his money back and I had to agree to see a youth counselor for a while to get my record cleaned up. The youth counselor shook his head at me and let me stop coming to my probation meetings before I was supposed to. He just waved his hand at me and said, "Get out of here," which I appreciated very much.

Over the course of that first year of my association with Dale, he managed to change course from getting me a record deal and being the guy who discovered me, to actually helping me and being my friend. A few cheesy, low-level music biz guys did come sniffing around, with and without Dale as their chaperone, but each time I saw it for what it was: a trap and a diversion from the street-level interface that I was seeking for my art. The act of sharing songs with people while looking straight into their eyes, that was what compelled me. I craved that feeling of trust and understanding that develops between people who are being totally real with each other. I was searching, through music, for the experience of family. It may have been one part pathetic but, as a singular motivation, it meant that there was nothing keeping me from being thrilled every time I connected myself to someone through music. Even if it was just one person. There was no need to long for something more.

That said, simply having a recording to sell propelled my life and my personal finances forward with a bound. I had taken part in some evenings of spoken word at Nietzsche's in Buffalo (another brainchild of Michael's) and on the bill was this tough punk-poet from Rochester named David Ripton. David was sexy and more than a little edgy and showed up in Buffalo wearing just long underwear. He told me he ran a weekly poetry slam at this place called Jazzberry's in Rochester and I should come and do a guest set. Dale drove me to Rochester that first time and I discovered that Jazzberry's was this terrific community arts space run by a cool lady named Susan Plunkett. They even cooked up good food there. Susan and her crew made sure young artists felt welcomed and nourished.

I didn't earn any money from the door that first night in Rochester but I sure did earn two hundred bucks selling twenty tapes. That was what is known as a game changer. Real money! I remember Dale put out a mailing list and I got tons of names and addresses, too. I never would have taken that mailing list thing seriously but he and Scot both insisted it was important. "Put it out!" they told me. As it happens, they were right and it made a big difference as I continued down a path towards a career in music. That mailing list was my pre-internet, direct outreach to each and every person in the world who gave a shit about my art. Each address was written down by hand and collected by hand (mine).

On the inside flap of my eponymous debut, we put an address for people to write to. We got a P.O. box in Buffalo to receive any potential correspondence and Dale became its overseer. I scribbled "Righteous Records" as the name on the P.O. box and I also scribbled it onto the tape jacket flap itself. The name came as a smirking response to all the patronizing questions of, "So, you're a singer, huh? You got a record deal?" It seemed the whole world considered a record deal to be the one barometer of success and legitimacy. Heck, maybe it was, but anyway, screw that, I thought. I hated the whole thing. When the "Babe" got added to the name later, the smirk got a little twinkle in the eye just above.

Mail did come in. More and more of it. Letters from college kids (mostly young women but guys, too) would arrive saying: I have a two-hundred-dollar entertainment budget, can Ani come play our Blahdy Blahfest? Such was the unfolding of my invitation to the road life. I would start out, boarding a train or bus with my sky-blue fifties suitcase from the Salvation Army full of tapes and my guitar in its brightly painted case, and I would end up exploring the whole continent in concentric circles. The painted guitar case was a security measure, so that even in a dark bar on a night with many performers, I would always notice my guitar walking by.

I stood at countless pay phones in countless places and dialed the 1-800 number at the *Buffalo News* to check in with Dale. He'd fill me in on the letters and gig offers and what indie record store had offered to take ten tapes on consignment. Then off I would go to play Blahdy Blahfest in New Brunswick, or a student union hall in Indiana or a take-back-the-night rally in Kalamazoo. Apparently, thankfully, the world still needed a folksinger and through the address on that first cassette, the world came and found me.

TRAVELING SALESMEN

I was such an anti-capitalist punk from the git-go that I could never bring myself to even tell an audience that I had tapes for sale. Dale and Scot both pleaded with me to do myself a favor and simply mention that I had tapes but something about it made me feel like a jerk. *I'm an artist*, I thought, *not a traveling salesman*. Besides, anyone who really wants a tape will ask. The label "entrepreneur" that media has pegged me with for twenty years really couldn't be more ironic . . . if you're me. Entrepreneurship (at least as an end in itself) could not have been further from the point. The point was not to conquer the world of business so much as to devise a way of having a career in music without having to engage the world of business at all. I came to represent the future of the music industry, but I meant only to avoid it.

Luckily for me, there was this whole underground world out there of little indie music stores and women's bookstores and I slowly but surely got plugged into my wing of the counterculture. The first people to step up to the plate and offer any semblance of distribution for my records beyond my direct consignment accounts were the two national women's music catalogues, Goldenrod and Ladyslipper. They produced these black and white newsprint mail-order publications wherein you could find all the records being made by women out there in the wild and woolly world beyond the top of the pops. They distributed the top of the pops too, though, and I'll bet a lot of conscious feminists made sure to buy their Madonna records from them.

Goldenrod and Ladyslipper were not-for-profit organizations of feminists trying to help the voices of women to find entry into the culture. In those days, if my records were available in record stores at all, they were generally racked in the "Women's Music" ghetto in the back corner. Yes, that's right, the "Women's Music" section. Who remembers that? It was usually one small row or a half a row of tapes and CDs by a myriad of feminists, mostly dykes. It's hard to even imagine now, only twenty-five years later, how little home in this world a voice like mine had. Chick singers were one thing, a feminist singing was a whole other matter.

My very first cassette could be found in the Goldenrod and Ladyslipper catalogues but not much of anywhere else. Same with my second album and my third . . . and so on. For many years, I traveled around and heard this sentence at every gig: "Where can I get your records? I can't find them anywhere!" My only answer was, ". . . uh, Goldenrod? Ladyslipper?" Of course, in this pre-internet world, this would-be buyer of my records would have to go into a women's bookstore, where they might have those catalogues on hand, and make a special order. Thank Goddess for those dedicated feminists at Goldenrod and Ladyslipper, who had my back long before any commercial music distribution companies ever looked my way! People did just that.

Demand before supply. That's the reality of my supposed entrepreneurial genius. It sucked to spend so many years hearing from people that they wanted to buy my records but couldn't. My audience and I were locked into a lose/lose situation because of my anti-capitalist convictions and I had to wake up and remind myself every day, *Okay, right . . . why have I chosen this path, again? What the fuck is my point?* I had to employ a decade's worth of patience, until enough people had walked into enough record stores asking for my records that word actually got back to distributors. First stores were looking for my stuff, asking their distributors, and then the distributors were looking for me. When major distribution companies did come calling, I went with the biggest indie that was not under the umbrella of a major. It was a joint called Koch.

In the meantime, I'd heard about this famous folk club in Saratoga Springs by the name of Caffè Lena so I mailed my cassette there with a note. Rather than spend money on a padded envelope, I reused one that I had received mail in. "Di Franco Recycling Corp," I wrote on the package along with jokes like: "Warning! Hazardous folk materials inside." The woman who booked the place said my package and my cassette made an impression on her so she offered me a gig.

Dale drove with me to Saratoga Springs that first time and I played for a handful of people in the tiniest room imaginable. (This is the famous folk club?!) I remember Ingeri's father and brother Julian came. They had driven there from Albany where Julian now resided. That was the magic of the mailing list right there. A few other people drove from a few other places. Luckily, the room was so small that ten people felt like a decent crowd. Once again, the tape sales kept me afloat.

After that first Caffè Lena hit, Dale and I had an uncomfortable moment standing at the check-in desk of a nearby motel. We had decided to spring for a room in Saratoga Springs instead of driving the five hours back to Buffalo that night. The lady behind the desk asked us if we wanted a room with one bed or two and we both died inside while Dale chuckled nervously and said "two."

PAY TO PLAY

Back in New York, I made a list of every downtown club that might plausibly give me a gig and I started walking into each of them in the afternoon, tape in hand. I'd ask who booked the joint and then I'd try to convince that person that they should hire me. Whatever I was offered, my answer was always yes. I took any sorry-ass gig I could find, including pay-to-play situations. Pay to play is exactly as it sounds: You are given a slot but only after you buy a bunch of tickets to your own show which you are then responsible for selling, to get your own money back.

One such night, at a forgettable club, I split a night with a band of preppy boys called Spo-De-O-Dee. For some reason that band name burned itself into my brain. They were nice boys who seemed fascinated by the feral little animal that was me and they invited me to hang out with them at one of their (parents') abodes afterwards. It was an amazing journey, in a car of all things, uptown to a uniformed doorman high-rise the likes of which I'd never entered before. I'm not sure if the place qualified as a penthouse but it felt like one to me. The guys offered to drive me back home afterwards so, in the wee hours, we all piled back into their car and headed back downtown.

When we pulled up in front of the triangle building they were hesitant to drop me off. "You sure you're okay?" I looked through their eyes at my building and was struck anew by its indelible creepiness. "Yeah, I'm cool, thanks you guys!" They drove away never to be seen again. That is, except for their lead singer, Jesse Harris, who would return to my awareness many years later as the successful songwriter who penned most of Norah Jones's early hits. It took me a minute to remember that night and his face when our paths crossed again a decade later. The band name brought it all back.

I found myself battling a generalized depression brought on by the city itself. The coldness and anonymity that allowed a metropolis of this scale to function seemed to hurt my feelings on a daily basis. The perma-smile that my face had shown up with got wiped away daily until it finally sputtered out and a more appropriately noncommittal expression took its place. Watching people battle each other, dismiss and step over each other, watching them lean on their horns to get one another out of the way, it all left me with a melancholy that I had to work to overcome. But then, as I paused to look up at some artful wrought iron, a man leaning on a signpost would say to me, "Beautiful, ain't it, sweetheart?" and the moment of our eyes meeting would be a reprieve from my loneliness. Swinging, weightless, between fleeting points of connection, I navigated the urban jungle like Tarzan.

The original Knitting Factory on Houston gave me a few gigs, mostly in that tiny room downstairs called the Knot Room. That little club on Third Avenue by St. Marks Place, The Continental Divide, they gave me some gigs. The Wetlands was super supportive and started offering me opening slots whenever they had one unfilled. Slowly, I found allies and kindred spirits in and amongst the cold, impersonal terrain. I got so I could sense when, soundchecking in an empty barroom in the afternoon, my guitar was making me a new friend. A bar-back or bartender would pause his set-up work when I hit my first few chords and rock back on his heels to squint at me. Fellow guitar players came out of the woodwork and punctured my isolation with little pin pricks of camaraderie.

Of course, there were also men who tried to pick fights with me wherever I went. There were dudes everywhere unaccustomed to hearing a voice like mine singing words like those and their hackles would go up. As soon as I exited the stage they'd be there to sign me up for debate club. And then there were the sound guys in whose hands my whole show rested. My well-practiced smile came in handy with them and I tried to kill each house sound guy with kindness in hopes that I could work him around to considering me more amusing than annoying.

Between the content of my lyrics and my insistence that each sound engineer do something he'd never done before, I seemed to be running up against every defensive male ego there was.

I had already developed a conception of the acoustic guitar that was contrary to the scritchy, bright sound most people assigned to the instrument so I was in a position, night after night, of trying to convince the sound guy to deviate from what he always did. I was simply requesting that they dump all the high end on the guitar EQ and pump the low end until it was somewhere in the vicinity of massive. This facilitated my ability to be a one-woman band. My scene was to literally low-pass the guitar, starting the roll-off at about 6 kHz, and then crank up the bottom at 100, 80, even down to 60 kHz (a sub-harmonic frequency usually reserved for bass and kick drums). That's when they would really balk. "60?!" Sound guys will go from aghast to angry in worse than no time. They will resist.

It became imperative that I grow a thicker skin or at least learn a few more coping mechanisms than I'd had in Buffalo, where everyone just thought of me as harmless little Ani. My skin became . . . not so much tougher but more elastic. I learned to absorb people's anger and bounce it back into the world in the form of poems and songs. I learned to focus my sights, like a scientist squinting down a microscope, at the glimmers of support and connection. Because those moments sustained me, I worked like a mule for them.

STRAYS

When the triangle building sublet (courtesy of Suzi's brother) was up, I moved straight south onto the western edge of the Village, on Greenwich Street. It was a basement apartment inhabited by two young, upwardly mobile Jewish boys who put on shirts and ties each morning and went off to imitate their parents. One of them was really nice and did things like take me up to Westchester on a lovely autumnal Sunday afternoon. "You need to get outta here," he said. "You wanna go for a drive?"

That basement apartment was not only windowless (because it was underground, of course) but it was Grand Central Station for all the vermin in the building. Mice (rats?) ran across my feet at night while I lay on my futon (don't throw food away in your wastebasket, stupid!) and roaches of every type were just simply everywhere. There were so many roaches you couldn't even try to kill them. That would have amounted to a full-time job. You just had to bang on the kitchen counters after turning on the light, to scatter them long enough to make a sandwich. I got so used to roaches that I would no longer jump or startle even when they were on me. I remember brushing my teeth one night and looking in the bathroom mirror to see a huge one on my shoulder, his antenna checking out the side of my face. I just flicked it off and kept brushing my teeth. It's amazing how adaptable human beings can be.

The living room was a narrow cave just big enough for a huge flatscreen TV along one side wall, which was the prize possession of my other housemate. It was the first flatscreen TV I or anyone had ever seen and it was bigger than anyone thought possible. The room itself was not that big and you couldn't really get far enough away from the damn thing to comfortably watch it, if you asked me, but there those two would be, eating cereal and watching the game, heads moving side to side to take in the action. I stayed in that apartment underground as little as possible.

One day my friend Daniel, a gay dancer whom I'd worked with back in Buffalo, called to say he was moving to New York and could he crash with me until he found a place? He slept on our couch with his big feet hanging off the first night but then the next night he asked, "Can I just sleep in your bed with you?" "Oh! Okay!" was all I could think to say. And so it went that Daniel and I spent a few weeks spooning on my futon while he reinvented his life in The City.

One day we were sitting in a diner eating greasy eggs and he let out a tiny squeak like a little pink balloon. I looked up and he was making crazy eyeballs at me, whispering: Don't look, but the dude in the next booth is a porn star. Of course, I looked. When we got home he revealed to me a magazine centerfold featuring the man from the diner. The dude was waxed completely hairless and spread-eagled for the camera. "Yow! Cocks and balls look so weird without hair!" I said. "Yeah," Daniel agreed, giggling.

Daniel had a habit of buying and consuming a pint of Häagen-Dazs ice cream every evening and unfortunately, when we were running partners, I fell into this habit with him. He was a six-foot-four strapping young man and his body made quick work of it but my body got overwhelmed. I gained weight and my face was suddenly covered in acne. It was years before I would catch on that dairy was not a thing that my skin can deal with. My face becomes an oil slick. I had many very humbling experiences of standing on stages with zits all over my face in the meantime. Very, very humbling. I want to tap the shoulders of people with pimples and just whisper into their ear, "One word: dairy. Doctors don't know shit. Stop eating it completely for at least four months . . . to reset your system . . . maybe six . . . just trust me."

Daniel eventually got his own place but I was not done eating Häagen-Dazs or taking in strays. One night I ended up at some apartment that seemed to be populated with an assortment of drug-addled, dubious characters and also several generations of unneutered and unspayed cats. There were multiple litters of skinny kittens, some with foggy eyes, all with fleas. "What happens to all these kittens?" I asked someone. They'll kill them soon, was basically the answer. After taking in the scene, my response was to pick up the smallest runt I could see and walk out the door. A questionable move at best. On a whim, I had tied my fate to that of a tiny, helpless little black kitten. The runt with the chip on her shoulder no less. Now there were two of us.

Stella moved around New York with me on foot as frequently as every few months. She was always the last "load" on moving day and she clung to my neck with her paws as we walked down the street together. Out on the terrifying streets she would treat me as friend and protector but as soon as we got to our new digs, she turned back into psycho kitty. Despite all my attempts to mother her, she never was more than one scratch beyond feral.

I tried to pawn Stella off on many a housemate and lover in the fifteen years that followed but each time she came back to me. We would look at each other and she would look away, ever victorious. Eventually, I ended up bringing her to Buffalo and dumping her on Scot. He took care of her until she finally, grudgingly, died in his arms at the ripe old age of fuck-you-all.

TOO GOOD TO BE TRUE

It was a child's school desk, the kind that has the chair attached, and it was on the curb with the trash outside a grammar school in the West Village. The desk top and chair seat were made of wood and they were connected by a metal frame. The whole thing was built for a tiny person, but I stared at this desk, trying to convince myself that I was a tiny person and that this desk could be mine. I sat in it, I stood up and stared at it some more, I sat in it again. Trouble was . . . how was I gonna get it home? It was then that I realized a man was standing next to me. "I have a hand truck you could use to get that home," he said when I turned. A middle-aged man, white, tall, was smiling at me. "Really?" I said.

The man lived just a few blocks away, so I walked with him to retrieve his hand truck. His apartment was at the end of a quaint little alley street, the kind that makes tourists in New York stop and take pictures. To get to it, you had to approach from the main street, walk through the lobby of one building, then through a courtyard and into his building and up some beautifully tiled stairs. I was enchanted. The enchanted part ended when he opened the door to his apartment. It was dirty and cluttered and crammed high with junk. It became clear he was one of those Village eccentrics that had been living in a rent-controlled place for so long that he could swing being poor and crazy in what was now an affluent and spiffy zone. His dandruffy cat came and rubbed against my legs.

I took the hand truck and moved the desk seven blocks to my underground lair (not easy) and when I returned, sweaty and steamy, to the dump on quaint street, the man began telling me things. He explained why his abode was the way it was, he had all kinds of excuses, including a wife who'd abandoned him and other turns of bad luck. He showed me around, such as he could. In his messy bedroom was carved out just enough space for his smelly bed and in the other bedroom there was one path by which you could reach the other side of the room and the large windows overlooking the pretty lane. I told him he was lucky to live in such a beautiful apartment and he should really clean it out. I told him that I lived underground and would kill to live in a place like this. It was then he made his offer.

If I was willing to clean out this second bedroom, he said, he would rent it out to me for what I was paying for my current apartment. That's what he said. I could feel the weight of his craziness but I was so covetous of the space and so eager to get out from underground that I went against my better judgment and agreed. He actually pointed out that there was a lock on the bedroom door so I could keep my room locked if I wanted. That is what I will do, I thought. It'll be fine.

It was not easy cleaning out that room, that's for sure. Luckily, the man seemed to have no particular attachment to all this stuff he'd been hoarding and was more than happy to watch me bust ass and haul it all out to the street. I did it, all of it, right down to mopping the floor and sponge cleaning the baseboards and windowsills. Then I moved in my futon, my guitar, my boom box, and Stella and bam! We were living the high life! Stella did not have the issues with other cats that she did with bipeds, so she was happy enough there. Every night, I locked the door to our room, pushed aside the feelings of creepiness, and listened to her purr.

The thing with my door lock was that it only worked from the inside, so I could lock myself in when I was home but I couldn't keep him out of my room when I was gone. I soon began to discover my stuff perturbed every time I returned. In fact, it became clear that when I left town on my little trips he would sleep in my bed. He didn't try to hide this, instead he seemed to make sure I knew about it, leaving the most obvious signs around. He apparently relished this bit of suggestion and intimidation and enjoyed watching me politely squirm, my hands tied by the person who was now effectively my landlord. I was going to have to reckon for my deadly sin. Thou shalt not covet thy neighbor's apartment.

NOW VOYAGER

On the back page of the *Village Voice*, my eyes found themselves lingering on ads for travel companies with names like Now Voyager. They were advertising plane tickets to Europe for a couple hundred dollars. The catch was, the seats were first purchased by a mail or freight company of some kind so the traveler was allowed to bring only carry-on luggage. They were closed tickets that usually had a return in a week. *First*, I thought, *I need to get a passport.*

I bought a Now Voyager ticket to London because I figured at least in England people speak the language my songs are written in. Since I would need to sweet talk my guitar onto the plane with me, I didn't want to push it by also carrying a backpack so all I brought beyond my guitar was a fanny pack around my waist. That is what's known as traveling light. The ticket turned out to be on Air India.

I was sitting at Kennedy Airport, writing excitedly in my journal, when one of the only other white people in sight, a young man, sat down next to me. His name, amusingly, was James Bond and he was from a little English town called Maulden. He was taking a break from injecting soybeans at the University of Whatever to return home for a short visit. James chatted me up until the plane started boarding and then he told me how nice it had been to meet me and went off to prepare to board himself. Guitar safely stashed in the plane's rear closet, I was sitting in my window seat watching the activity on the tarmac when up walked James again. His seat was next to mine.

We talked the whole way across the Atlantic and when the pilot announced our descent into Heathrow, I excused myself and made my way to the back of the plane like I was making one final trip to the bathroom. I looked around and when no eyes were upon me I got into the closet with my guitar and closed the accordion curtain behind me. I knew that if we landed and everyone emptied into the aisle of the huge jetliner it would be days before I could make it all the way to the back of the plane to get my axe. It seemed like a fittingly anarchistic move given the scene on the plane with all the passengers sitting cross-legged in their seats, eating rice with their hands or wandering the aisles in their saris, rocking babies. I loved Air India. The curry was delicious.

At baggage claim, James and I hugged goodbye and I walked off, having all my luggage already on my person. I headed through the exit door into the outer lobby and looked around, then I sat down in the nearest chair to think. I didn't know a soul in England. I had absolutely no place to go. "Do you have someplace to go?" a voice asked from behind me. It was James, now flanked by Mr. and Mrs. Bond. Before I knew it, I was squeezing hilariously into the smallest car I'd ever seen with the entire Bond family, my guitar, and James's luggage for the hour-and-a-half drive to Maulden. When we arrived, Mrs. Bond showed me immediately to a little spare bedroom for a nap and woke me up a couple of hours later with my first cup of proper English tea. The Bonds really couldn't have been sweeter.

That evening I was sitting at a picnic table outside a pub drinking a pint with James and his mates and marveling at my surroundings when up drove The Redheaded One in his convertible. I don't need to disguise the redheaded fellow's name because I've forgotten it, but he ended up being the next, somewhat less heartwarming stop on my adventure. Turns out he was going on a two-week holiday to Spain in a few days and James straight up said to his face, "You should let Ani stay in your room while you're gone!" The Redheaded One cast a sneer in my not-the-babe-he-was-looking-for direction but reluctantly, he agreed. I had a shaved head, mind you, and an "earring through my nose" as people called it in those days. I was not putting off an air of babe-osity but soon enough, I was riding shotgun in his red convertible, speeding down the left side of the roadway towards London.

That first night he rolled over and gave me half of his bed to sleep on but by the second night, reprehensible as it seemed, he insisted I use my body to pay him rent. A little send-off. It is hard to know sometimes what constitutes "rape." Rape is a black dot in the center of a dark smudge in the center of a very big grey cloud that dissipates and pales at the edges. I have found myself in various gradations of powerlessness around that dark center and never quite known what the name is for where I am. I imagine most women have looked down at some point in their life and not been able to see their own hands in the fog. Where am I? Am I here? . . . or here?

Landing a two-week crash pad meant of course that I did not use that return plane ticket. Instead, I made friends with all the other inhabitants of The Redheaded One's flat in Camberwell and soon after arriving, I cooked them all a spaghetti dinner which blew their minds. They all gathered around the cutting board and marveled at the amount of garlic I was chopping. They were terrified and amazed.

My first move was to suss out all the open mics in town and start showing up. One of my flatmates was a political radical and a music fan and turned on immediately to the cassette I gave him. According to him, young people in England were lazy and listless and whiling away their time on the dole while Americans were busy making revolutionary art and shattering the status quo. He loved this burgeoning thing called rap music and he respected me. He instantly became my guide to the club scene, directing me to all the open mics that count and all the right venues to hit up for a gig.

Unfortunately, the return of The Redheaded One from Spain put a hard expiration date on those most hospitable digs. I needed to get out of there before he came back. On the day of his return, I picked some flowers in a nearby park, wrote a note of thanks to the flatmates, and off I went with only that night's open mic as a destination.

It was an Irish bar, like most of the open mics, and whether because of that or simply because the spirit of the Irish seemed to mesh more seamlessly with my own, most of my friends in England from then on would actually be Irish. I played my two songs on stage that night and then, in an unprecedented move, I said, "Okay! I have nowhere to stay tonight! Who wants to take me home?" There were a few laughs and a "Hear, hear!" and, of the couple of offers I received back at the bar afterwards, I chose the one that came from a woman.

Allie was a hilarious husky-voiced drunk with blonde hair, red lipstick, and a vague connection to the music industry. We hit it off just fine and after taking me in out of the kindness of her heart, she quickly mutated the deal into renting me the spare room in her flat in Finsbury Park. "You should have a record deal," she would tell me in slightly slurred speech. "I can help you."

She introduced me to her friends in a popular Irish band called The Fat Lady Sings who were on a major label and were mixing it up in the tiny, accessible music industry of Britain. One of them became my champion and set me up a few meetings with record company people. "I am going to make you a star!" he would say with a leprechaun twinkle in his eye. I had heard it before.

I had meetings in nice offices and in restaurants over "Mexican" food (does this guacamole have mayonnaise in it?!) and various other strange settings that were apparently thought to be appealing to an American. It is a funny thing to think back now to the world before the internet, when even the most similar countries were still deeply distinct and so many of the world's little cultural details retained a penchant for being lost in translation. I personally loved that more quirky and charming world and mourn its loss in the age of global sophistication.

Pretty quickly I did receive some interest from labels and I flirted with the possibility of signing a recording contract right then and there, but once again, my instincts told me no. The most compelling offer I received was from an indie label called Cooking Vinyl, which had had success breaking another exotic American folkstress named Michelle Shocked (*oh wow, her again*). It felt like they understood my culture and, as I got to know them, I didn't find them creepy or skeezy at all. I called home to Dale and to Scot and told them of the exciting new developments. Dale, in particular, was excited.

As it happens, even the contract from Cooking Vinyl, the cool little guys, felt like indentured servitude to me. I realized I'd be answering to them for a long time in exchange for them backing me up, if they even could back me up, so instead of signing a deal, I said a polite "Sorry, never mind" to all my champions and went back to scaring up gigs. I wrote a song called "Gratitude" about my experience with The Redheaded One and I played it at the first-ever legit gig I scored at a venue called The Mean Fiddler. My former Camberwell flatmates came to the gig, save for Red Riding Hood himself, and it was a somewhat satisfying experience to call him out, if only in front of his friends.

That first gig at The Mean Fiddler was memorable for several other reasons as well, one being that, as I spoke to the club booker over the phone in advance of the show, I kept having to repeat my name to him (no, that's Ahhhhhnee, yes, Ahhhh . . . Kneeeee) and was confused momentarily when he asked me, "Isn't that a bloke's name?" "Uh, well . . . no," I said, "that's *my* name." When I showed up at the club on the night of the show I got a lesson in dialect because on the marquee it read: Arne Di Franco.

That gig also happened to be a shared bill with some red-haired girl who wheeled the piano into the middle of the barroom and played very dramatically to the indifferent and chatty crowd. I remember cowering from the tension as she stopped in the middle of a song once to chastise the disrespectful audience. I had such a self-effacing way of approaching an audience myself, I would just try to trick them into listening, and here she was approaching the challenge from the other direction. Her name was Tori Amos and at least *her* name was spelled correctly on the marquee.

Not long after that night, I was perusing *Time Out* (the cultural rag of London) and I saw an ad for the Cambridge Folk Festival. My interest was piqued. Not only was it the biggest and most prestigious gathering of folk music in the country, I noticed that my old pal Suzanne Vega was on the bill. I decided to spring for a train ticket out to Cambridge to make the scene. Of course, I didn't have enough money for an actual ticket to the festival and I had no plan as to how exactly I was gonna "make the scene" but I went for it anyway and got on the train.

It amazes me to this day that I pulled it off. Like some scene from a movie, I put the Vulcan mind meld on the security and ticket people and strutted right through the entrance gates with my guitar on my back and a look on my face like I owned the place. It worked. Safely and miraculously through the gates, I wandered about, taking in all the Celtic acts and balladeers and then I made my way to where Suzanne was signing autographs at a merchandise tent.

I stood in a very long line until finally it was my turn at the table. She stared at me blankly as I had nothing in my hands for her to sign. I must have looked very different from the nine-year-old she'd last seen in Buffalo ten years earlier. I was wearing army pants and flannel, I had a pierced nose and a bandanna around my head. After a few seconds, I said, "Hi, Suzanne, it's Ani." "Oh!" she said, "You have a bandanna on your head!" We exchanged a few awkward words and that was that, on to the next signing. No warm embrace, no "What the hell are you doing here?," no invitation to stick around. *That was ten years ago, Ani. She is famous now. What exactly were you expecting?*

That night lives in my memory as one of the bleakest I've experienced in my traveling life. It was high summer but summertime in Cambridge, England, when you have missed the last train back to shelter and are spending the night on the street can be fucking cold. I had worn layers when I boarded Air India as my own walking suitcase, but every layer I had was not enough to keep me warm that night. There were no subterranean vents spewing hot air like in New York, there were no all-night establishments of any kind to take refuge in, there was just the cold ground and an occasional cold bench. I would lie down to sleep, start to quake, and have to get up and walk again. By dawn I was a zombie, walking and walking in a trance about the small burg, waiting for the light to come on in the train station. It was then I made up my mind: I'm going home.

THE NEW SCHOOL FOR SOCIAL RESEARCH

The New School for Social Research, that's what the banner read. Walking down West Eleventh Street one day, I paused underneath that banner and tried to peer past my reflection into the windows. I liked that series of words so much that I pushed open the door and went in. I found myself standing in a quiet lobby and beyond that, in the center of the block between Eleventh and Twelfth streets, I could see a sunny courtyard with some modern sculptures and a few people seated here and there, talking or reading. I picked up an informational pamphlet and learned that I had entered a university for political and social studies founded after World War II by Jewish intellectuals who had fled Europe. I was intrigued and went to find an office where I could ask some questions.

Classes at the New School were small and took place in circles around tables instead of audience-and-performer style. They were meant to be discussions, not lectures. I applied for another round of student loans and signed up for a couple of courses. Some of the students I encountered there would sigh like high schoolers and grudgingly fulfill their duties, but I, who had come of my own volition and was paying my own way, could not have been more enthusiastic. Most everyone in the place was a counterculture devotee and politically engaged to some degree. The teachers were active writers and artists and one of them in particular was to become my life's new spiritual guide. In the series of seminars that I chose to take at the New School over the next few years, the template of my life emerged. I started with creative writing and feminism 101.

In that first class on feminism, I was introduced to the writings of Zora Neale Hurston, Audre Lorde, Bell Hooks, Alice Walker, Adrienne Rich, Ntozake Shange, and Carol Gilligan. I can't remember the teacher, but she sure curated a killer class. My mind busted wide open with those writers' wisdom and an explosion of awareness came flooding in. Every single thing I read in that class was met with a resounding *yes* in my body and as soon as their words entered my mind it was as though I'd always known them. The time before my awareness of being immersed in patriarchy was vanished from my memory and I was reborn into full consciousness.

I knew it right away: I am a part of the feminist continuum. I am entering myself. The political radical that I was born to be was finding context, changing shape . . . becoming female. And now that I'd finally stepped beyond patriarchal paradigms, my passion for social change became heightened. Like any human, I needed to see my own truth reflected back at me before I could know it in myself. It is telling to note that most of those feminist writers, these astute social critics who named everything for me, were African-American women. Those who sit furthest from the center of power, see it the clearest.

There was also an African-American poet named Lucille Clifton, born in Buffalo thirty years before me, whose words touched my life when I was young, especially with a poem she wrote called "lost baby poem," about having an (illegal) abortion. My experience with my own abortion at eighteen remained locked inside me and did not enter into my writing, did not leave my lips, until I read Lucille's poem. It was her voice that unstuck mine. Included on my eponymous debut was a song I'd written called "Lost Woman Song," which I dedicated to her. I used to recite Lucille's poem on stage as an invocation to playing my song and began talking publicly about how women have the power to shake each other awake and animate each other's voices. Feminism 101 cemented my will to become a part of that process of breaking silences and challenging the code of resignation surrounding patriarchy.

BOOPHA

One of the girls in feminism 101 whom I met had a standard-issue name but I took to calling her Boopha for reasons I can't explain. I think the incongruity pleased me and it fit the ludicrous humor the two of us had going. Immediately upon meeting, we recognized in each other a potential accomplice. We had also both signed up for a gay and lesbian literature class and together we read everyone from James Baldwin to Jeanette Winterson. I remember her showing up at the New School with a low-slung swagger and a queer-as-I-wanna-be air about her. Little did I know, when she'd boarded the train in Kentucky, she was just as unsure of herself as I. She had come to New York, like the rest of us, to reinvent herself.

We wrote notes in class with doodles in them and then we went and tattooed those doodles on our bodies. She took me to dyke bars and to the Clit Club, a women-only dance club in the Meatpacking District, where women were dancing in cages much like the one that had been in my old room, just a block away. I stood there in the pulsing leather and rubber-clad darkness marveling that there was even such a thing as women dancing in cages for other women. It looked to me like a parody of patriarchal objectification without the men. I kept trying to take it seriously but I couldn't deny the whole thing felt a little silly.

The Clit Club was a rare gig for female strippers, to be in a woman-only context, and was probably a genuine opportunity for some real fun, so I should shut up. Boopha and a whole slew of my friends would soon become strippers and sex workers of various stripes, and though they all hovered around queer themselves, they generally worked in the one place there was to work: the world of men. I would wonder many times over if I shouldn't follow suit, since these friends always seemed to be making way more money than I was, but I couldn't bring myself to. I needed hope more than I needed money. Among my stripper friends, there were drug habits and rapes and things broken and things lost. They all seemed to descend into dark times, despite their best efforts to beat patriarchy at its own game and come out laughing.

Boopha was smart, smart enough to draw me. She leveled her eyes at me and I held her gaze without refusing or encouraging it. I held us suspended while I gauged the distance to the ground below me and the strength of the rope I was holding on to. I still had a boyfriend back in Buffalo. Monogamy was an assumption that seemed to come in the box with each lover. I'd only had two lovers so far, both men, but that seemed to be the way of it. How was this different? Was I supposed to call Scot now and ask permission? For what?

It would be many years before I would begin to have the capacity to effectively buck the subliminal system of sexual possession. Sex (heterosexual sex at least) involves ownership, that's one of the first things you learn when you come of age. Open, mutually respectful polyamory has remained mostly theoretical in my life and has felt almost too radical to fathom, let alone pull off, in the culture I was born into. Instead of dedicating myself immediately and wholeheartedly to resisting automatic sexual possession, I just taught myself to quietly slip through the terrain in between fences. Like people do. I built myself a lot of trapdoors in order to not feel trapped.

But monogamy as a free choice feels like a ruse when possession is a vampire that comes and bites you while you're sleeping. Before you can even wake up in the morning with someone, there is an invisible pact to be passively complied with or actively counteracted. The tools of counteraction (direct and open communication, confidence, clarity . . .) never seemed to be in my toolbox when I needed them. It didn't help that my brain had a habit of panicking and shutting down whenever it was stressed. Never in my life have I known what to say until at least three blocks or three days later. It also didn't help that I could always feel what the other person wanted more acutely than I could feel my own self. That really doesn't help at all.

Youth and monogamy seem inherently contradictory to me. Religion aside. It is widely understood that exploration and play are how human beings learn and grow, and we are encouraged to experiment and engage with so many things. We are, in fact, forced into schools eight hours a day, five days a week, for twelve years in order that we sufficiently explore every aspect of our world. Then we are asked to sideline our sexuality, compartmentalize that part of ourselves somehow, and hold ignorance and lack of curiosity up as virtues.

Sex is a dangerous field of study, true. Special equipment and great precautions are necessary. But to say that any of it—celibacy, monogamy, or even heterosexuality—is a "choice" and the alternatives can simply be opted out of, is to fundamentally disrespect the supremacy of Natural Law over patriarchal religions. The forces that drive sexuality are bigger and more powerful than any man-made religious doctrine. *They are more real*. Individuals can adhere to man-made doctrines up to a point, but Nature operates like any other casino: The house always comes out on top. Whosoever thinks they can overrule Natural Law with their spiel is fooling no one. Is not all of Nature pushing young bodies together with a force stronger than words?

Boopha offered herself to me as my laboratory and I accepted. I experimented the way all young people experiment, to discover the underlying physics of love. There were baking soda volcanoes to make erupt and liquids to turn into gasses before I could say I even vaguely understood. We were meeting in a place far from the lover-as-owner-protector thing, that's all I knew. In fact, I could tell if I wasn't careful, this girl was gonna take me down with her. Boopha was careening down darker and darker alleys and, for my own self-preservation, I eventually turned and left her there.

Luckily, I was not the only one messing around outside of my boyfriend-girlfriend relationship. Scot was also young and we lived in two different cities, increasingly in two different worlds. We wordlessly adopted a don't-ask-don't-tell policy and, every now and then, our bubble of monogamy would burst dramatically and need to be mended. We weren't able to define our relationship for ourselves so we struggled within traditional paradigms and we struggled within ourselves. We postponed our day of reckoning.

The jealousy between Scot and Boopha ran deep and burned white hot, though, that much seemed unfixable. The tension was so thick every time Scot visited me in New York that I just tried to avoid having the two of them in the same room. When Scot came, I hung out exclusively with him. But sometimes that scheme didn't work. Like the time when Boopha insisted on coming to one of my gigs, though Scot was in town and had offered himself as tape seller for the night.

Boopha described for me later a scene that happened behind my back. Scot was banging things around on a table in the back of the room, setting up my mailing list and tapes, while Boopha leaned in a doorway watching him. Finding his banging amusing, she asked amusedly, "What are you doing?" He stopped, locked eyes with her, and replied slowly, "I'm making myself indispensable."

SEKOU

Of all the many wonderful people who came into my life via The New School, Sekou Sundiata came bearing the greatest gifts. I signed up for a poetry class of some kind and there he suddenly was, his long graceful arms and hands flowing as he spoke, his dark, handsome face bejeweled with two quiet eyes in a constant state of observation. He was smooth and soulful and dapper, at turns Pan-African and ultra-cool. I picture him, fedora cocked, walking with the skipping lilt of the trickster god. His walk said, "I have one foot in heaven, one on earth," and indeed he did.

Sekou showed me that poetry is a way of seeing and that a poet is not so much a person skilled with words as a person who recognizes the poetry that exists all the time all around us. I saw him perform with his band Dadedoodada and saw that, like myself, he'd hung his hat at the intersection of poetry and music. He did not sing or play an instrument himself but he had an ear and a deep relationship with music. His words had music in them.

One night we both wound up on stage at the old Knitting Factory on Houston Street at a poetry slam that he had challenged his students to show up to. Afterwards he said, "You should give me your number, I have some projects that might interest you." I pulled out my pen and wrote "For a good time call" next to my number on a little piece of paper. I was trying to be funny. Why am I always trying to be funny? I cursed myself over and over with each step home. *Oh my god, you idiot! You are such a fool! Why couldn't you have at least written, "For a good rhyme call"?!* I remained, first and always, a nervous fan in Sekou's presence.

One project that he would try to rope me into revolved around the

Nuyorican Poets Café over on East Third Street. At that time, the Nuyorican was the slam poets' coliseum. Bob Holman, a bigwig around there, was scouting talent for a public television series that he was curating about this new craze called "the spoken word." Sekou told Bob he should check me out so I went over to East Third Street to stand outside the place in front of a graffitied wall and audition for him in front of a camera. He did not choose to include me in his PBS special but Sekou's endorsement meant more to me than Bob's rejection.

I suppose I was too timid for Bob. Strutting and scowling was the fashionable stance of the day. It was obvious from all the poetry slams that everyone was supposed to project Urban Tough and do their part to help poetry escape its fey, antiquated box labeled "irrelevant art forms of the past." It's funny to say, but I was never much of a performer. I would just show up with some poems and songs in my head and deliver them with the sincere energy that I possessed in that moment. That energy was often hesitant at first and might only dive deeper and start swimming the breast stroke after coming to trust in an audience, and they me.

I always felt bad about my lack of bravado or command or whatever until one day, many years later, I was watching a documentary about Thelonious Monk. Monk is a hero of mine, one of the musicians who visited this planet who speaks deepest to my soul. Something about the queer, awkward, self-deprecating strut of his hands, his level of I-actually-don't-give-a-fuck-what-you-think . . . it just kills me. Kills me like when your spirit is finally, gratefully, released from your body. So, there I was, watching some other musician who played a lot with Monk talking about how his performances were like conversations. Monk would enter a room and sit down at the piano (this guy was recalling) and the first thing his hands would say was, "Hello. My name is Thelonious."

Yes! Art is a conversation! Yes. That's how I like it, too. Who starts a conversation with, "I rule you! I am all powerful! Hello!" Well . . . maybe some people.

In Sekou's class my voice would shake when I spoke. There seemed to be nothing I could do about it. Sekou had a way of initiating discussion, saying nothing for a long time, and then dropping one thought on the room that lingered. After that first semester, and for the rest of my brief tenure at the New School, I signed up for every class he taught. The classes ranged from creative writing to one called "Malcolm X, A Hero's Journey," which was a reading of *The Autobiography of Malcolm X* through the lens of Joseph Campbell's work *The Hero with a Thousand Faces*.

That class was a minefield of intense debate better described as argument. Accusations flew. The racially charged tension in the room kept me quiet and cowering in a corner most of the time. Sekou, for his part, listened calmly and interjected with great precision. This was the early nineties and identity politics had only just begun to run away with us. We were the radical youth. We understood the true power of our diversity, we knew the meaning of intersectionality, and we were, each in our own way, anguished by the ongoing hypocrisies of America. The belief that America was making social progress, that it was moving forward, withered and died at our feet in the eighties. We were the first guard in the age of disillusionment. Enter the competition of oppressions. Begin the infighting. Spike Lee's *Do the Right Thing* said it all. There is really nowhere to go but down in flames . . . so everybody go ahead and pick up a torch.

In that Malcolm X class, black kids sat on one side of the room and white kids sat on the other. When I walked into the room the first day, I reluctantly joined the ranks of the oppressor and sat on my designated side. I noticed there was one fair-skinned girl with a majestic mane of blonde hair who sat in amongst the black kids and I instantly admired her courage. Sekou asked us to go around the room and to each say why we were here, what had brought us to the class. The pretty blonde said something about Malcolm being an important part of her own history that she wanted to know more about and she got nods from the dark-skinned girls to her left and to her right. Wow! Why didn't I have the courage to say that? That's exactly why I'm here, too! Look at how confidently she crossed the color divide and claimed her place as a student of American history, a student of radical activism, political organizing and agitation, and look at how she was affirmed and accepted by the African-American students simply for having that level of self-possession!

Of course, I later learned that she had a father who was "black" (which in America is anything other than a hundred percent Swedish) and that is where her confidence and sense of inclusion came from. When I learned that factoid, I felt another moment of thrilling transcendence and hope crushed inside me.

It would be a long and humbling journey for me to a more nuanced understanding of how perpetual racial inequality and oppression takes its toll on each of us and cannot simply be opted out of. Each ensuing generation must inherit the anger, resentment, outrage, disunity, fear, guilt, pain, denial, pain, pain . . . until the wound is actually and truly healed at its source. Through great attention and care. Through the laying on of hands. Through penance and reparations and truth telling and uncomfortable confrontations. I was too young to understand, sitting there in Sekou's class, how collective pain sets its traps for each new batch of Americans and has the power to defeat even the most lofty of individuals, making a mockery of their free will. Racism does not recognize the humanity or actual character of a dark-skinned person, so why should it recognize mine? It is a force that, by its very nature, erases us.

Patriarchy is a spring at the source of many rivers. Racism is one of the many tributaries. Domination and submission, competition, aggression, hierarchy, these are fundamental traits of the masculine design. Walking down Fifth Avenue one day, I decided on a whim to enter a big church and take quiet refuge in one of the pews. I absorbed the air in the place and took in the sights and sounds for a few minutes before I looked down and saw the Bible in the back of the seat in front of me. I picked it up with an open heart and started reading from page one. In the beginning, God created heaven and earth and then he made all this other stuff and then he made man and said, "All this shit is yours to rule over, even that chick over there. I made all of this to serve you." *Look at this society. What other words could possibly be at its bedrock?* Outraged, I put the book down.

I was embarking on a journey to discover patriarchy as not just the force that subordinates women but as the underlying imbalance sewn into the fabric of human society which can only beget greater imbalance. Peace cannot be created from imbalance. Study natural law and you will find *that* in the preamble! Turmoil, conflict, and disease are products of imbalance, whether it be in an organism, an ecosystem, or a society . . . Yes, *peace is a function of balance.* To start with the grand imbalance of global patriarchy and achieve a sustaining peace on earth is impossible. This was the truth I was beginning to know.

Human nature, like all of nature, involves the relationship of opposing forces. These forces must be similarly weighted to achieve stability and resonance. When masculine and feminine nature achieve an equivalent gravitational pull on all the mechanisms of government, culture, and society, peace will begin to become possible. We can find a path then, through all the other social diseases, a path towards realizing our potential as a species.

Everything which looks to be still is spinning.

In my better moments, I will learn to take all the social dramas less personally, but only after countless instances of being newly trapped in defeat and disappointment. The artist possesses an immense power to remake the world for herself . . . but not an absolute power.

RACIST BULLSHIT

One day, at Parsons School of Design (another undergraduate college under the New School umbrella), there was an exhibit by some Japanese graphic designer whose name I've forgotten. It was mostly a display of Japanese product design including a washing powder that featured a black-faced Sambo figure with that goofy Sambo smile on the cover of the box. I remember taking note of it as I strolled through the exhibit and thinking hmm . . . they must not get it over in Japan. The denigrating weight of that image got lost in translation. I moved on.

A few days later, a buzz went through the whole university and rumor spread of what Sekou had done. I went back to the gallery and sure enough there it was: *This is racist bullshit* was scrawled across the print in Sharpie, and underneath it, he'd signed his name. A school-wide debate ensued and people heatedly took sides. Sekou was a badass and that was his way: to quietly get people talking about what matters most. My esteem for him grew.

The simple act of shaving my head in 1989 (a time when there was little cultural context for a white chick to be sporting such a lid outside of "skinhead") became something of a lesson in prejudice for me. In the absence of my hair, my antenna started picking up a distant message beaming-in to me from society. I became unable to escape the awareness that I suddenly made the majority of people around me uncomfortable. I stopped getting inquiries from strangers on the street of, "Can you tell me the time?" (a pre-cellphone world, mind you) though I was wearing the same big bulky wristwatch and open countenance as before. I felt a palpable uneasiness from salespeople behind counters, from fellow standers on subway platforms, I even witnessed someone crossing the street once in order to not walk past me. *What the hell is wrong with people?!* I began to quietly seethe. *Can't they even see me anymore?* With a shaved head, my actual character had become invisible and a menacing presence was perceived in its place.

After a time, even the most polite uncomfortable person served to quietly enrage me. It was then I began to take it in . . . my pseudo experience of atmospheric prejudice. I mean, atmospheric like when somebody is barbecuing pork two blocks away and the faintest whiff sneaks past your nose. In that moment comes a palpable desire, you notice. Yes, I could grow my hair back in an instant and the depth of my privilege, even while walking around looking like public enemy number one, will always be unfathomable to me . . . but something in my core humanity took notice. I had felt the beginnings of my very own reaction to a force, not the force of full-on oppression, but of its tiny seedling: fear.

I had shaved my head with a much different purpose in mind (to become less of a sex object) and it had worked, but here was something else about society trying to show itself to me. I realized that it is one thing to believe in something with your mind and it is another thing entirely to experience it. Experiencing even a passing shudder which momentarily stirs you from your sleep is . . . more than nothing. While I lay dreaming, my subconscious was detecting the signal of a deeper truth in code. It felt like this: My god, the rage! *Of course: the rage.* There is really nothing more rational and honest (let alone inevitable), in the body of the oppressed, than rage. The first of many burdens becomes the task of moving through it, transforming it into something that does not eat you alive.

I felt empathy blow through me. How would I deal with this over time if I were Black in America? Never mind the possible upscaling to extremes of poverty, violence, and collective, multi-generational suffering. How would even this most minuscule of factors influence who I would become? What if I were male and had testosterone coursing through my body? What would my rage look like then?

In my dream, behind each Black man who I would never be stood his mother and she was looking right through me. Her eyes said, *Don't forget this.*

ACTIVATION

Mike Doughty, who would later become the front man of the band Soul Coughing, was in that first poetry class of Sekou's, too, and a few subsequent ones with me. He seemed to position himself as my direct competition and we were friendly enough but never really bonded. Doughty was a rare beast amongst the school's student body in that he was somewhat apolitical. I, on the other hand, typified the sort of radical activist that the school attracted in spades. As the first Gulf War was being initiated by Bush senior and his right-hand man Dickface Cheney, I got involved with the War Resisters League and with a student group we dubbed "Hands Off Sam."

Sam Lwin, a Burmese-American student who was a Marine reservist, was against the war, too, and he decided to go out on a limb and declare himself a conscientious objector. That, of course, is easier said than done. Sam got locked up and messed with for a long time in order to resist going to Iraq and shooting people for the oil under their feet. I found myself, more than once, up at the Marine armory in the Bronx, demonstrating and leafleting on Sam's behalf and against the war in principle. Six other reservists in the Bronx Fox Company joined Sam in his conscientious objection thanks to our efforts. An amazing mutiny, really. They all caught hell but at least none of them was deployed to participate in Bush's invasion.

We also did a lot of busing down to D.C. to protest the war, when we were not taking to the streets of Manhattan. My fondest memories of the yellow school bus brigades to our nation's capital were the counterculture takeovers of the highway rest stops along the way. Flooded with buses of tired activists, the rest stops looked like some young, dreamy America where no one is fooled and everybody actually gives a shit. If only Virginia looked like this all the time!

Back in New York, I was organizing benefit concerts at the ruffian hangout down on Rivington Street called ABC No Rio, at the New School, and at St. Mark's Church. I was stomping around Union Square trying to educate people against the manufacture of consent by a complicit media. I was taking the train up to Spanish Harlem to discuss the nonviolent possibilities for civil disobedience. I was stationed at the cigarette smoke–filled New School student union hall on Eleventh Street having heated debates and planning actions.

It was at the New School that I really learned the art of political engagement. I learned that with any heart, and with a solid basis of mutual respect, you can go toe to toe in fierce debate with someone and then shift gears when the meeting or class is over and relate once again as friends. I came to relish this new exercise of social tension and release, of engaging in difficult and troublesome realities without breaking connections or forfeiting one another. Speaking up and being true to oneself, meeting and challenging one another, and then ultimately accepting differences and forgiving trespasses felt . . . so much better than the alternative.

The idea that conflict does not need to result in pushing each other down or away was a relief to me beyond words. It was like the antidote to all the poisonous silences that I had inhaled growing up. We can make room for each other to make mistakes, we can enter uncomfortable and even adversarial spaces, and then we can come back to a hand-shaking stasis and even laugh together. We can exercise mutual respect. We can be, at the very least, united in our humanity and in our passionate concern.

All people meet truths that are different from their own with resistance, but to allow them simply to air, in all their wrongness, becomes the first step on the path of social evolution. New truths take their time being heard and switching lanes is done gradually, on a diagonal that utilizes the flow of time and space. Abrupt turns are not natural or practical in a world that's happening so fast, a world so trafficked with identity and ego. I was learning to trust the time it takes and the imperfections of the process. I was learning to use my speaking voice and my listening ears without fear. I was learning that the process of democracy is not some sort of automatic reflex but a skill, even an art, that must be practiced and modeled for one another in order to exist at all.

I signed up for an internship at the El Salvador Sister Cities Project and walked three times a week down to Lower Broadway to put in after-noons receiving faxes from the front lines of the conflict in that tiny, war-ravaged country. The American government was fighting commu-nism in El Salvador by arming a brutal military dictatorship and many a peasant farmer's name was daily being added to the lists of the "disap-peared." Because I was well spoken (thanks mom) it soon became my job to phone up congressional aides and entreat them to push their bosses to stop arming the dictatorship. I made the case that the FMLN was not a group of violent communist thugs (as the American media was happy to portray them) but a haphazard coalition of everyday people sim-ply trying to achieve justice, peace, and some basic human rights in their own country.

The Sister Cities Project was an organization that linked up cities in the United States with repopulated peasant communities and villages in the Salvadoran countryside. The idea was to focus bringing aid, safety, and attention from one community to the other. The American-sponsored violence was best kept in check, ironically, by the presence of American citizens on the ground in El Salvador, so we sent frequent delegations down from our sister cities to temporarily quell the Salvadoran military's tendency to slaughter their own people. Several times, I had planned to go down myself on a delegation but gigs got in the way. Unfortunately, I always opted for the gig and have yet to see El Salvador.

"From each according to their ability, to each according to their needs" seems like a pretty cool idea to me. I've never understood America's utter vilification of communism. I read Karl Marx, I read Engels, we all did. *The Communist Manifesto* was joked to be the best pick-up bait at the New School. Sit yourself someplace conspicuous, open your copy, and pretend to read it very studiously if you want to reel in a New School babe. I read it earnestly, with no purpose other than to unravel a mys-tery, like the way I read the Bible. So, what is all the fuss about?

Right away it seemed obvious to me that there was more going on with America's anti-communist fervor than the "good versus evil" story that so many seemed to be selling and so many others seem to be buying. The global battle between communist countries and democratic/capitalist ones appeared to me as just another one of history's many pissing contests. Each ethos had its merits and each raised its share of issues, but in truth, and in practice, both are mired in patriarchy and hence unable to manifest in the world their highest intentions.

I was soon to meet many Wobblies, labor unionists, socialists, community activists, and class-conscious people of all kinds as I began to burrow my way into the folk music underground. I was already calling myself a socialist when I showed up at my first folk festival so, though I represented a strange new mutation, I fit right in. The old folkies who were able to look beyond the difference of my uniform—the shaved head, jack boots, and nose piercing—welcomed me with open arms.

PETE SEEGER

For all the years I knew Pete, his presence never faltered and his power never waned. Of course, I met him as an old man and he had his shit pretty dialed in, the clutches of youthful desire and ego having long since released him. Having been blacklisted and put out of commission for many of the prime years of his career for his affiliation with the Communist Party, he had bounced back to prove, ultimately, that all his years were prime years. He was in his early seventies when our paths first crossed but even into his nineties he was keen and at the ready. Long after his voice got shaky, his heart and mind were coming through loud and clear.

His was an unassuming power that came from a calm sense of purpose and a palpable lack of fear. It seemed to be at the core of his teaching to act as a conduit for something bigger and more meaningful than himself and, guided by this motivation, he moved with a grace through the world. He would reach around behind the heads of people he was talking to and turn off the spotlight they had trained on him, quieting the elevation of saviors and refocusing people back onto their potential to each be a savior of something . . . of each other.

Further down the road, I would meet a man named Bob Dylan and feel the opposite sensation from him. Bob felt like a man who lived in fear that someone would discover and expose him as a fraud. I am not saying he is a fraud. On the contrary, I believe his art to be a great gift. I'm just saying there is a difference between open and closed. The man forced to guard his legend carefully in order that he always have something to hide behind, no matter how brilliant he is, is not as powerful to me as the man who stands out in the open, naked and unarmed.

Pete seemed to recognize me as a good ally and I recognized him as a great feminist. I remember watching him give a press conference once where he performed an act of mental jujitsu on the whole room and it was like we all lay momentarily stunned on our backs looking up at the buzzing overhead lights. "Mr. Seeger," the journalist began, "you have been inducted into the Songwriters Hall of Fame and the Rock and Roll Hall of Fame, you are the recipient of a Grammy Lifetime Achievement Award, a Kennedy Center Honor, and a National Medal of the Arts, your songs have become hits for artists like Peter, Paul and Mary and The Byrds, and you have contributed to the civil rights, labor, and environmental movements . . . tell us, sir, what are you most proud of?" Pete paused in his way and smiled and said, "I stayed married to the best woman I ever met and we had three children and six grandchildren." *Take that, oh hierarchical world of masculine "accomplishment"! Relationship. A successful life is one spent in loving relationship with others.* Pete had a way of just quietly putting it down right where everyone could see it. I loved watching him work.

The first time I showed up at his Hudson Clearwater Revival in the early nineties, I made an impression. Mostly because I brought with me a cadre of fist-in-the-air teenagers. Pete and his wife, Toshi, had founded the festival to help benefit the clean-up of the Hudson River (so horribly polluted by GE) but after many years, the festival itself was struggling. Like many folk festivals, the audiences were slowly aging and precious little new blood was mixing in. I had built a word-of-mouth following of radical youth in the New York area and when they reassembled themselves at Clearwater, Pete beamed.

I have always felt like a suspension bridge in the long road of American folk music. One that spanned the dry, cracked creek bed of the late eighties and nineties, between the old era evaporating behind me drop by precious drop, and the new deluge which had yet to be dreamed up in the clouds. The culture was moving from "folksinger" to "singer-songwriter" and abandoning ties to the radical politics of its forbears. But to me the radical politics were the coolest part, so I was swimming upstream. Elvis Costello's recording of Nick Lowe's "What's So Funny 'Bout Peace Love and Understanding?" was like my anthem. I became determined to fly the flag of Woody Guthrie in an era when it couldn't have been less cool.

"Alarming happy," a snide Kurt Loder called me on MTV back when it still ruled the boob tube, making of my earnestness a joke. I was always falling short of pop-culture cool but my indie success would get me noticed in the pop music world and I would eventually find myself at music festivals where actual young people went. I had ample opportunity to compare ecosystems. I found I generally preferred the old leftie, radical-activist types who stood charmingly and unfashionably on the side of substance. Their world would ultimately feel more like a home to me than any of the hip scenes I was invited to visit along the journey.

Folk festivals were an entree into a new world for me and represented the dawning of a national audience for my music. They were also my grand introduction to many of the architects of my profession. I was met with my share of resistance for my punk and hard-core feminist leanings, but I was also met with a lot of affirming nods and warm hugs. Pete,

Nora Guthrie, Tom Paxton, Odetta, Peter Yarrow, my future friend and collaborator Utah Phillips, along with next-generation artists like Greg Brown, John Gorka, and Dar Williams (and even some peripheral stars like Stephen Stills) were warm and welcomed me into the fray. Interestingly, the womyn's music contingent at the folk festivals (the dykes) seemed somewhat wary of me and tended to eye me with suspicion. It was a fine line that I walked between the charge of "man hater" from defensive dudes and the role of alien interloper assigned to me by the old-school feminists. Gingerly, I made my way.

I think my one shining gift in life has been to know who my teachers are and to follow them around looking for ways to be at their service. It was easy for me to turn down record deals because I didn't find any of my teachers in music industry spheres. It was also easy to say, "How high?" every time Pete called and said "Ani! Jump!" And call Pete did. Or he would write to me with a pen in his own shaking hand. Pete showed me that an effective activist is one who goes forward right now with a good idea and goes directly. Nobody seemed to take care of his calls or correspondence for him, at least not when it mattered. He was like a walking list of things to do with a bunch of check marks on it. He got excited about stuff and it made him tireless. My willingness to be of service to him was secretly selfish because it meant more time for me in his presence.

I picture him strolling up to me in a muddy field at Clearwater on what was probably my fifth appearance there, clad as always in his work boots and flannel shirt, saying, "Hey, you know that benefit for Leonard Peltier in November I wrote to you about? I think we're gonna move it to . . ." Okay, so for context, this is at *his* festival, a setting where he was subject to an endless barrage of faces talking at him all day long, he's older than the hills at this point, *and* his wife has just recently died, poor fellow. All circumstances that would have been dizzying handicaps to me and my ability to know who's who and what's what. But not Pete. He spotted me from fifty paces and strode up to relay all the details of the change in plans pertaining to our last correspondence, the details of which I barely remembered myself.

As he approached me, I observed his limbs were moving as freely as his mind. He looked like he was still chopping his share of wood. Pete's was a powerful life force, bright and shining to its last.

four

THE NEW FRONTIER

Scot decided to go to law school. His father was a lawyer and he had the brain for it so why not? If nothing else, it was a way out of the construction business while he was still in possession of all his fingers. He enrolled himself in the University of Buffalo Law School and nervously anticipated his new life. By the time September rolled around, however, I managed to compromise his entry into his new life in a way that foreshadowed his future relationship with the law: Folksingers come first.

We were up at the lake together, staying in the cabin on the island, and it was a particularly rainy late summer. As the trees began to show their colors, the rain poured into our primitive abode with such force that we ran out of buckets and basins to put under all the leaks. The cabin, which had been built Lincoln-Log style of stacked timbers with an asphalt shingle roof, had had precious few repairs done to it in eighty years. Logs were rotting everywhere and huge carpenter ants made piles of sawdust around us while we slept. The roof was a disaster. A week before law school orientation, the weather broke and Scot said, "We gotta put a new roof on this thing. We can do it in a week. You and me." Roofing was not heretofore in my construction skill set but I was game, grateful for any assistance in keeping my family's legacy from slipping quietly back into the earth.

We canoed over to the mainland and drove into town to buy shingles, roofing nails, and tar. Bundles of asphalt shingles are damn heavy but we managed to get them, boatload by boatload, back to the island and then one by one up onto the roof. From the roof of the cabin we were visited by great blue herons as they temporarily came to roost in the tall pines on the island's windward helm. Flocks of geese flew high overhead on their way to South America, their distant honking conversation barely audible in between our hammering. We watched the loons fishing the waters in the lee of the island and mink playing along the shore. Occasionally the slap of a beaver's tail. The sun crossed the whole sky as we hammered away, one wide-headed roofing nail after another.

The job, like all construction jobs, proved to be more difficult and take more time than anticipated and we started putting in longer and longer days as the week drew on. We came down off the roof only to eat or visit the outhouse. Law school was to start the very next day and we were still working. Our food supply had all but run out but we were under so much pressure that we didn't want to take the time to go into town to buy more. We took to eating plain pasta and something I affectionately dubbed "griddle biscuits." Griddle biscuits are made of a paste of flour, water, and salt, fried in a pan and served with jelly. Brutal. I also learned during this charrette that pasta must absolutely be cooked in boiling water. Not wanting to take time out to stoke the fire in the stove to the boiling point, I experimented with slowly simmering it into a meal. How pasta can become utterly inedible when cooked at the wrong temperature, I will never quite understand. We settled for another meal of griddle biscuits.

In the end, Scot was a week late to start law school but it didn't seem to matter. He caught up with and surpassed most of his fellows quickly. Among the dry, boring studies he was made to endure (tort law, contract law . . .), criminal law showed itself instantly and enduringly to be his passion. That passion was driven by his criminal law professor, a career public defender by the name of Palmer Singleton.

Palmer was an eccentric character to say the least. Raised Quaker, he was a pacifist with a toughness and a real-worldness that put all those sheltered law school babies to shame. A bona fide loner, he lived with his pack of rescue dogs in somewhat feral conditions himself and shined up only for court appearances. He'd had an aneurysm in court once and had taken a city bus to the hospital where he was immediately whisked into brain surgery. I imagined that this was why a little bit of drool always leaked out from around the pipe that was a permanent fixture in his mouth.

(Palmer described the experience of having the top of his skull cut off while sitting up, totally conscious, as a hell that he would not undergo twice. A brain under such trauma wants to go to sleep and often stays asleep forever, so he was given only a local anesthetic and made to stay awake during the whole surgery. He said he yelled at the person whose job it was to keep him talking and answering questions the whole time. He said he looked upon the little kids with cancer that he met in the hospital, who had undergone multiple brain surgeries themselves, as stronger and braver than himself.)

Temporarily burnt-out on his career as a public defender and anti–death penalty advocate, Palmer had come to Buffalo to try his hand at grooming the next generation of socially conscious lawyers at UB but it didn't last long. He was loath to suffer all the self-serving fools that populated the student body of the law school and was known to bellow reproach at his classes and even to storm out in disgust. He latched on to Scot as one of the few students with a level of ideology to match his own and he steered Scot into the realm of public service. He showed him how he could use the law to do good.

Would you want to be judged solely on your worst moment? No. Then that is not the way you should judge others. That is the wisdom of the defense attorney. You have to be able to see the value and the humanity of every person, even those who mess up bad. You have to be able to access the profoundly spiritual understanding that people's actions, even their very identity, are not the whole truth of who they are. Palmer was a true pacifist, who simply did not indulge in the world of coercion, domination, and hierarchy. He showed all his clients (the innocents and the serial murderers) basic human respect. His mission was to bring cycles of violence to an end, not to judge the fallen amongst us.

Even before I understood what Palmer had spent his life doing, I experienced his commitment to nonviolence as a vibe thing. I don't know a lot about Buddhism, but I think of him as having Buddha nature. A sort of cranky version. Space has to be made in this world for consciousness to experience itself, to reconnect with itself when it has been broken or severed. I have managed to meet a few of these precious space holders in my day, these connecter people. There's Palmer and Pete . . . and um . . . Sister Helen Prejan, and well, maybe that's about it. I hear the Dalai Lama has it down. In the case of Palmer, he seemed clear that the best way to begin healing the violence of society was by extending a hand to the people on the very bottom, the ones living in cages with little to no human rights. The ones facing their own deaths at the hands of the state.

Poverty is violent, economic oppression is violent, misogyny and racism are violent. These fundamental structures cannot but claim victims. Human beings become cogs in violent machines. When men fall off the bottom of the world, it is easy to paint them as monsters and turn away, but more likely they were just the men who happened to be closest to the edge. We blame them, we blame their families, but really the blame should be spread across the shoulders of everyone who still refuses to admit the world is round. No one should ever fall off.

By the time the spring semester came to a close, Palmer had had enough of his experiment of playing law professor so Scot and I helped move him to the next stop on his journey, the Roxbury Public Defender's Office in Boston. We loaded up Scot's pickup truck with the other half of Palmer's possessions and followed his station wagon down the I-90 to Massachusetts. The apartment he'd leased in Roxbury was a three-story walk-up so it was quite the moving job, his only possessions being boxes of books and files . . . and dog food.

After moving Palmer, our journey stretched thrillingly south and west to Texas. Scot had taken on a summer internship at the Death Penalty Resource Center in Austin, one of Palmer's former places of employ. The resource center was a place where public interest lawyers tried to prevent executions by filing appeals whenever an execution date was set. Their job amounted to trying to convince the governor that there was reason to have mercy on a prisoner and allow him to live. I had never been south of the Mason-Dixon line myself, and I certainly had never been out west, so I was very excited to go. Dale had been to Austin several times for the South by Southwest music conference and called ahead to a lady there who promised she could help me find work in the "live music capital of the world."

Journeying into the American South for the first time altered me. Scot and I rode, windows open, in the cab of his air-condition-less 1980 shit-brown Chevy pickup and camped at night in an old canvas tent, so our connection to the landscape was intense. The South entered me through lungs and pores and heart on that trip and has never left. We camped at Mammoth Cave in Kentucky and woke up to a din of cicadas like I couldn't believe. I'd grown up with cicadas in Buffalo but never like this. The trees were swarming with the large insects and their deafening symphony embedded itself in my imagination and has remained forever-more one of my absolute favorite sounds.

We stood and gazed up at the balcony of the Lorraine Motel in Memphis where Martin Luther King took his last breath and then we ate barbecue that required a whole roll of paper towels for damage control. We saw an old bluesman named Johnny Shines play in Montgomery and we rode to Selma just to stand at the foot of the bridge which Dr. King and company crossed twice in the forward-and-back march of civil rights.

The specter of slavery was suddenly haunting the landscape, from the plantations on the outskirts, to the Confederate generals whose names were plastered all over town. I had underestimated the proximity of slavery and now here it was suddenly leaping out of the history books and morphing into an ever-present living atmosphere. The cicadas began composing a soundtrack entitled *Seething Rage Versus Languid Resignation* as the wounds of slavery revealed themselves to me as redder and more raw then I'd previously understood. For the first time, I wondered if there might just be a deadly infection still burning underneath the skin.

Crossing the border into Louisiana, we were greeted by a huge David Duke billboard. I had heard about this Klansman who was gaining political power in Louisiana and now here he was, advertised larger-than-life as a form of welcome to the state. It was a warning sign. A threat. You may be out of Alabama, but you aren't out of the woods yet, it said. I had never beheld racism so bold and unapologetic. I had also never beheld the look of profound weariness and rugged perseverance in the faces of the black folks who walked amongst these ominous signs and mortal dangers. People who, when I looked at them, looked right through me, weighing my privilege and my ignorance against my humility and sincerity. I had never felt so thoroughly and instantaneously sized up.

Like Mark Twain before me, my alteration became complete when I reached the mouth of the Mississippi. We got to New Orleans and I was dumbstruck. The architect's daughter in me was swooning at the visually poetic urban landscape. I could picture my mother pointing here and there saying, "Just look at the scale of this!" The monkey in me approached, in reverence, each majestic Live Oak Tree. I mean, oak trees in Buffalo are towering monuments of symmetry and virility, but these southern live oaks . . . these were mythical and awe-inspiring. Meanwhile, the musician in me thrilled to each musical expression of freedom and strength of character, each expression of resistance to oppression and defeat.

Here was a city with more than its share of mystery and inspiration. Here was a human cultural epicenter: a swirl. A city where, for one thing, African slaves and their descendants succeeded in using European culture as just another tool, this time to beam messages of transcendence out to the rest of humanity. The bubbling and steaming laboratory where jazz was invented and where so much of American music came to be made and remade . . . New Orleans, I should have known I would return to you someday and wade, waist deep, into your murky, sophisticated magic.

THE LONE STAR STATE

By the time we reached Austin, Scot and I were more than ready to get out of the truck and land in our sublet apartment near Barton Springs. The lawyers at the Texas Resource Center were the first lefty lawyers that I'd ever met beyond Palmer. When an execution date was set, they worked around the clock researching the case, looking for any and all avenues of appeal. They did so with an understanding that the criminal justice system in America is deeply flawed and only a system much more perfect than ours should ever consider itself capable of deciding who should live and who should die. They did so with an awareness that an execution does not represent the end of a cycle of violence, but a continuation of it.

Scot had a T-shirt that read on the front something like: "It's expensive, it's violent, it's racist, it's arbitrary, it makes mistakes," and then on the back it said, "The death penalty—abolish it." Boy, that shirt was a conversation starter in the jolly old state of Texas! I mean, Austin was full of progressive people but you couldn't really get away from the fact that the dominant culture was gung-ho for capital punishment. With George W. Bush as governor, Texas was executing more people than any other state by far.

I could feel in the energy and the collective spirit of those pacifist lawyers at the resource center that they really had it right. Compassion and forgiveness is the only kryptonite that can bring violence, finally and truly, to its knees. Executions bloom out their compounded trauma through whole families and communities and only ever result in deeper social fracturing. Did you ever look to see in which states the death penalty is even legal? It is predominately in the South. The former slave states and their cultural equivalents. Just sayin'. In Texas, you can get executed for driving the getaway car if they don't like the looks of you. And we all know which looks they favor.

Capital punishment has proven that it is not a path to peace. The families and communities of neither victim nor perpetrator are served. It also does not function as a deterrent to future crime, despite what its proponents might have you believe. Both of those lies have been statistically and empirically disproven. The purposes that capital punishment supposedly serves are all fabrications and inventions. They are so many excuses for man to exorcize the most negative aspects of a very ancient mode of tribalism. They are excuses for the dopamine rush of domination and revenge.

While I was going scrounging around Austin for gigs, Scot was driving to these little far-flung towns, to interview the mother, the brother, the arresting officer, of a man who had shot someone point-blank or a man who had hogtied and cut another man's throat. In each story that culminates in a death sentence, a whole lot of things have gone wrong. Everywhere you looked, people had failed each other and violence begat more violence. From the violence and oppression in the history of the impoverished, to the eleventh-hour performances of drunk lawyers and racist or apathetic judges, it becomes clear: Human beings are neither good nor evil, humans are human and subject to many forces. We fail each other in ways that have more to do with our lot in life than with our "selves" and we seek redemption in the same way.

I felt humbled bearing witness to a depth of suffering (on every side) far greater than I'd experienced in my own life and also witnessing a depth of service I could scarcely approach, either. These lawyers at the resource center seemed endlessly dedicated though there was very little in the way of tangible reward for their work. They sure didn't get applause, like me. They would sit at the office together on the night of an execution, praying that the phone would ring and it would be the governor with a reprieve but the phone almost never rang. At midnight, the clock would click over and they would lower their heads, silently saying goodbye to a human being whom they had come to know and care for. I was startled to learn that all executions take place at midnight: an appropriately medieval-feeling custom surrounding this form of "justice."

It would be some time before I would become hip to the philosophy and practice of Restorative Justice, a true alternative to our current system which promotes and even incentivizes execution and imprisonment on a mass scale. If you trace the lineage of mass incarceration in America, you can't escape its connections to slavery and white supremacy. Incarceration, touted understandably in bygone eras as a progressive alternative to torture and hanging, was, in reality, used as a tool of control and exploitation of the poor since its inception. The layman's notion of "rehabilitation" in the prison system in America has proven misguided or, at least, outdated. Still, I couldn't imagine what a structural alternative could be until I became acquainted with the Restorative Justice movement.

Restorative Justice brings victims and perpetrators together in guided mediation and dialogue. It re-envisions the relationship between government and communities in response to crime. The role of government becomes not to run punitive systems based on punishment and isolation but to maintain order while facilitating communities in doing the hard work of reparation, restoration, and healing. After violence has occurred, amends must be made and true accountability is achieved not with human sacrifice but with communication, penance, mutual understanding, and acts of repair.

Restorative Justice has actually been instituted and practiced to great effect all over the world, revolutionizing the criminal justice system in places like New Zealand and helping populations recover from mass crimes and genocide in places like Rwanda and South Africa. In a Restorative Justice system people on all sides are provided a path to regaining peace of mind. Cycles of violence become transformed and people are released from living out the rest of their lives in pain and anger.

Palmer would remain a teacher and comrade to me for many years and through him I would become involved with the Southern Center for Human Rights and meet other inspirational lawyers like Stephen Bright. I would discover MVFR (Murder Victims' Families for Reconciliation) and intersect with Tim Robbins and Susan Sarandon in time to participate in the *Dead Man Walking* benefit concert. I would discover the Innocence Project, the Moratorium Campaign, and the Prison Music Project and I would come to know, beyond a doubt, that one of the vanguards of revolutionary love in our country exists in the vast community of people who dedicate themselves to the reform of our criminal justice system.

In the meantime, it would seem like the music culture of Austin should have been a natural fit for me and my acoustic, song-driven music, but somehow it wasn't. I managed to get some work (mostly at dyke bars) but the cult of the cowboy that dominated the Texas culture leered sideways at me without ever really bothering to turn its head. The little bit of attention from the Austin music press that I did manage to score was condescending. Still, I followed my guitar around that town plenty. I tried on and off for years to win a place in Austin's heart.

UNWELCOME HOME

When autumn came, we left Texas without ceremony, Scot returned to law school in Buffalo, and I went back to New York. I discovered my room on Quaint Lane totally violated and I felt violated, too. Crazy dude had taken up residency there and seemed hesitant to leave. His cum was all over my sheets and his condoms and cigarettes were all around my bed. I'm talking *used* condoms. Cowering behind my locked door, with Stella drooling on my lap, I was consumed with the urge to escape.

My immediate solution was to just hang around the New School after all the classes were over and take my repose upstairs in the undergraduate building. I waited in a dark classroom until everybody had left the building except for the security guard downstairs and then I slipped onto a table and slept all night with my head on my backpack. Not comfortable, but safe enough.

The next night I jumped the gun and the last student walking out caught sight of me there, lying on a table in a dark room. To my massive good fortune, that student was Sung Joon and he went and told his girlfriend Oriane who came back upstairs to talk to me. Did I not have a place to live? Because (Ori told me) she and her friend Sheila were looking for a third housemate to share their apartment over on East Twelfth Street. Bingo! Our stars aligned. I had a new home complete with two new friends. This time, Sheila was the one sleeping behind the curtain in the living room and I had a room with a door to close, albeit one that scraped my futon on the way by.

Daniel went back with me to reclaim my bed, my boombox, and Stella from the crazy house and I never saw that dude again. Come to think of it, I never saw Daniel again, either. His trajectory was Midtown and deeper into the world of dancers and mine was to the Lower East Side and Brooklyn and points unknown. Also that year, Sung Joon, a

Korean exchange student, would drown tragically in a river in Connecticut and so no one would ever see him again, either. You don't know sometimes, when people make an exit, that they are really exiting. Let alone exiting-exiting. I still shudder to think of Sung Joon's parents flying to America to collect his body. I, myself, was headed towards an unexpected plot twist of my own. I was pregnant again.

ONCE MORE WITH FEELING

To my children, whom I signed for at a time when I would've signed anything," that's what Adrienne Rich said when Oriane and I went to see her give a reading uptown one night. Those words followed me home. Mother Nature insists on wanton procreation and Mother Nature and society together collude to insure that only females are held accountable. Only females are shamed for sexual activity outside of "wedlock." Only females are condemned for unwanted pregnancies.

Nature pushes in a female's door and insists that she feed its relentless pursuit for immortality. It pursues her ravenously from within and without her skin. Does patriarchal culture really imagine she should be some sort of self-taught Jedi at any age? Prepared for a sudden swordfight and a daring escape? Ready to stand as one individual against all the forces of the living, breathing, physical, chemical, mammalian reality? Nothing could be sillier.

As a female, should you not be a self-taught Jedi and find yourself with an unwanted pregnancy, society has a ready-made verdict for you: You are a slut who forces others to suffer for your carelessness and stupidity. You are a bad girl, a fallen woman, an irresponsible and cheap human being. Patriarchal culture will spin a force that is bigger than all of us into your own personal character flaw and your mistake will be your own. Oh, and because of this mistake, your life is no longer rightfully yours.

Having an abortion will make you a thief at best, walking around in a stolen life.

It is ludicrous to me that I was thrust into the world with a reproductive system not really knowing anything about the intentions it had for me, the methods it would use, the challenges I could expect. Waterfront School's "sex ed" class in the ninth grade was a charming effort but didn't really count. We all knew where babies come from. The vast arena of feminine knowledge and wisdom that lay beyond that, I would have to discover for myself over the course of the next thirty years. I had to reinvent the goddamn wheel. I'm only really getting a handle on my relationship with my reproductive system now, on the brink of menopause. Where were all these tools when I was building my life?

Finding myself with another unwanted pregnancy at the age of twenty, I returned to Buffalo to have another abortion. I was administered some kind of gas and remember muttering things on my way from and back to full consciousness. I was mortified at this. What did I say? The very next night I was on stage in a whole other town, playing guitar with a dull ache in my gut where my tissues had been sucked from me. I had already committed Lucille Clifton's "lost baby poem" to heart and I cried while I recited it. I cried secretly behind my singing. I had experienced a physical and emotional upheaval and again the trauma was compounded by the shaming and condemnation. I shared lots of things with the audience that night but fear of more shame and condemnation kept me from sharing the one biggest thing.

Here's the truth: I have had two abortions, I have borne two children, I think I had an early miscarriage once, and of course, I've had more periods than I care to count. From experience, here's what I know to be true: Life does not begin at conception. It begins before.

It is written in patriarchal texts that the man carries the seed and that he sows it in the world, but that's more of that classic patriarchal flip-of-the-script if you ask me. It's not the man who carries the seed, it's woman. The human ovum, by far the largest cell in a human body, is the seed of a person. In every seed, even before fertilization, there resides a powerful dream. It is the dream of becoming. Seeds are, by their very nature, full of hope and longing. They are very much alive.

Every girl baby is born with a basket of tender seeds. Her birth is fractal, her being is fractal, and from there stems the revolutionary consciousness that feminism, at its best, can offer the world. Only in relationship with one another do we actually exist. Autonomy is an illusion. Your blood *is* my blood, my body *is* your body. Such is the lived truth of the mother. The advancement of feminism and the emancipation of women is necessary if only to break the masculine trance of separateness and individuality. Or at least to provide an adequate counterweight.

As a female, you can claim your individuality but also there is the macro experience which I will call being a part of the Great Mother Spirit, which you cannot opt out of. Even should you choose not to personally reproduce, there are still sacrifices to be made. The first of which is that, when you become a woman, you will be asked to start letting go of your seeds. You will be asked to serve the cause of life by participating in its brutal inner mechanisms of natural selection and death.

The death of each unfertilized ovum, in the days prior to menstruation, is also the death of a potential human being. On some level, it is felt as such by the woman whose death it also is. When a human seed gives up its dream of life and dies, there is some measure of reckoning to be done by the Great Mother Spirit. If, in this moment, you are she, the everyday cell death that is a function of growth and being-hood can magnify in your heart to a scale that feels unbearable. The world spins dark. The woman whose job it is to reach into her basket of dreams and let one die every month may become angry and resentful. She may rage at the world. She may sob.

In medical science, this physical and spiritual experience of grief is called PMS and culturally it is seen as proof of woman's irrationality and hyper-emotionalism. In truth, I think it is more a function of our collective misunderstanding of the whole phenomenon, which is crazy-making. It is the default setting of disrespect and disregard, or seeking to pathologize and control the feminine experience that becomes maddening.

There is difficulty in the menstrual cycle, yes, even darkness, but if we could collectively comprehend it enough to depersonalize it, I believe it would make a lot more sense to us all. How could the "miracle" of creation not come at an equally profound cost? A cost not simply exacted in one seismic moment of childbirth. A cost not even exacted just from women. We should have respect for the Great Mother Spirit even as rumbling storm clouds and lightning move through her mortal servants. We should listen closely to the messages her servants bring back from the fire. We should respect the grief and the suffering, for they are inherent to the fires of creation. They are the handmaidens of renewal.

Watch the woman who holds a seed's hand as it rides a roller coaster from high hopes and an unbridled lust for existence, down the dizzying dive of the fallopian tubes, to abandonment, rejection, and death in the womb. One minute that woman is ovulating and irresistible, exuding all the force and beauty of life itself, and the next she is twisted around her bitterness. But how could she not rage at the world when all of nature is using her eyes to cry? Afterwards, she will bleed and shed the loss and disappointment and the process will begin again. She will reopen herself again and again to the dream of becoming. With or without cultural conformation, this is the reality women live every day.

Some seeds give up their dream and reintegrate into the cosmos easier than others, maybe they weren't convinced about the whole undertaking to begin with? Others can drive you horny-toads with their willfulness and then slay you with their disappointment when they get shit-canned. The fertilized ovum that dies in an abortion is a seed that managed to get a little further along (it really thought it had it this time!)

but one abundant rain of spermatozoa does not a whole human being make. Making a full-fledged human being is actually a long, complicated and arduous process, not an instant miracle from God.

The seed of a tree falls from the safety of its branch onto concrete. Another finds ground but there is no rain. Another is chewed up and eaten by an animal. Another is so lucky as to sprout but then is thwarted under a falling log. None of these things is a tree. The seedlings of animals, including humans, are no less voluminous and their deaths no more tragic. This process of selection is repeated naturally and necessarily for every actualized human being as for every mighty oak. For every tree in the forest, there are thousands of tree dreams deferred. To pull out the hearse and have a funeral for every aborted fetus is indicative of man's will towards exceptionality. His quest for superiority and mastery over all other beings, including women.

Until a human fetus is viable and can live and breathe in the world, it is a thing synonymous with woman, just as the walnut is part of the walnut tree. I know I'm working this tree metaphor a little hard here but, seriously . . . it is just so damn simple! The woman is the tree, dude! Her branches have been waving and waving all this time, shouting, "Up here!" while the patriarchal gaze looks right past her, unseeing, and projects its ego like a laser into her gut. War is mass murder, capital punishment is murder, murder is murder. Abortion is part of the eternal process of natural selection, one that women have been engaging in since long before medical science came along to offer any compensation for the entrapments of the modern social design. When a woman chooses whether or not to reproduce, the earth itself is choosing. With or without confirmation from man, this is the reality that the earth lives every day.

I used to periodically count the ages that my first two children would've been if they had entered the world as such. It wasn't that I was wistful that maybe I should've borne children at eighteen and twenty years old (not at all), more that I was in awe that the life inside me had the power to overtake me at any moment and jump from my clutches into the hands of another. It was an exercise in the terrifying math of the near miss. *Your life as you envisioned it could have effectively ended three, five . . . ten years ago. Just imagine. What kind of shell of your former dreams would you be now?*

And now, having happily carried two children to term, I can also tell you this about pregnancy: At first it is something that happens to you, then it becomes something you do, then, many months after that, it becomes a relationship between you and "someone else." Taking the position that a two-celled zygote has more liberty and agency, more of a right to become itself than the woman who carries it, *that* is the real tragedy. The real murder. For man to be unable to acknowledge the full humanity of a woman and instead to project his own ego onto a partially formed fetus hidden in the lining of her most central core being, shows the deep deficiency of perception created by patriarchy. Only in a world so thoroughly immersed in patriarchy would this whole farce of enforced reproduction (or enforced sterilization) even be possible. Men dictating to women when and how they shall give birth is treason.

Granted, another woman might have a totally different relationship with her basket of seeds than I do. She might have lived it all differently and her truth will be equally true. Contextual thinking is another hallmark of feminism. There really are no absolutes. Another woman might feel so much compassion for each tiny little green shoot that she might immediately and eternally scratch abortion off her list of remote possibilities. This seems entirely understandable and sweet to me. I respect maternal nature in all its forms.

Women make these calls based on so many things that men can only begin to speculate about. Every situation is unique and every woman is right when she decides what is right for herself. At the core of a belief in reproductive freedom is an affirmation of diversity. The right to our human diversity, more than the right to privacy, is what we're really talking about when we talk about the freedom of choice. Like religious freedom and the freedom of speech, reproductive freedom in America should be understood as a fundamental right of reasonable people to be different from one another and to understand things differently. Our freedom to have differences of opinion and perception and to be allowed to live and express those perceptions is at the supposed core of the American state. Reproductive freedom must be understood as a civil right.

Meanwhile, each and every aborted seed is simply hurled back into the infinite field of possibility, death not being an ending, but a life process. The first law of thermodynamics (one of the classical properties of our earthly existence) is that energy cannot be created or destroyed. Why should humans be different? Where does the dream of life go when it is unable to manifest into a particular (temporary, finite) human form? It goes somewhere else. It goes into another, wanted, welcome, and supported form. It moves to the left and to the right and becomes that dragonfly, that mountain, that happy, cherished baby right there. *Trust women and fear not. All of consciousness is manifesting, no matter who gives birth to what.*

The Slant

a building settling
around me my
figure female framed crookedly
in the threshold
of the room
door scraping floor boards with every opening, carving
a rough history of bedroom scenes
the plot hard to follow
the text obscured
in the folds of sheets slowly gathering the stains
of seasons spent lying there
red and brown, like leaves fallen

the colors of an eternal cycle
fading
with the wash cycle
and the rinse cycle
again an (un)familiar smell
like my name misspelled
or misspoken
a cycle broken

the sound of them strong stalking
talking about their prey like the way
hammer meets nail
pounding they say
pounding out the rhythms of attraction
like a woman was a drum
like a body was a weapon
like there was something more they wanted
than the journey
like it was owed to them
steel toed they walk and i'm wondering why
this fear of men?
maybe, it's because i'm hungry
and like a baby i'm dependent on them
to feed me
i am a work in progress
dressed in the fabric of a world unfolding
offering me intricate patterns of questions
rhythms that never come clean
and strengths
that you still haven't seen

My IQ

when i was four years old they tried to test my IQ
they showed me this picture of three oranges and a pear
they asked me, "which one is different and does not belong?"
they taught me different
is wrong

but when i was thirteen years old
i woke up one morning
thighs covered in blood
like a war, like a warning
that i live in a breakable, take-able body
an ever increasingly valuable body
that a woman had come in the night to replace me
deface me

see my body is borrowed, i got it on loan
for the time in between my mom and some maggots
i don't need anyone to hold me, i can hold my own
i got highways for stretchmarks
see where i've grown?

and i sing sometimes like my life is at stake
cuz you're only as loud as the noises you make
i'm learning to laugh as hard as i can listen
cuz silence is violence in women and poor people
if more people were screaming
then i could relax
but a good brain ain't diddly
if you don't have the facts

we live in a breakable, take-able world
an ever available, possible world
and we can make music
like we can make do
genius is in a backbeat
back seat to nothing if you're dancing
especially something stupid
like IQ

for every lie i unlearn
i learn something new

and i sing sometimes
for the war that i fight
cuz every tool is a weapon
if you hold it right

BEAUTY AND THE BEAST

The lady who Dale hooked me up with in Austin was a middle-aged party chick named Silvia who was attempting to parlay her party-chick skills into a job in the music biz. She fancied herself a promoter and took me around town, trying to educate me about Texas music culture like it was the most important thing anybody could know. Nothing much came of our association. I got more gigs on my own, but after I left town, she and Dale devised an idea for how to get me back down to Texas. Silvia paired me with a songwriter of Mexican descent that I'll call Darkness Rodriguez, and she dubbed our little Texas tour "Beauty and the Beast." Darkness and I joked often about who was who, but we gamely played bars together in San Antonio and Dallas as well as a few shows in and around Austin.

Most of these shows were attended only by the drinkers and pool players who happened to be in the place anyway, but I can remember reaching through the din one night in San Antonio and touching a drunk woman out there floating in the flock of ten-gallon hats. This woman started to tune in to me and then slowly I could feel her energy focus on what I was putting down. At the end of my set (a moment that went unnoticed by some, heckled by others) she raised a fist in the air and let out a long guttural hoot that really made my night.

Some of the gigs with Darkness involved us sitting on stage together, trading songs. His songs were long, literary ballads with social commentary built into their carefully crafted verses. In his mid-forties, he was also a lawyer and had grown up well educated and comfortable but his songs were from the perspective of the working class and the immigrant Mexican. He would amble on stage with a lurching gait, the two aluminum canes that he used to walk fastened around his elbows and his guitar slung over his back.

A bout with polio as a child had left one of his legs crooked as a tree branch and that one he used mainly for balance. The other leg was thin and limp so it was strapped into a rigid thigh-to-ankle brace. That one was the pillar on which he stood. Darkness was not exactly kind, but I gave him the benefit of the doubt that having your legs swept out from underneath you as a child could leave you with a bitterness that I shouldn't judge. He was also barely taller than I was myself and we made an interesting couple and an interesting show really . . . for anyone bothering to pay attention.

I made Darkness laugh a lot and he seemed to not be a laughing kind of guy. We started hanging out outside of the shows and I was introduced, one by one, to all the people who fed him the material for his songs. They were a tribe of gun-packing Chicano outlaws and they each had a silent girlfriend who was impossible to get to know, at least in

English . . . at least by me. I was a human oddity in their scene and probably considered no more a real woman there than I was in the white
cowboy equivalent. With my shaved head, my army boots, and my insistence on participating in all the political debates with the men, I stood
out, so I settled into the old familiar role of weirdo.

My curiosity propelled me to slip into the role of Darkness's lover,
though he was twice my age and there was no actual love between us.
He apparently had had a wife and kids once, but they seemed to be nowhere to be found. The one activity I refused to join his crew in was
their cocaine consumption. I stayed in the living room smiling awkwardly at the silent girlfriends while the men retreated to the bedroom
for more fuel for their big talk.

One day, I called Dale and he informed me that a girl at UC Santa
Cruz had written to invite me to come play there. California! Now, that
was further than I'd ever been. Besides, I needed to get out of Texas.
Darkness had a little beater car and I told him if he wanted to go with
me I would pay for the gas and I could do most of the driving. Much to
my surprise, he said yes. Turns out, he had never been outside of Texas
before.

Two things should have tipped me off that this journey was not going
to be a walk in the park. One was that Darkness snorted his last cocaine
bump on his way out the door, and the other was that we had to jump the
car to get it started.

CALIFORNIIAY

We had three random cassette tapes on the journey, brought by
me, and we wore them plumb out. One was a Robert Johnson
compilation, one was Prince's *Purple Rain* and one was Bob Dylan's latest record, *Oh Mercy*, which Silvia had laid on me as I was leaving. Every

new stretch of landscape reminded Darkness of a Clint Eastwood movie and the differences between us grew starker with the terrain. I navigated the car among the towering red buttes of Utah and we both gasped as they lurched up around us. Darkness spontaneously hollered, "I'm sorry!" at the channel of blue sky overhead but, actually, he sounded like he always sounded: like he didn't really give a shit. He was not sorry for how he treated me anyway, that's for sure, and his demeanor grew colder and more forbidding as we went. Maybe it was just the cocaine withdrawal.

One night, in the high desert of New Mexico, we decided to pull over to take in the infinity of stars that had consumed the sky. Not only was there an endless tapestry of stars above us, they were raining down and burning out, one after the other, right over the hood of our car. Darkness was driving and, in his inexperience, he pulled over too far onto the snow-packed shoulder. This was not the first time he'd gotten us stuck. The world of Clint Eastwood was more textural and viscous than it appeared on the big screen. Having the only working legs in our operation, it was my job to push us out again but this time, as it turns out, we were really stuck. I dug with my hands in front of each tire and I rocked that bumper with all I had but the wheels just spun deeper into the snow.

We waited for a long time on the empty road, silently watching shooting stars as it got colder and colder inside the car. Then, over the ridge, appeared the headlights of a pickup truck. Not wanting to fuck around, I did jumping jacks in the middle of the road to make sure it stopped. The truck stopped with its headlights on me and out lumbered a huge Native American man in silhouette looking like Nicholson's sidekick in *One Flew Over the Cuckoo's Nest*. I turned to Darkness and knew exactly what he was thinking.

The man looked from me to Darkness and back again, silently assessing the situation. I met his eyes and watched as volumes of unspoken words floated strangely in the air between us. He nodded and got behind the back bumper with me, signaling to Darkness to hit the gas. The car still didn't budge so the man went and got two flat boards out of the back of his truck and we wedged them in front of each of the front tires. That did the trick and I hooted my joy as I reached out to shake one of his big hands in both of my tiny frozen ones. A faint smile crossed his lips and more flakes of unspoken words floated silently down onto the snow between our feet.

Coming down off the Sierra Nevadas into the fertile bowl of the Pacific for the first time was another sensory experience like I will never forget. How rapturous the Pacific air after so many miles of rock and sand! No wonder everybody and their cousin was moving to California! This was ridiculous. Avocados and mangos dripped from the sky into my mouth and waves lapped seductively at my toes. People everywhere padded around in their sandy bare feet while day after beatific day dawned breezy and balmy around them. I was almost mad at these people who had the gall to live in paradise instead of in the real world. The whole place seemed inappropriately sublime.

By the time I made it to the UC Santa Cruz radio station, where I was scheduled to do an interview, Darkness and I were more than ready to say goodbye to each other. I told him to just go, that I could take it from here, having no idea where I was actually going to sleep that night or what I was going to do after that. He turned and lurched away and I never saw him again.

I did the on-air interview, played a couple tunes, and then I bid goodbye to the DJ in his booth. I sat down in a chair in the front room of the radio station to contemplate my next bold move. Before I could get too mired in contemplation, two young blonde women appeared, both of them beautiful and tanned with California written all over them. They had heard me on the radio and had come to find me. They asked me if I wanted to go kayaking with them. "Yes," I answered, amazed. "That is precisely what I want to do."

Floating out on the ocean, breathing in the briny wind, I became acquainted with the girl who would become my running partner for years. Her name was Shawnee and her California sandy feet walked just as independent a path as my black New York boots did. I had to give it to her: Her thinking stood in constant challenge to everything she was ever told. Plus, her free-spirited bare-footedness was very seductive. She was voluptuous and uncontainable and I was not the only human to be attracted. Marvel Comics could have drawn my story up to this point but R. Crumb would have needed to step in here to draw Shawnee. Crumb would portray her accidentally crushing buildings under her feet with lots of tiny little men running out of them. He would draw her, face and tits upcast, laughing at the sky.

Shawnee and I were to become defectors together, periodically dropping out of society and into a world of our own devising. We would become confidants and even lovers but all that didn't happen yet. On this day, she just took me kayaking on the ocean and then back underneath the redwoods for my show at the university. My sweet cousin Julie had also heard me on the radio that day and showed up to the show. I used to see Julie up at the lake in Quebec every summer and now here she was, living in Santa Cruz. By the time the show was over, I was swept up in a swirl of awesome women and my journey out to California was all but forgotten. Life can change fast.

REVERSE OBJECTIFICATION

Shawnee had a jalopy painted a reassuringly similar color to the rust that covered its lower half, and we used it to make the scene. She took me to the nude beach north of town where men crouched low over the dunes with binoculars and she took me down to the boardwalk to ride the rickety roller coaster and laugh at ourselves in the funhouse mirrors. I noticed the amount of catcalls in my daily life increased exponentially with Venus de Milo by my side. I couldn't help but remark at the desperation men seemed to exhibit for a bodacious blonde with big tits. It was simply incessant.

We got to wondering what men would do if we flipped the script and treated them in that way so we decided to do a social experiment. We saddled up in the relative safety of the orange bomber and drove all around town. We slowed down by groups of men and also by men walking alone. We catcalled young men, middle-aged men, and old men. We tried to be thorough and scientific while mentally recording our findings. Here are the basic results of our reverse objectification study:

Young men = confused
Middle-aged men = angry
Old men = elated

Groups of men tended towards the aggressive and veered towards anger but men walking alone exhibited more humor and curiosity. No one was intimidated.

I hatched a plan to buy a car myself and drive back east. I had just about enough money saved with the addition of my life savings wired by Western Union from Buffalo. I was advised that L.A. was the best place to find a car for cheap so I said goodbye to Shawnee and took the bus there. I stayed with Scot's friend Mike in Redondo Beach while looking through the swap sheets and making calls. Sure enough, with Mike's help, I found a 1969 Volkswagen Beetle with my name on it and soon I was waving goodbye to California.

I had only just exited L.A., heading east, when I looked down and realized my gas gauge had plummeted to empty. I panicked. Wait, wasn't it full when I left? I must have a leak or something! I pulled over and whipped out the dog-eared VW fix-it bible that had come with the car and started poring through its pages. Then I looked up and laughed out loud. I was actually hundreds of miles from L.A. and I had just driven for three hours. With my shit-eating grin plastered to the inside of my windshield, it had felt like ten minutes. Time really does fly when you're having fun. I looked around and realized I'd never felt so free. I had my own car and I could point it in any direction I chose.

The only problem with driving for thousands of miles by yourself is that you can't play guitar. There was no tape deck in that Beetle, either, so I found myself doing some deep FM and AM spelunking. I sang backup with all the raucous Mexican music and the country and pop music stations, too. Still, I missed my guitar and experimented with trying to play it behind the wheel but even on the wide-open highways of the West, off hours, I determined beyond a doubt that driving and playing guitar is not feasible. Let alone a good idea. Out of desperation, I wrote an a capella song called "Every State Line" and sang it over and over as I drove.

UP A NOTCH

Unfortunately, I sold that '69 Beetle in Buffalo for more than I paid for it and downgraded to an eighties Hyundai. Scot had gotten it in his head that '69 was not the proper vintage automobile for a young woman to be traversing in back and forth across the country alone (a thing I planned to do again as soon as possible). My success in Santa Cruz had won me a return engagement and Dale was helping me to cobble together a random handful of gigs between the east and west coasts to justify another long journey.

That poor Hyundai was a shaking, rattling, hot mess from the git-go, nonetheless, it was to become my main mode of transportation and my official residence for the next few years. Tired of paying New York rents for apartments I rarely visited, I dumped Stella on Scot and officially traded in my zip code for a license plate number. Goodbye New York. I painted and collaged every inch of that Hyundai's surface, inside and out, on my endless journey, carrying art supplies with me and working as I went. Home improvements. That was before I understood that green hair and a wildly painted car were like neon signs blinking out there on the high plains of middle America, saying "Pull me over! I'm just the kind of anti-authoritarian punk you're dying to fuck with!"

I pointed the rolling artmobile west and my first stop past Buffalo was this little club outside of Cleveland, a gig that would have been entirely unmemorable except that some bigwig booking agent guy was supposed to be showing up to check me out. Dale had gotten a call from said booking agent after I tore up the Mariposa Folk Festival a month earlier in Toronto. Dale's Toronto connection had scored me a few workshops and a day stage set at Mariposa and by the end of the weekend I had sold more tapes than any other artist. An audible buzz ensued in the folk underground. "This is the biggest folk booking agency in the country!" Dale told me excitedly over the phone. "He said he's been hearing about you!"

The agent did show up that night in Cleveland, his name was Jim Fleming, and he struck me as a stand-up guy. I did not have a decent turnout to impress him with, there was only a handful of people in the room, but something in my songs caught his ear. To his credit, he cared more about good songs than he did impressive turnouts and he was not a man afraid to put in the time it takes to build a career. We sat in his car after the show and he told me about his booking agency and his history in music. He told me about his life and his family as though I were a trusted friend and I was inspired to do the same. After talking for a while, he offered to be my agent on the spot. I was psyched and immediately said yes. He said well, we'd better adhere to protocol and I should just officially think about it. He would call Dale.

I never had a map or much knowledge of the unfamiliar territory that this career-in-music thing was pushing me into, it all happened too fast. As each fork in the road presented itself, I just followed my instincts and rarely broke speed. As long as my mind was working unconflicted and receiving messages clearly from my gut, my gut served me well.

Jim gave me a cassette of a brand-new album from another artist on his roster that he had been listening to on the drive down. It was Greg Brown's *Down in There* and I traded him for one of my cassettes, which he did not have yet. He drove off listening to my eponymous debut and I drove off listening to Greg. (At least that lil' Hyundai had a tape deck.) I felt good and I suppose I would've felt even better had I known that Jim was to become an enduring friend and ally and also my dedicated booking agent for the next twenty-five years.

All I knew at the time was that I needed to drive quite a ways to an ill-advised gig in Minneapolis, my first ever in that town. The gig was a few blocks from the wonderful Cedar Cultural Center but at the time they didn't know I existed and vice versa. Jim would change all that. This day, I was playing for tips in some café, much to the chagrin of the waitstaff. During my set break one of the waiters asked me to please turn down. "I didn't think I was playing that loud," I said. "Well, see, this is not really a music venue," the dude explained. I slunk back to my corner to finish out my appointed duties quietly, as background music.

As is turns out, though, several people had actually come there to hear me play, thanks to the handful of postcards I had sent out, so I played just to them while they leaned in to listen through the restaurant din. One of them was a man who bought my cassette with four two-dollar bills and two Susan B. Anthony coins. I was impressed. Another was a dyke who looked me in the eye afterwards and said, "MJ in Austin says you are welcome to stay with her anytime." ". . . What?" I blinked. "You remember MJ in Austin?" "Yes." "She wants you to know you are welcome to stay with her any time."

MJ was a singer-songwriter I'd met at the Cactus Café when I had first arrived in Austin. She was running the open mic there. I had showed up at her open mic a few times and before you knew it, MJ and I were teaming up to split a few nights in the Cactus's upstairs room. MJ was easygoing and understated. Gentlemanly. Come to think of it, we did have a kind of flirtatious vibe. I thought about her offer as I packed up my stuff in the Minneapolis café. I wondered if she would think it was funny if I pulled up outside her door in the exact amount of time it would take me to drive to Texas after receiving her message. I eked a cup of coffee out of the café and pulled onto I-35 South.

I can't remember where my next gig was but it wasn't for at least a week. Why not hang out in good ole Austin? I drove south without sleeping and went directly to MJ's house, stopping only for gas and once to save a goddamn puppy. An ill-advised move. But what could I do? I was cruising down some busy six-lane divided highway through some big town and I caught sight of this little black puppy running down the goddamn median. *What the fuck?!* I checked the rearview to verify. There he was, his little furry black body bounding through the tall grass.

I got off at the next exit and drove back along the service road until I spotted him again. Then I hopped the fence and played chicken across the highway with my heart in my throat. When the little guy spotted me, he started running in the other direction. "Comeer you little fool!" I yelled over the din of passing semis, running in hot pursuit, thinking, *Great, just great, Ani! Now, exactly what you were trying to avoid happening, is going to happen right in front of your face!*

I overtook him and scooped him up and the first thing he did was shit soupy diarrhea all down the front of me. I ran back across the road, covered in shit and clutching his little quaking body. Then we had a fine time scaling the fence together. I cleaned us up the best I could (new shirt for me, shit shirt for him) and off we went to the nearest restroom to do a better job.

By the time we got to a restroom, I realized I had a beset puppy on my hands. He was scratching and scratching himself silly in the wheel well of my car, flinging shitty shit everywhere and yelping at his own flagellations.

I discovered, after I washed him clean, that there were places where his fur was scratched bare. He must have some bad fleas, I thought.

I went and procured some food for him and he ate ravenously. Having no idea what to do, I made him a bed of a flannel shirt and left him in the ladies room at a nearby train station with a note asking someone to please help him find shelter and care. It was the best I could do. I drove away with a sinking feeling in my belly and the windows of my car open to air out the smell. I was trying to reassure myself that some kind woman would take it from here. At least he was not roadkill.

TYPHOID MARY

I made my way to Austin and MJ's house and she welcomed me into her life and into her bed. It was strange to be in Austin again, but this time I managed not to intersect with any of the people from my former time there. MJ and I palled around for a week and then I said it was time for me to head west. On a whim, I asked her if she wanted to come and her answer was yes. She unstitched herself from her life and off we went. Luckily for me, she was game for sleeping in the car or out under the stars at night with no tent. The Southwest was a wonder to behold and this time, with kind company and a feeling like we were in it together, I could actually enjoy it.

Around the time that MJ jumped in, the bushing around the gearshift broke in the Hyundai (it was a standard) and the car ceased to go in reverse. *No going back*, my poet's brain chuckled to itself. The inability to go in reverse did actually present a startling amount of difficulty in our travels, however. You eventually develop an instinct for not pointing yourself into dead ends and you get good at things like using gravity to park. That game gets a lot easier in San Francisco. We did have quite a few mishaps, though, and we got so we would jump out and push that car around without even having to speak about it.

As it turns out, that little black puppy had scabies. As it turns out, now so did I. And so did MJ. And her housemates back in Texas. When they informed us over the phone, they were not pleased. Scabies are harder than fleas to get rid of, harder than lice. It requires the laundering of every last bit of fabric one might own or ever think of owning and a prescription cream for the body. We were so screwed out there on the road. The rolling scabiemobile would claim more victims before this particular cross-country odyssey would come to an end. MJ jumped out in Santa Cruz and Shawnee jumped in for a few thousand miles. And, of course, Scot was waiting at the finish line.

THE CHANGING OF THE GUARD

Dale had been fielding the steady drip of snail-mail gig offers that trickled into the P.O. box and responding to all inquiries in the evenings from his desk at *The Buffalo News*. As a music critic, he worked nights in the 24/7 newsroom, staying until the wee hours in his little cubicle. Go see a gig, then go back to the office and write about it for print the next morning, that and reviewing albums was his life. Being nocturnal myself, this arrangement worked great for me because late was the best time for me to call. *The Buffalo News*'s 1-800 number was our lifeline. "Dale Anderson, please" was probably the sentence heard most by the night shift switchboard operator. We should have known trouble was coming.

Dale was treating *The Buffalo News* like it was our office, shipping my CDs out of their mailroom and making calls from his desk. He was not exactly savvy or discreet about it, like either he didn't understand the consequences or he just didn't get that there might be a conflict. For whatever reason, he was practicing a sort of honesty by default that I can relate to. I have been known to practice honesty by default myself. Basically, if you don't put any real energy into hiding, you will eventually be seen and then at least the place in the world that you shake down to will be an honest one. One day the word came down and Dale was demoted from rock critic to writing obituaries. It is a testament to the power of the union, I suppose, that he was not fired outright.

Meanwhile, with Jim Fleming on the case, my touring schedule had suddenly amped up and the demands on Dale had become more complicated. There was a contract to sign for every gig (two forty-five-minute sets with a fifteen-minute intermission) and a rider to send out (coffee *and* water backstage!). Payment came in the form of "guarantees" plus "percentages" and there was math to be done and records to be kept. There were more directions to be gotten and arrangements to be made. There were more and more people to respond to, pay, and get paid by. There were more and more cracks for the details to fall through.

Dale's inability to negotiate the world of the music business with much more aplomb than I was part of his charm and maybe even part of our connection but that charm was being lost on an increasing number of others. No sooner was the task of managing my affairs mutating into an actual (if meagerly) paying job, poor Dale was in over his head. The tension began building between him and Jim and I found myself caught in the middle. Jim had been through plenty of "first manager" types with his jazz and folk artists over the years. He knew the deal all too well.

My audience would eventually outgrow the folk circuit and Jim, himself, would be forced into new territory. He, too, would get pushed. But there seemed to be nothing he couldn't do. Somehow, Jim managed to book arenas and multiple bus tours the same way he did with coffeehouses, with integrity and heart and a sense of community at the fore. He was loyal to the little indie promoters, even the shitty ones, until sometimes I was just standing there looking at him, tapping my toe. That was the exact way I wanted to be represented in the world, though (with too much kindness), and he knew it, so he always had his ace in the hole.

One day a mistake Dale made resulted in a thousand-dollar fine for me which, at the time, really hurt. It was a hard blow. Then Dale and some guy he knew in England got together and booked me for a few gigs over there. It was to be my first triumphant return to England after my self-guided *Now Voyager* stint. We were very excited that my picture had even made it into the *Time Out* magazine of London, but Dale's associate had advised him that I didn't need a work permit, so that publicity quickly became a liability. When I got to Heathrow, the customs people pointed to my picture in *Time Out* and my lack of proper paperwork and shook their heads at me, denying me entry. After many long hours at the airport, I was turned around and put on the next plane back to New York with a stamp on my passport that would haunt me for the next ten years. My moment of reckoning with Dale had come.

I asked Dale to meet me at an ice cream shop on Elmwood Avenue in Buffalo where I had worked as a teenager. I thanked him for his help and his friendship but I told him I would not be renewing our year-long management contract when it was up in a few months. It had been almost two years and we'd had some fine adventures, but it was time for me to go it on my own again. I no longer needed what he had to offer. We cried and hugged and laughed together.

Dale was not about to quit his pension-paying job at the paper to be my manager for real. He and I both knew it. Not only did being my manager not come with a pension, it didn't even really come with a salary yet. Our contract stipulated that his 20 percent management commission didn't kick in until I grossed over twenty thousand dollars a year or something and that had barely happened. He reiterated that that's why our contract was only a year in length: so that we were both in it together only because we both wanted to be. He seemed to get it and even seemed a little relieved. We hugged again, we wished each other luck, we went our separate ways.

Dale had continued to go around with me, without pay, because we laughed a lot and because everywhere we went people got excited. He came because he, too, was a lover of music and adventure and I think he really needed to get out of his particular grind. In the beginning, he had seen me as a potential path to gold and glory, but soon enough, I had become just a fun diversion. Now that being my manager was threatening to mutate into a real job with a grind all its own, it was his stop.

Going it on my own is not exactly what happened next, however. Scot had been moving in from the periphery, providing organizational support where Dale's had been failing. Scot kept telling me that I needed to get my shit together before I got audited. My habit of hitting the road and transforming whatever funds came my way into greasy diner food for my belly and gas for my car, with no actual record of what was earned or spent, was viewed by him as unsustainable. It was maybe a bit premature, considering my income was barely at a taxable level, but still he had a point. Now that there were contracts being signed and actual W-2 forms being filled out with my name on them, I would need to step up my game.

Scot's first move in Dale's wake was to pull out two envelopes before I left on my next trip and hand them to me. On one he wrote "gig money" and on the other he wrote "tape money." He told me to keep a running tally of how many tapes I sold on the "tape money" envelope. And take money only out of the "gig money" envelope for expenses. And keep a running tally on the "gig money" envelope of expenses. And save receipts. In fact, here's another envelope labeled "receipts."

Scot began calling himself my "business manager" and it wasn't long before business manager just became manager and Jim had another inexperienced first-timer on his hands. This time, it was the dreaded boyfriend-manager. Jim was understandably skeptical but he gave Scot a chance and eventually Scot managed to rise to the occasion and earn his respect.

ANDY

There are a lot of Ukrainians in Canada. You notice this if you hang out there long enough. I guess migrating people like to stick to their latitude. In the family photo, Andy Stochansky's babushka'd grandma sits stoically in the middle of a clan of pale potato people, all thoroughly white and Eastern European except for Andy, sitting on his mother's lap, dark as all get-out. Like the Turkish postman dropped off a little package for his mom one day or something. Andy's hands alone, crossed on his own lap, looked like they belonged to a different family. "Blood of the wolf," his grandma would hiss under her breath while shuffling away, shaking her head at him.

I first heard Andy play at the Tralfamadore Café, a club commonly known as the Tralf, in downtown Buffalo. The evening was a split bill between myself and a Toronto-based pianist/singer named Anne Bourne. Andy was Anne's sensitive, back-up-singing, djembe-playing accompanist for the evening and he was very tasteful and vibey. His dark curls fell mysteriously around his eyes. *Hmm, that guy is good,* I thought and, after the show, I got his number.

We met above his grandma's grocery store on Queen Street in Toronto to jam together for the first time. I was pierced and jackbooted with a shaved head and his grandma didn't seem to much like the looks of me, either. Andy was so very Canadian, with his accent, his gentle manners, and his red and black flannel, I had little choice but to be charmed. We immediately felt each other when we played music together because we were both so dynamic and fluid with volume. Finally! Someone else who knows how to breathe with it! Here, finally, was someone I could really jam with.

I hired him immediately and we started gigging in and around our triumvirate of cities: New York, Buffalo, and Toronto. Andy had just started playing drum kit and before we could embark on too much road tripping, he needed to procure some cases. Instead of dropping any dough on legit cases, he and his father built some plywood jobbies and stuffed them with foam wedges and blankets. The wheels at the bottom were too small and they were tippy and tricky to roll. Any bump would invariably mean a shin-splintering disaster and a lengthy cleanup. At the top were angry latches sticking out everywhere that would gouge you as soon as look at you, but Andy had an affection for these cases because he and his dad had made them together. I had affection for them, too, actually, because I loved his dad. Our dads were a lot alike.

Andy could speak Ukrainian fluently and he used to work the waitresses at Veselka on Second Avenue in New York pretty hard. One day I walked in there to meet him for a bowl of borscht and when I sat down I got the full once-over from our matronly waitress. They were obviously tight already. She frowned at me and turned to Andy and I watched while they exchanged a few words. Cocking an eyebrow at Andy as she walked away, I inquired, "What did she say?" "She asked if you were one of ours," he informed me. "I told her no . . . but that you were just a friend."

I had made two recordings, my eponymous debut in November of 1990 and *Not So Soft* in November of 1991, but by the spring of 1992, I already had a pile of new songs so I enlisted the help of Andy and a ragtag collection of Buffalo musicians to make *Imperfectly*, my first record that was not just me alone. The album came out in June and I was off on my second gauntlet of summer folk festivals, this time with Andy by my side. He played drum kit and hand percussion and I played my one and only guitar. My playing was aggressive so I got good at telling stories and jokes while changing broken strings.

Andy's rig was pretty rickety so I also became proficient at launching into poems and stories while he duct-taped his world back together. One night, while I was doing a poem, there was a series of loud thumps and clanking sounds coming from his world. *He must be trying to fix that god-damn pedal*, I thought. "What the hell was happening during 'Not So Soft'?" I asked, sweaty and panting, as soon as we got back to the dressing room. He pouted at me and then replied impetuously, "I was painting with kick drum." "You were painting with *kick drum*?!" I squawked. "Since when is a kick drum something you paint with?" We looked at each other for a second and then we both laughed until we fell over.

That winter came another record, *Puddle Dive*, and Andy and I were clocking in long hours in rented minivans, dingy motels, and tiny dressing rooms together. We were touring more than we were not touring. There were no cellphones or computers, we were just out there together, becoming acquainted with the world, one town and one hole-in-the-wall at a time. The shared memories were piling up around us. After a certain number of miles, you become like war buddies, with unspoken reams of understanding between you. As the choo choo train passed the stage at the Christmas crafts fair (yours truly judiciously editing each one of my songs in real time) Andy and I would just have to look at each other and we'd both lose it. Fleming was booking me some pretty wack engagements in those days. The only strategy seemed to be: Get her out there and keep her out there. I was just happy to not be out there alone.

On stage, Andy started piping up more and more and our back-and-forth banter, always off the cuff and unscripted, was pretty hilarious. He started singing with me, too, and for the first time since my days with Michael, I found I didn't have to sing by myself. The presence of Andy on stage turned out to be an unintentionally useful theatrical device for my show, actually. Like the token white guy in a black band, Andy helped to build a psychic bridge between me and the audience, allowing them to overcome their fear.

Andy had more of a sense of theater than I did in general. I was a folksinger through and through and had only one mode: walk out on stage in the shirt you woke up in and start interacting with people. To premeditate anything was cowardly or false, in my book. Somewhere in me, I was biased to think that, if art is a dialogue, then to plan out what you're going to say or do when you meet an audience is to negate their presence and dishonor the ever-living Now. Andy brought my bumpkin folksinger approach into question, subtly at first, then more forcefully as he started to feel freer to voice his opinions and ideas. I tried on his theatrical ideas and had fun experimenting with my own shows and my own preconceived notions.

"What if we both come down through the audience playing hand drums, singing blahdy blah and then end up on stage at your microphone just for the last chorus?!" "What if we walk out in total darkness and tell the lighting guy to hit only backlights as we start singing in silhouette?" "What if you did that guitar feedback thing in 'In or Out' and then ended it by taking off your guitar and laying it down on the monitor while it's still massively feeding back?! Then you could stage dive into the audience and exit the room from the back! Like, disappear out the front door of the venue! I'll finish the show with a drum solo and tell the sound guy to cut the guitar feedback when I give him the signal!" And so on and so on . . .

Andy and I did a lot with a very little. It was the art of rubbing two sticks together to make a fire. I remember, when I played the song "Joyful Girl," he used to come up and stand next to me, drumming on the side of my guitar with his fingertips. Actually, it would be more accurate to say, I'd forgotten about that altogether but some chick walked up to me the other night (in public) and reminded me of it. She said she first saw me play in the early nineties and when Andy did that, it gave her chills.

When we rocked, we rocked with a balls-to-the-wall force. There was no steadiness or polish to what we were doing but there was an intensity and my old whisper-to-a-scream dynamic to hold audiences captive. Words tumbled, in avalanche after avalanche, from my mouth as my tongue and Andy's four limbs attempted to keep up with my right hand. I was already experiencing pushback from the world to the feminist challenge of my lyrics and my response seemed to be to push harder. I banged at the gates. I grabbed and rattled them. My singing voice abandoned its former attempts at prettiness and became more visceral and even cat-like at its jagged peak. Meanwhile, Andy and I were learning how to play, we were learning how to tour, we were learning how to grab an audience by the crotch and hold them there, making them laugh and cry until they forgot all about being scared.

With my penchants for cranking the low end on my acoustic guitar and playing bass lines in and amongst my chording, we sounded like a band. Over the course of the next few years, the question asked most frequently of the dudes running sound at our gigs was, "So . . . is there a bass player?" (as in: I hear one but I don't see one) or, "Are you playing bass tracks?" People would walk away not really believing the answer that the sound guy had given them.

WATER WATER EVERYWHERE

At those early shows there were girls, girls, girls. Many of them were either queer or trying on lesbianism for the evening, though, so poor heterosexual Andy lived an ironic life. He was surrounded by young women stretching into their joy, their lust, their power . . . but not for him. Luckily, he was too nice a guy to take advantage on those occasions when he would get some hottie all the way to a bedroom and then find himself comforting her as she sobbed on his shoulder, confessing that it was me she really loved. It was another one of our running jokes and the joke, it seemed, was on him.

For myself, I had no interest whatsoever in sleeping with fans. It sounded like a combination of being under a microscope and being on top of a screwy power dynamic. It was bad enough that people had cameras in their eyes and recording devices in their ears when they talked to me. It's a bummer trying to make casual conversation with someone who is busy acquiring a story to tell. Going to bed with those cameras and microphones would've just been an even bigger bummer.

I can kind of relate to the lives of the mega-famous. People like Bob Dylan don't have an easy row to hoe, that's for sure. I should really try to cut that guy more slack. Truth is, I can understand why he recoils from the people of the world out there gathering Bob Dylan stories. But I do know others—Bruce Springsteen, Susan Sarandon, Tim Robbins . . . Pete—who have shown me what it means to be practiced in deflection. Downplaying fanaticism and wringing a few drops of humanity out of the dry towel of stargazers is a skill that does not come easy. Stardom is something you have to meet head-on or it will go ahead and make a lunch of you. Robert Plant is another one who's got the skill. Truth is, it's exhausting and who knows, if I was deified by the time I was twenty-five, I might just say *fuck it*, too, and build a Bob-style wall. At a certain level, hysteria must become an insurmountable wall all its own, the likes of which can cloister the Dylans, the Beatles, the Stones, without their even trying. One thing's for sure, fame ain't gonna make a people person of you if you don't dig people already.

The thing about fanatics is, it's often the ones that "love" you the most that will turn and stick a knife right through you when you piss them off or disappoint them in some way. I say "that" instead of "who" because it is not really a human-to-human thing I'm talking about. It is a relationship between a projector and a screen and, as the screen, I have felt my humanity thoroughly erased many times. At those times, I re-mind myself: *Ani, this is why you can't rely on the affirmation of others for your own self-worth. If you are counting on the big thumbs-up from the world to get by, you leave yourself open to getting slain.* It's one thing to tell yourself that, though, and it's another thing to live it.

Women, especially, can be emotionally intense. The letters and gifts that came backstage, the portraits and paintings and jewelry, the signed books and demo tapes, the typed resumes and handwritten manifestas, the invitations for me and Andy to go to someone's house after the show for "homemade lesbian porn and tea." It was all very sweet and funny . . . until it wasn't. I was entering an era of celebrity and becoming acquainted with some of the accompanying hysteria myself. Andy helped me to make plenty of running, ducking, wheel-screeching escapes from women that seemed to want to eat me alive. The very people that I spent my life defending had a tendency to make my life really hard. I was surrounded by the "support" of other young women, but after a while, it became clear that I'd better run and hide. Andy would not be the only one leading an ironic life.

Luckily, that dynamic would eventually abate and a degree of sanity would reappear in my life. It was exciting for my career to be on the way up, yes, but in many ways, it got better on the way down. The hysteria waned and the loving reciprocation between me and my audience was able to open up then and ripen into itself like wine. I wouldn't trade where I am now for all the mega-fame and fortune in the world. Instead of feeling like a constant sucking sensation, my relationship with the public is now one of extended family and beloved allies in the struggle. Their presence in this world, the gifts they give me back, their eyes that meet mine, each one holds and accompanies me. Gives me hope. Not only is my relationship with my "fans" back to being a human-to-human thing, I believe it to be one of the very best human-to-human things.

IS CHICAGO, IS NOT CHICAGO

We played in Chicago and some chicks invited us to a dance club after the show. There were a lot of post-Ani show dance parties back in the day and sometimes Andy and I would turn up. The trouble with getting our boogie on this particular night was that we needed to be in Bloomington, Indiana, early the next day and, theoretically, sleep needed to occur at some point in between. It was an impossibility we chose to ignore.

That night, supposedly, I met my future bosom buddy Animal on the dance floor though my memory of the whole thing is sketchy. Then, supposedly, we all took our shirts off and danced half-naked. The shirtless thing happened so often in those days that it's no wonder it didn't stand out in my memory. A bunch of young women whipping off their tops and dirty dancing with each other is A. sexy, and B. a delicious challenge to the patriarchal objectification of our bodies. Two birds. Plus, if you're me, hitting it hard on the dance floor leads to a slippery puddle of sweat at your feet, so it's a good way to have a dry shirt to walk out of the place in. We would create an atmosphere of freedom and triumph and the goddesses would laugh as tits went swinging everywhere . . . or we'd all get kicked out of the place. The waters begged to be tested.

I eventually confronted the math of our drive and went looking for Andy in the pulsing darkness. I dragged him out of the Chitown party and back to the minivan. Then I drove the rest of the night to Bloomington while he lay snoring in the backseat. The gig was a women's music festival so Andy was headed for a night off while I played one solo. It was a women-only affair but the festival was being held on the University of Indiana campus so they couldn't actually prevent men from being there. School was not in session and the performers and audience members alike were staying in the women's dorms. Andy was billeted in the men's dorm with the one creepy hippie dude who insisted on attending the festival because he could.

When I opened the sliding door of the van, Andy sat up drool-stained and disheveled, squinting into the morning sun. I saw his bleary eyes take in the scene and then come to rest on me. "Keep it in your pants," I said, pulling him out of the van. The bearded lady who received us at the artist's check-in table handed me my credentials and then looked Andy up and down. "How does your friend identify?" she asked me. I turned to hairy-ass, bleary Andy and said, "Um, I don't know, how do you identify?" He looked at me, he looked at the bearded lady, "Uh . . . I'm a boy?" He phrased it like a question. A moment that would live on in infamy.

Andy slipped in and watched me play that night from the back of the room. It almost made me nervous to see him there. It's funny the things that make one nervous, it's not necessarily the things you'd think. It has never been a good thing, necessarily, for me to know when there is somebody I know in an audience. It can be hard to get them out of my mind, wondering what they might be thinking or feeling in any given moment. Submitting oneself to judgment is a big part of being a performer and fear of judgment gets more potent and distracting when it's personal. If you can't handle judgment, you learn to, or you gotta go do something else.

I can't count the number of times I've been crushed by a heckler, a review, or simply by my own brain as I dissect my performance all night instead of sleeping. Worse than the din of the peanut gallery is the tinnitus of self-loathing that is always there, ringing away in the background, should the peanut gallery subside. Scot would always find me slumped over after shows and chastise me, "How come tons of people can be screaming and cheering and the one who shouts something stupid is the only one you seem to hear?" I don't know. I wish I knew the answer to that one. I wish I could slay my vulnerability like a stupid green dragon. I wish I could cease to care when judging voices come tromping with their big, heavy boots into my wet cement. Maybe there is no one shouting anything mean. Maybe I am just shouting mean things at myself. I seem to be forever dissatisfied with how well I was able to sing this or say that. Why didn't I follow through with that point there? Or cut that off there? What I meant to say was . . .

I only pray that all the time I've spent flogging myself after shows and walking around haunted by my public failures has served to help me hone my skills as a communicator across time. These days, when somebody describes me as eloquent or articulate, I tell myself that all those sleepless nights are why, that they were not for naught. It makes me feel better to think that my occasional eloquence is the cumulative effect of thirty years of obsessive: *Dammit, Ani. What you should've said was . . .*

I.R.S.

I.R.S. Records (distributed by EMI) was a perfectly fine label which took a shine to me as I started to make some quakes out there in the wilds of the indie underground. They were flying people around to check me and my audience out, in the clubs and crevices I was playing with Andy. Whole groups of them started turning up. Andy and I would hang out with them and laugh nervously, kicking the ground after the show.

When I was out in L.A., they invited me over to their headquarters in Hollywood to meet everybody. They had a big fancy building and they were obviously legit players in the industry with the power to take me to the next level. They seemed serious about getting behind me and I was excited by their attention. It was the mid-nineties and I was still just out there scrapping around. *They are so nice . . . I mean maybe, just maybe . . . I mean . . . there is quite likely only so far a person can go in music on their own . . .*

It looked like this was really my chance to jump into the big time and I felt the gravitational pull of ambition. But then . . . I saw myself inside that sparkly, showy world that I disdained and I tried to picture myself playing along. I just couldn't. I don't want to care about my image. I don't want to kiss the camera and work it. *You don't need anybody*, I told myself once again and I took a deep breath and walked away from that building in Hollywood. I went back to my scrappy little life.

My utter conviction that I don't need anyone or anything but myself to do what I need to do got me through childhood and, though it is in many ways misguided, it has also been the essence of my superpower. Something inside me seemed to need to flex my powers often, too, if only to prove to myself that I still possessed them. Like the time some fan over at *Spin* magazine called Righteous Babe with a generous offer of free ad space. They were about to go to print and still had a big half-page ad unfilled, a thing that would normally cost several grand. They offered it to me just because they were into me and what I was doing. What could be cooler than that?

My peeps over at RBR got busy designing an advertisement for my latest record or my upcoming tours or some such, but when they told me about the opportunity and ran the ad by me, I balked. I told Scot I just wanted block letters that read EAT PUSSY, NOT COWS to fill the ad space. I thought it would be funny (and refreshingly irreverent towards the very idea of advertisement). Scot was unimpressed. He tried to talk some sense into me but he knew from experience that that was unlikely. "Can we at least put our logo at the bottom?" he asked helplessly. "Okay," I said, "but just a little logo."

As it turns out, the magazine declined to print my submission and offered the ad space to someone else. Someone more rational.

RENDEZVOUS

My phone rang on December 17 and it was Shawnee saying, "Let's go to Mexico for Christmas!" I couldn't refuse. Her plan, she informed me, was to hop freight trains from Santa Cruz to El Paso, which she insisted she could do in a week. She had met a dude in Santa Cruz who'd done some riding on the rails and this dude agreed to accompany her all the way to El Paso, showing her the train-hopping ropes. He told her they'd need a week to get there. We agreed to meet at the bridge to Juárez at sunset, Christmas Eve. From there we just planned to cross the border on foot and follow our noses. "Okay. Sunset, Christmas Eve, at the base of the bridge. See you there! Good luck!" What could go wrong?

I can't remember how I got to El Paso because that memory was eclipsed entirely by what followed. Shawnee and I had no way to communicate with each other once she set off, so we were going on faith with our little plan. I had a backpack slung over one shoulder and a guitar over the other. It was a tiny guitar, just a fretboard that hangs off your neck with a string. It sounded like a tin can but it was light and it did the trick.

I arrived early, in mid-afternoon, and sat down amongst the vendors plying their wares on blankets laid out on the sidewalk that swoops down from the bridge. There was an endless stream of foot traffic passing by. It was sunny and brisk and Christmas decorations were everywhere. A choir of carolers sang on the steps of the church and the Salvation Army bell rang away in the background. After a while, I struck up a conversation with this Mexican dude named Victor. His English was pretty good and his smile seemed to express a kind heart. I can't remember what Victor said his deal was, but it involved crossing the bridge every day, back and forth, back and forth. I was amazed at how many people did so, in either direction. A vibrant border indeed. I told Victor my story and he seemed amused. We chatted while I waited for Shawnee and he waited for whatever he was waiting for.

The afternoon wore on and the sun began to set. No Shawnee. People started to pack up their trinkets in their blankets and go home. The priest from the church across the way walked over to me and invited me to Christmas Eve dinner in the house of the Lord. He also told me about a teen shelter nearby. I thanked him and pulled my flannel shirt out of my pack to keep from getting chilled. I wasn't giving up yet. I wasn't about to leave this spot. When it started to get dark it occurred to me that maybe I should've considered a plan B.

Victor, who had gone off to take care of something, came back. "What are you going to do now?" he asked me. "I'm not sure," I replied. He said he knew a place on the Mexican side where we could get a clean room to sleep in for cheap, much cheaper than here. He said if I was willing to spend fifteen bucks he would take me there and we could share the room. I looked at him, I looked around, "Okay," I said.

We crossed the bridge with the twinkling lights of El Paso behind us and descended into the dimmer streets of Juárez. Victor led me down narrow, twisting alleys with laundry floating above us like ghosts, spooking me like a racehorse in the dark. We made a left, a right, several more lefts, and rights. I was getting nervous. Where the hell are we going? Am I really such a good judge of character that I should be following this strange man down dark streets in a place where no one even knows I am? Logic began to question trust, pacing the courtroom of my mind in its trim suit, mounting ever more convincing arguments.

We turned into an unmarked door and down a narrow corridor, coming out into an empty courtyard with a dirt floor. He talked to a lady sitting on a folding chair whom I could barely see in the darkness and after I gave her my money we went up a dark staircase to another hallway and a door. There were two cots inside and to my relief Victor settled himself on one as I claimed the other. *Everything is going to be all right*, I told myself as I lay awake listening to a series of strange, muffled sounds. Sounds from a whole other country and culture! I am in Mexico! Eventually the sounds were accompanied by Victor's snoring and I fell asleep, too.

On Christmas morning, Victor and I ate fritters from a street vendor and drank instant coffee together and then we wound our way back to the bridge. The twisting back streets of Juárez were no less wondrous in the light of day (such a different world than just the other side of the border!) but they had lost all menacing aspect. Now, I was just captivated. My faith in my instincts and the goodness of humanity had restored itself. Victor was my friend.

We paused briefly at the apex of the bridge to inhale deeply and survey the known world until the flow of pedestrian traffic pushed us onward. Even on Christmas morning, the activity on the bridge was undeterred. We retook our position along the wall on the American side and spent the day talking and laughing. I played him songs on my tinny little guitar. I didn't pry into the nature of his business, he had no blanket and no trinkets, instead we spoke of more intimate things, our families, our loves, that which was close to our hearts.

Finally, it was late afternoon and my hopes began to rise. Then it was sunset once again and just when I was starting to become pessimistic, up pranced Shawnee with her companion, both of them covered in dark grey soot. All things considered, a day late is pretty damn prompt when you've just ridden freight trains and camped out under the stars for a thousand miles. The grey soot smeared on their faces made them look like high school kids playing "hobos" in their school play. Underneath the ash, though, were these queer characters who didn't belong in anyone's high school play. Shawnee and I squealed and embraced each other and the two men stood back eyeing each other.

Shawnee's partner was in his forties with a dyed black, punk rock tousle of hair and piercings here and there. There was a pale protuberance where his eyebrows should've been. Shaved eyebrows give a real strangeness to a face. Victor was well put together (albeit, in the same clothes he was wearing yesterday, the clothes he'd also slept in) and his appearance was distinct from all the people he was suddenly associating with. He had invested in the story of me, though, so, uncomfortable as he might have been, he stuck around to see how the story ended. We all crossed the bridge together then and got a room for four.

By morning, the bubble in which Shawnee and I existed had reformed around us and the men were visibly excluded. Victor shrugged in understanding and bid me a fond farewell as we parted company but Shawnee's guy, who was obviously in love with her, narrowed his eyes at me and petitioned her to continue their adventure in some other direction.

Her laughter trilled down like a bird's, from a perch high above him, and she patted him before walking off.

I'm not sure what in Shawnee's history had given her the bitterness she carried with her, but I ended up running a lot of damage control during our reign. Inside her, a little girl crouched, waiting to pounce, hissing at the world of men. The interface that she had found with men was most likely experienced by them as "a tease." She had a habit of drawing them in with gorgeous batting eyelashes and then flipping the switch to fierce resentment when they started trying to suckle on her life force. I had to admit, I could relate to her discord. She never seemed all-the-way-crazy to me, just . . . damaged in a way that I vaguely understood even though I didn't. On this day, though, there was no damage control by me, I just shrugged and waved goodbye to Mr. Punk Rock Hobo.

MEXICO

We decided to go to the bus station and take a bus as far south as we felt we could afford. That ended up being the city of Chihuahua. We just wanted to get away from the border. My head was partially shaved (the lower half) and the hair on the upper half was dyed a dark blue, but on the way to Chihuahua, I decided I wanted the blue part to stand up in spikes and that some sort of glue was most likely the right styling tool. Shawnee's Spanish was perfunctory and didn't include the word for "glue" so, when we got off the bus, we had quite a time trying to ask people where one might procure this stuff, you know (hand gesture, hand gesture, fingers pulling apart to represent viscosity). After many ridiculous interactions, we learned that the commonly used word for glue is "gloo." Right. We found our way to a hardware store and I executed the hairstyle of my dreams in a public restroom.

Despite my curious appearance, Shawnee's blonde goddessness drew a steady stream of suitors once she had finally washed the soot off herself, and our journey became structured around a series of gentlemen callers. We wordlessly developed a code that went like this: When men ask our names, we look at each other and the first one to answer sets the stage for the characters we then play. If I said "Mickey," she said "Jo Jo" and that meant: *Make no mistake, we are dykes and we would like for you to fuck off as soon as possible.* If she said "Mona," I said "Lu Lu" and that meant, *This one's cute, a little flirting is in order, back me up.* If we used our real names, that meant, *This feels real. Let's be real and make real friends.*

Our favorites were the two soldiers who showed us around, even sneaking us onto their base and into their digs. Their digs were basically a freestanding plywood box that they slept in, like the rest of their fellows, two by two. Those army guys were the sweetest and most sincere men that we met on the whole trip. Go figure. We went with them to their plywood box as Ani and Shawnee and left with their address to write to. We also stayed at the house of a young man who showed us around his town with his friends and then offered us his parents' spare room for the night. In the morning, the baby was passed around and everybody took turns touching Shawnee's hair and mine, too. We had an amazing home-cooked breakfast and left feeling so grateful to the whole family, it hurt. When it all got too overwhelming and we were socially exhausted, we sprang for a rented room.

Shawnee was big in every way and her expansiveness made me seem reserved by comparison. It didn't help that I couldn't speak the language and so was rendered mute most of the time we were in Mexico. We became lovers on that trip and I discovered sex with her could border on the symphonic. More than once, we found ourselves giggling and scurrying through the sand, away from a modest room that we had just rented, before we had to meet eyes with anybody in the morning light. She was also an ejaculator and tended to leave us and everything around us in need of a good washing every time she met her pleasure. I was in charge of damage control in that area, too.

I called home once on that trip, home being Scot. I wanted to say, happy new year and, don't worry, I'm alive. To make an international call, I had to go to a calling center that was just a small, spare storefront room with a guy sitting behind a desk and a sort of phone-boothy thing in the corner. With all the rigmarole, it took me a long time to get this task accomplished and Shawnee got bored waiting outside. I was already struggling to hear Scot over the dim line when a mariachi band came right up and surrounded the booth, playing and singing very loudly. Shawnee had paid them to serenade me. Behind them, I could see her laughing out on the corner as I raised my arm in a mortified "What the fuck?!"

With the exception of our initial bus ride, our main modes of transportation were walking and hitchhiking, but if I have one takeaway from this book to impart to my daughter, it's this: It's all okay but the hitchhiking. That shit's just too dangerous. I had a knife that I carried and Shawnee had pepper spray and we practiced quickly accessing them, but still the feeling of being at some stranger's mercy while hitchhiking was real.

Once we accepted a ride in a semi but as soon as I climbed into the truck's cab I felt a sense of dread. Our driver was big and burly, with hairy everything and a smile that wasn't warm. I looked down and noticed the handle of a baseball bat sticking out from under his seat. He began to ask us creepy questions like, do we have boyfriends and how much money do we have, all of which Shawnee was translating for me as she struggled to answer in a way that was neither incriminating nor encouraging. We were driving further and further down a two-lane highway to nowhere and we were seeing no other cars.

At some point, I made a big show of having a full bladder and asked Shawnee to ask our driver to please pull over so I could relieve myself. I was sitting between them, so I knew Shawnee would have to get out to let me out. I shoved our stuff out with me as I jumped down and when my boots hit the ground I hissed, "Run!" We tore off down the road in the direction from which we'd come. As soon as we heard the truck pull onto the road again, we slowed down and then, when it finally disappeared, we stopped to catch our breath. We couldn't remember exactly how far back the last signs of life had been so we just started walking and laughing and exhaling out our fear and tension. After a little while, a vehicle appeared coming towards us. It was a small pickup truck marked "Policia."

The cab of the truck was full with two men and there were a handful of men riding in the back, too, each uniformed and armed. Some had shotguns. For a moment, we contemplated asking for assistance but as they slowed down to take in the sight of us, the men in the back began to catcall, saying things that I understood even though I didn't know the words. I had been harassed by policemen before, in my own country, but out here, outnumbered and isolated, our fear returned to us. This was just not our day. Luckily, they rolled on and left us to the relative peace of our walk. We agreed that the first thing we were going to spend money on when we reached civilization was a beer.

We made it as far as Topolobampo and ate fish tacos on the beach. Then we started to talk about going home. We felt exhausted and our appetite for gentleman callers was at an all-time low. Were we ever going to meet any women on this trip? We realized that we had hardly encountered any women at all except for the street vendors who'd handed us food. We'd only really seen them out and about in groups with kids or with men. We had come across no young women like us, just walking around together. On our way back north, we hung out in a lot of public restrooms. It was our last-ditch effort to try to shift the gender of our Mexican adventure. We didn't actually make any female friends but at least we cut down on the gentleman callers. Women in Mexico apparently don't go to public restrooms to make friends with weird wayfaring gringas. In fact, speaking with strangers at all seemed to be not their thing.

There are many songs that remind me of Shawnee from *Puddle Dive* and *Out of Range* but none more than "If He Tries Anything." That tune I wrote about our grand Mexican adventure.

five

MISH

I was invited to play the biggest and longest-running women's music festival in the country, the Michigan Womyn's Music Festival, and I went there all eager beaver excited. This was a festival run entirely and exclusively by and for women. The whole staff, from security to sanitation to hospitality to the stage and tech crews, the performers, the audience: all women. Where else was that ever gonna happen? Like . . . nowhere! I had high expectations.

But from the very first parking attendant, it became apparent that this was not the laid-back folk festival scene that I was used to. In fact, there were more rules and people enforcing those rules than I'd ever seen. I met some cool women at Mish and I got the feeling that the festival existed on many levels, the best of which I might not necessarily be accessing, but mostly I just kept rubbing up against the whole thing. All those damn rules. I came looking for a feminist nirvana and found myself trapped in a world where everything was suddenly a big deal.

Both Shawnee and MJ went that year, too. Shawnee had slipped into the role of my number-one gal pal and was attending as my guest and MJ was heading there with a little crew from Texas so we just planned to meet up. In fact, we had only just met up when I said something like, "I gotta go do my soundcheck, I'll meet you guys over at the hospitality tent after," and some woman wheeled around and admonished me for using "male-centric language." I looked at her, taking a second to even understand that she was referring to my use of "you guys." MJ was then asked to take off or turn inside-out her T-shirt with a picture of the Texas Tornados, a band of, gulp, you guessed it, men on the front. All this and we were barely in the front gates. Everywhere we went, some woman seemed to be dedicating herself to protecting some other theoretical woman who might be triggered or feel tacitly oppressed by some tiny detail of the known universe. There seemed to be no details left unattended.

Soundchecking that afternoon, I was reassured to find the engineers and stage crew friendly, competent, and professional. I had a moment standing there on the main stage, looking out at all the infrastructure, the stages and sound systems, the towers and tents and showers and canteens, when I felt suddenly overwhelmed by the fact that all of this had been made by women alone. One becomes so used to the fact that men, white men to be exact, run and control everything, that to remind oneself that there are even places on the globe that are built and run entirely by men of different hues is hard enough, let alone to imagine that the world can keep turning without any men at all. It is surprising, even for a female who believes herself no less capable, to actually experience a world built and run by women. When you've never experienced something, it has the subliminal effect of making you believe it is not possible.

Of course, no sooner had I inhaled the beauty of my empowering moment than I noticed all these thin strings crisscrossing the field in front of me where the audience would later be seated. After soundcheck, I walked out to investigate. I found that the audience area had been divided into many sections so that no one audience member would have to suffer the proximity of someone else who might disturb them. There were children-welcome zones and no-children zones, dancing and no-dancing zones, smoking and non-smoking, even a zone designated perfume or "scent" free! *What. The. Fuck? Why can't we all just get along?*

The quest to make everyone happy all the time seemed to have led to a world of micromanagement in this place. Extreme inclusion had circled back onto itself and become its opposite. (Big shout out to the ole yin yang symbol here, perhaps the most profound and astute rendering made by the human hand!) I mean, maybe highly designed, intentional communities serve good purposes and I was just in the wrong one for me or maybe it was just their style of delivery but, in any case, I wanted to get the hell out of there. I never missed the male *huh, wha?* approach to the emotional landscape so much. The masculine ability to just focus on a task without getting all up in your feels, in the absence of gender oppression, showed itself to me as a kind of grace.

Of course, women have had precious little opportunity to develop and refine any worlds of their own making. In that sense, women haven't had a chance to achieve the level of confidence and ease that comes with being fully and undeniably in charge for eons. I imagine part of the uptightness of this mini-society-without-men could have stemmed from the fact that it was first and foremost a brief and tenuous thing. No one could really relax into it. I have played plenty of brand-new venues in my touring life and I can tell you this: When a facility has just opened, the staff are very uptight and heavily invested in enforcing all the rules. After a venue has been around for a long time and is run by a seasoned veteran crew, ease reigns.

I happened to go straight from Michigan to the Winnipeg Folk Festival, which is a gathering even larger and more elaborate. At night, in front of the main stage, an audience of ten thousand or more bumped and jostled one another. Children and adults and smokers and dancers and sit-and-listeners and perfume-wearers all worked it out together and had a peaceful, happy time. I stood there watching, feeling sad and consumed by my inward reassessments. Utopia seemed indeed more complicated than just the absence of patriarchy. The subliminal effect of never actually experiencing something can also be to think that it will be better than it is. One thing seems undeniable: Utopia does not look the same for all of us.

I made the mistake of shit-talking the Michigan Womyn's Music Festival after I left there, spinning as I was in my disappointment. I made some enemies in doing so. I have since learned some things that have helped me to empathize more fully with the struggles that those women were facing. To say it was an uphill battle to do what they were doing would be an understatement. They operated under a constant threat of violence from their redneck neighbors and were openly terrorized by pickup trucks full of shotgun-wielding homophobes. The women had to covertly bury their power transformers in secret locations and plant trees to remind themselves where they were because men would sneak on the land and blow them up.

I also see now that what those women were creating was a culture so foreign to me that, like any foreign culture, it should naturally take time for me to acclimate. My lack of patience and openness to the process of learning and adjustment was an inhibiting factor but I was a punk kid and rebellion was my default setting. From this distance, I can appreciate that while there were many new rules to be abided by in order to live harmoniously within the Mish community, there were also other rules suddenly, gloriously absent. Rules about women's bodies and behavior, rules about our very safety, which normally inhibit and control our lives every day.

I empathize with them especially now that their festival is gone after coming under heavy fire for ten years from the people directly to their left and to their right. And no, I don't mean the rednecks. Mish was an institution that survived for forty years and provided a space for women to feel unashamed and unafraid for one week every year but it became most heavily criticized by a transgender movement that protested its "womyn-born-womyn" admission policy. The festival's mission statement of being a space for "womyn-born-womyn" remained unchanged despite fierce protestations. Trans activists mounted a boycott of the fest and set up a trans camp down the road. They even began boycotting individual artists who played at the festival. A dark cloud of strife and infighting descended and the skies would never again be clear.

I personally find that the saddest and most depressing fact of all. I sympathize with both sides and can't help but mourn the tendency of people to lean towards absolutism and mutual destruction. I understand the need for trans women to find community with and be accepted by other women, and I understand the need for people with reproductive systems, perceived female from birth, to make space to process their particular relationship to patriarchy.

We still live in a rape culture. We live in a world where people with ovaries do not own their own bodies or possess all of their basic civil rights. Girls are born into this world as objects or, at best, second-class citizens. Girls are subordinated and subverted so universally that it just seems normal. Patriarchy is so deep inside us all that we let women be dominated, controlled, violated, and treated as less than equal (less than human) all the world over and we turn away in politeness and "cultural sensitivity." When I hear from trans friends that gender is how you feel, I say yes, I hear that truth. But this is a world of many, varied, and sometimes conflicting truths. Gender, like everything else, is many things to many people.

Gender seems to me to be complex and reflective of the interplay of lots of things. Measurable things like male and female sex genes and hormones and also unquantifiable things like the spirits and energies that live through us. The swirl of masculine and feminine within each person (that profound and ever-present yin/yang), in addition to presenting a vast field of possibility within, exhibits a complex interface with culture and experience on the outside. Gender orients itself among a myriad of coordinates, resulting, ultimately, in an infinity born of two. Nature's math seems to me to be possessed of a profoundly simple grace:

$$1 = 0$$
$$2 = \infty$$

As in: There really is no such thing as a singularity (a thing operating outside of relationship) and two is always the springboard to infinity. I do not believe it's necessary to denigrate or deny any of nature's persistent binary themes in order to understand gender as a spectrum. Binary systems in nature possess infinite potential.

When you think of binary in terms of relationship instead of the number two, it becomes not about either/or but about both always. It's about a world in dialogue with itself. To think that the binary system of masculine and feminine is threatening to the recognition of gender diversity is to have succumbed to an idea of "binary" that is fixed, finite, and man-made. An either/or, black/white reduction is a highly unnatural thing, indeed. Binary systems in nature are in motion. They are fluid and spinning and overlapping and interconnected and, from moment to moment, they evolve. It's not that there is no such thing as the duality of masculine and feminine, it's that there is no such thing as a world in which they are fixed or mutually exclusive.

But just because gender is a spectrum and has fluidity doesn't mean oppression ain't oppression. Oppression is another thing entirely. Within the binary swirl of masculine and feminine, where and how is oppression played out? Where does the great and abiding social imbalance initiate? Gender "nonconformity" comes with a high probability of oppression, too, and yes, those Mish women might have done well to abandon some of their rules, but at the end of the day, I support their right to their lived truth and to an exclusive space to process it. Why not make another women's festival with a broader admissions policy? We need more safe spaces for women of all kinds to process their experiences, not less.

I believe the closer we can bring ourselves to collectively acknowledging and addressing the fundament of patriarchy, the better off we will be in all our social movements.

FOLK FESTIVALS

The world of the folk festival is rich and varied, at least it was when I was making my living on the scene. Going way beyond singer-songwriters in scope, these events are often celebrations of roots music from all over the world. The Canadian festivals, in Vancouver, Edmonton, Calgary, Winnipeg, and beyond, were particularly epic, each one a global convergence of musicians fostering good old-fashioned friendship and understanding between disparate cultures and people. There were a few big stars who rode in and out on their tour buses and played one main stage set (I would one day become one of those) but most of us stayed all weekend and made lots of little appearances. Workshops threw people on stage together during the day and some remarkable musical bridges were constructed on the spot. Then, back at the performer hotel at night, the dance parties and jam sessions didn't stop. By morning, all of the world's borders would have been rendered null and void.

Spending whole summers making the rounds of folk festivals also meant repeatedly seeing the other musicians who were playing the same circuit. By summer's end, I would have traded addresses with a band of gypsies from France, a Malian guitar player, a percussionist from Uruguay, and some Tuvan throat singers. The West African guitar players and I would look at each other when the playing started. There was something about the circular loops of grooved patterns that I made with my guitar that was related to how they played. Me and the African dudes recognized one another as members of the same extended guitar family.

"You must come to Senegal!" my new friend told me one night with a big smile. "They will love you there!"

A good weekend at a folk festival can leave you marveling at the very magic of music. This thing with the power to put us all back together after the world has torn us apart. So many times now, I have watched music make family of strangers and still it never ceases to amaze me. I especially loved the Vancouver Folk Festival because Gary Cristall, who was in charge at the time, had a particularly keen dedication to global diversity, even going so far as to hire 50 percent female performers across the board. A little intention goes a long way.

One summer I became pals with the beautiful singer Celina Carroll, originally from Barbados, who fronted the Toronto band Mother Tongue, and we laughed upon meeting each other because we were sporting the same implausible haircut. Both our heads were shaved except for a small circle at the crown where a yarmulke would go. Hers grew out from there into a braid and mine was like the top of a pineapple. It was the hairdo I'd perfected in Mexico. One day, having a few hours to kill between the afternoon workshops and the evening's festivities, Celina and I decided to sneak down to the hotel hot tub together and have a soak. Neither of us had bathing suits so we had a bra-and-underwear thing going on underneath our towels. When we got to the pool, we found we had been beaten there by the Tuvans and had to squeeze into the tub between five dudes who were also donning their Fruit of the Looms.

Shaved everywhere except for the crown of the head is apparently a common haircut in Tuva, because we looked around and realized there were now a startling number of people in this hot tub with our patented hairdo. It didn't take long before we were all having a good laugh at this coincidence. The one Russian-y-looking guy who spoke a little broken English explained to us that, in Tuva, this was a man's hairdo. We explained that, in North America, this was a freak's hairdo.

I have to say, there is nothing quite so rapturous as five people throat singing in a cavernous, tiled hotel pool room. They kindly obliged our

The Di Franco family. I'm the little guy.

They didn't have a graduation gown small enough for my dad.

Little tomboy

Ingeri and me

LEFT: Classic stuff, huh?

RIGHT: Unfortunately, I don't have an uncropped version of this picture of me and Michael, because Ingeri is on my other side.

Michael and I much, much later.
Around the time we made his one and only record.

1980

1986? Yes. That's a perm.

At the lake in 1988

Before moving to New York

After

Scot

Scot as Vladimir Lenin

The Now Voyager in London

1990.
On duty in my engineer's cap.
I wore that cap out.

The girl traveling in the '69 Beetle

Protesting in D.C., 1991

Andy took this picture somewhere out there on our
endless drive. We toured for years in rented minivans
and I had a knack for attracting law enforcement.

This patented hairdo I dubbed "the unilock." I had about a finger's worth of hair that, when released, went down to my chin.

LEFT: A popular haircut in Tuva

BELOW: Painting the Hyundai

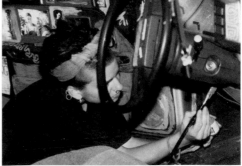

Me and Pete on stage at Clearwater, 1993

Me and Pete many years later, at the Sloop Club on the banks of the Hudson

Playing the Michigan Womyn's Music Festival

My first great trio, with Andy and Sara Lee on bass.
We moved up to a tour bus!

Cat girl

Lovin' on my Heidi Ho

A girl and her Goat

My dear friend Utah

The ghost of Utah and the ghost
of Goat making *Fellow Workers*.
Polaroids are not forever.

My second great trio, with my other beloved Canuck,
Jason Mercer, on bass, and open-mouthed Andy, and some
of the Rebirth Guys. That's Derrick over on the right.

Walkin' my man
Palmer in Atlanta

ABOVE: Me and Maceo at Red Rocks. That's Bruno there in the background.

RIGHT: A funky fresh feeling *was* felt by all

Performing with Sekou at the Apollo. That's Todd Sickafoose playin' bass.

My favorite rock-and-roll photographer ever, Danny Clinch,
took this picture of me and my head full of dreads
makin' friends on the streets of New York.

request for a private performance and we turned off the jets to make it quiet. I closed my eyes and my spirit lifted as they dialed us in to the deeply vibrating earth with their voices. Next to ten bazillion cicadas waking up on a fecund Kentucky morning, it was one of the most amazing sounds I've ever heard.

UTAH

Utah Phillips, originally from Salt Lake City, had been denied a U.S. passport because of his tax resister status but Canada was still letting him amble on in. This was pre-9/11 and America's subsequent clampdown on immigration, which made everyone else, including Canada, turn around and clamp down on us. Every summer, Utah was still setting out from his home in Nevada City, California, to putt over the border with a driver's license and a nod and play the Vancouver Folk Festival.

Jim Fleming introduced us there, at an after-party and bingo, I was smitten. Utah was about forty years my senior and looked like a cross between Santa Claus and a rail-hoppin' hobo (the latter part being true) but we were also very much alike in some elusive way. We were the same combination of angry, grateful, and defiant. We were both gonna reinvent the world for ourselves or die trying. I tried to fill my pockets with all the stories, quotes, and life lessons he was constantly imparting, but mostly they just slipped through my fingers before they even got to my pockets. Where I failed as an understudy, I hopefully made up for as a fan.

Turns out, Utah and I employed a lot of the same techniques on stage, which is to say, we liked to get people laughing and then, when their heads were thrown back in an open-mouthed guffaw, we'd slip a little kernel of truth in there. It seemed, in our separate laboratories, we'd both discovered it: That's how you get people to swallow shit. My dad had taken me to see *Richard Pryor: Live in Concert* when it came out in movie theaters in 1979. I was nine at the time so he walked me out of there pretty quick but the fact that he'd even taken me said it all. He loved Richard Pryor and soon, so would I. Lenny Bruce, Pryor . . . later Bill Hicks, all would serve as great inspirations to me. Sometimes I think I have more in common with the social commentary comedians than I do with singer-songwriters. I think the same was true of Utah.

Though we were similar, Utah was on the scripted end of stage artists where I was more extemporaneous. I was the say-the-first-thing-that-comes-to-your-mind type and he was rehearsed and methodical, with a well-kept arsenal of bits, gaffes, and comebacks. Needless to say, neither of us would have considered it sufficient to just stand there and grind through tunes. A show should be a show, dammit, with an arc. A beginning, a middle, and an end.

Utah was an old-school folksinger and oral historian whose stories and songs connected a lot of the dots of the people's history and people's songs in North America. He sang and played guitar but it was his storytelling that was the most profound and compelling element of his art, if you asked me. His stories would wrap you in the rich, colorful quilt of America and all the radical history that they never taught you in grammar school. The songs were the part of the show where you'd sit back and take in what you'd just heard . . . have a little laugh or cry about it. They were the moments of release where you'd be invited to open up your face and take part in the singing.

I became compelled to capture Utah's stories on record, lest a big part of his life's work get buried with him. Storytelling is not the kind of thing that usually gets recorded, except maybe by the Smithsonian, but I had my own damn record company so I decided to be Utah's Smithsonian. Sort of. I made an album called *The Past Didn't Go Anywhere*, where I constructed a journey through some of Utah's classic tales (all garnered from cassettes of his live shows) and then, to make it more listenable, I set the stories to sampled drum beats and musical accompaniment courtesy of me. I was like the Smithsonian with a crude sampler and a graffiti artist's irreverence.

Luckily for both of us, whatever it was I was trying to do seemed to work. Teenagers started showing up to Utah's gigs and he enjoyed a late-life renaissance of his career. His words and wisdom were connecting with more young ears and minds so I was happy. In fact, I was so encouraged, I decided to do it again. I made another record of Utah's yarn-spinning only the second time, we actually worked together, performing the stories-with-a-soundtrack thing live in the studio. That second album we called *Fellow Workers* and Howard Zinn, bless his heart, wrote the liner notes for it.

Utah was conscripted in the army as a young man and got sent to fight in the Korean War but then he freaked out over in Korea and deserted the army. He tells the story of his epiphany and desertion on *The Past Didn't Go Anywhere* and that story of transformation from soldier in the army to soldier of peace and justice (which on the record I just called "Korea") is one of my favorites of his stories. So many dots connected. But then Utah came home after the war and spent years drunk, bumming around on the rails. One day he found his way to the Joe Hill House and to Ammon Hennacy and that's when his transformation finally clicked into place. Under Ammon's tutelage, he evolved into the fully formed pacifist, anarchist, one-man-revolution that I knew him as.

He resumed traveling the country, only this time he did so with a guitar and a purpose. Refusing, ever since the war, to fly on airplanes, he came into each town slowly and got to know the place. He became a dedicated student of history, particularly the history of every place he went, walking around for a day or two and talking to people in anticipation of every show. The way he conceived of it, his job as folksinger had a research component to it and it began the moment he stepped off the train. He took the time to make each of his shows personal and relevant to the community he was in. He made it his gig to sow the seeds of critical thinking and he did so through a street-level awareness of history and oral tradition.

Though the rest of his near and dear all called him by his given name, Bruce, I called him by his public name, Utah, because even after we became close, he always seemed to be performing for me. He was like a formal father, eager to impart everything he knew, so we stuck with the roles of master and apprentice though our friendship existed on many levels. I recognized that Utah had something to offer the world and he recognized that I had something to offer him. I brought to him a whole new, enthusiastic audience, and he provided me with the rarest of things: camaraderie and inspiration in the making of politically radical art. Company.

Over the course of our friendship, I wrote him letters and he took to sending me back cassette tapes with spoken letters in return. I loved my private broadcasts from his study in Nevada City, his voice intimate and relaxed, wandering . . . cat purring on his lap. That cat of his was a wonder. She was a Siamese who sat at the dinner table each night on her own stool. There was no mischief or tomfoolery at the table, she was not given any scraps, she just sat there enjoying the company of people, turning her head to look thoughtfully at the face of each person who was talking. It was unnerving how she did that.

Utah, so stylish and funny, such a study in bullheaded conviction and radical critique. Utah, keeping the people's history alive beyond all those stuffy halls filled with the official histories of the wars and the warlords. So extremely skeptical (for good reason) about the imperial system and its justifications for war. Such an ardent advocate for the 99 percent and their need to find solidarity with one another in standing up to the boss class. A card-carrying member of the IWW and a patriot who was fond of quoting Mark Twain often: "Loyalty to the country always. Loyalty to the government when it deserves it."

It ain't easy being a tax refuser but Utah was able to prove that his life had evolved into one big long protest against the dumping of our tax dollars into the military-industrial complex and into lining the pockets of the rich. He was able to prove his utter dedication to pacifism and his studied belief in the principles of anarchy. Of course, tax refuser or no, he always lived hand to mouth himself and I watched it become harder for him to get by as he got older, there being no pension plan for retiring folksingers. He started a hospitality house for the homeless in his hometown and he had a weekly show at the local community radio station but he was just getting by. Once I had to bail him out so he didn't lose his house.

As an anarchist, Utah chose to forgo voting, instead "using his body as his ballot and casting it on the side of peace and justice every day." We disagreed about that one. I, personally, put my radical ideals and disdain for politicians aside when it comes time to knuckle down and vote. I have seen the difference between Republican and Democratic appointees in the criminal justice system alone. The "lesser of two evils" can mean the difference between life and death for a person embroiled in the system. From local police chiefs to federal judges, all those ripple-effect appointees make huge differences in people's lives, huge differences in the carriage of justice. I see my vote as a duty I perform for my society, imperfect as it is, not as another avenue of self-expression. I believe a vote is just as important to cast even when there is no personal satisfaction or glory in doing so. Maybe even more so. The very nature of a vote contains within it a recognition that you are part of something bigger than yourself.

But I gave you a pass, old man. Because you really did bust your ass on behalf of your country and cast your body as your ballot every day. But only you, Utah, only you! Besides . . . I happen to know that you registered and voted against George W. Bush in his bid for reelection in 2004. Enough was fucking enough. Bless you, my ever vigilant, ever evolving friend, for keeping your ears and your mind open. That was only shortly before you died. I'm so sorry that you did not live to see Obama . . . though you would've railed at him, too, you ornery cuss.

THE ALPHABET VS THE GODDESS

The medium is the message" (a concept first articulated by Marshall McLuhan): Now that's an idea that really hit me by degrees. You have to tap into some elemental shit before you can get the full effect there. The idea being basically: Any medium, by its very nature, is prone to express certain things. Like say . . . heavy metal music expresses what it is to be a young, disenfranchised white dude. Beyond all the surface minutiae of a heavy metal song, it is essentially about young-disenfranchised-white-dudeness. Okay, maybe that's not the best example, but you get the idea. Go with me on this.

If you train your eye, I believe you can follow this concept quite far into the heart of things, this concept that each medium defines, or at least sets the parameters around, what it does and does not communicate. On some essential level, I believe this has something to do with, *Why music?* for me, and more specifically, *Why live music?*

Many humans seem to concur that God sits detached in heaven or thereabouts, head in the proverbial clouds, while Goddesses (plural), if they exist at all, are beings in and of the earth. Patriarchal religions and the cultures they spawned can't help but acknowledge that it is through the female that humanity is tethered to the earth. Her body is the rope. Because of her "bearer" role, the female evolved, over many eons, to excel in feeling and synthesizing sensory information, unable for reasons of simple biology to engage in the dispassionate, mono-focus pursuits of either hunt or battle. That part of our collective intelligence that thin slices and intuits, the part that cannot explain logically how it knows what it knows, that was the intelligence prioritized by the primeval mother. Our feminine side if you will. This is also the part of our intelligence that is the wellspring of art.

The linear and logical capacities of our intelligence, with its linguistics and mathematics, all of our systems, categories, methods, and plans, were the intelligence prioritized by the primeval hunter. The intellect that focuses and achieves ever increasing degrees of specialization is widely considered synonymous with "intelligence" in patriarchal society but really, it is but one aspect of our schizophrenic cognitive abilities. Each of us is employing radically different types of intelligence in any given moment. The masculine and the feminine sensibilities ever busy with their interplay within us. The monkey brain, the midbrain, and the famous high-falutin' prefrontal cortex ultimately speak with two tongues and have two distinct voices when they step up to the mic. Each of them has drawn its own conclusions.

As individuals, we emerge through our own personalized brand of free-flowing interaction between the detachment of intellect and the connectedness of feeling and intuition. Though some of our individual talents and natures may tip heavily in one direction or another, ultimately, the collective intelligence of our species is maximized, I believe, when we strike a balance between the masculine and feminine sensibilities amongst us. In any case, logic and detachment (out in front for so long now) have proven that they have downsides.

Music, the universal language of the feminine brain, operates in the world like an antidote to detachment. It is a medium that necessitates connectedness, starting down at the bottom with the resonant frequency of the earth itself. At some point, the rhythmic syncopations and overtones of the subharmonic breathing earth become so fast that we interpret them as drumbeats and then, as they get even faster, we experience them as notes. Such is the dazzling geometry of sound that our animal ears comprehend easily, discerning beautiful patterns from randomness, harmony from dissonance. Our bodies know a groove from a bunch of people making sounds simultaneously and can interpret the emotional nuance in the relationship between human and drum, drummer and other musicians. Music employs intuition. Also: interaction, mutual awareness, and cooperation. Music results in deep empathy for one another and therefore a feeling of wholeness within ourselves.

Just about anyone can be moved to tears by music or be moved to re-enter their body and dance. Music contains a celebration not only of the living present moment, but of the whole of life with its endless repetitions. When it is really happening, music is a medium that transcends culture and speaks to the very core of our aesthetic souls, connecting us with nothing less than the beauty of being alive together. It touches a place below the logical and linguistic frame and draws from a well even older than the stories we tell.

But what of the stories we tell? Language, specifically the written word, is another ridiculously powerful medium, guiding our thoughts and pushing its message to the forefront of human history and society. The alphabet, when it was invented, ushered in an age of global literacy and idea sharing. It was this powerful tool that could make ideas stand still long enough to be put into great big piles. These piles of ideas brought humanity great advancements, they brought us everything that you see around you (unless you are sitting out in nature right now, in which case, Goddess bless you!), but there was a downside to the evolutionary leap of the alphabet. The downside is patriarchy. Stay with me. The medium of the alphabet, being masculine in nature, is prone to express our collective masculinity. More essential, therefore, to the history of patriarchy than even the might-makes-right relationship of male and female bodies, is the advent of The Word.

In the footprints of the written word, so has humanity gone. It has meant, for one thing, a long journey away from being in active relationship with the earth and with all of consciousness and towards living in a house of mirrors. A world of our own invention. These piles of written words have surrounded us with an echo chamber of our own (masculinized) voice and gotten so high as to even block out the most basic elements of what's actually happening, like sunlight and breeze. Most of us live wholly convinced and distracted now, within the folds of our own fabrications. Man-made notions like "past" and "future" consume us. Simply put, the nature of the alphabet is abstraction and the direction it has carried us is further into abstraction.

Our ability to tell the kind of story that lives unchanged forever has made us godlike. The written word has paved the way to another level of perceived supremacy. To break down the known world into parts and give each part a name has given us a sense of power and control. The feminine principle has, over time, been subordinated by greater and greater volumes of logical argument. The ability to be present in the sensual, animal, interconnected now, for many of us, returns only with things like music. In this very fundamental sense, even those heavy metal dudes are accessing their feminine side when they speak the language of music. You gotta love that one!

Damn you, oh written word! My great love! My liberator! How can it be that you are also the purveyor of humanity's most deep and abiding curse?! . . . The Great Mother laughs now and pauses to gaze pityingly at me until she finally turns away. "How could it not be so?" she deadpans, looking off at something I can't see. "Everything for you humans is always so simple . . . But in the center of light is darkness, child, and in the center of darkness . . . a light."

This probably won't surprise you, but I believe that all the greatest leaps of human cultural evolution involve the true resonance of the masculine and feminine sensibilities within us. Albert Einstein, or any other revolutionary scientist, can go only so far with logic. At some point, intuition must kick in and inform the process for it to become transcendent. Similarly, this dance takes place inside the great artist. After pushing relentlessly, step by step, through the linear discipline of craft, the artist frees themself, like John Coltrane with his horn, to make an expansive leap into someplace entirely illogical and intuitive. Ground is broken.

MAKING SONGS 3

I'm often asked what my songs are about. The closer in the people, the more directly they feel licensed to inquire. "What are you trying to achieve with this work?" is a question asked by a journalist. "Who (exactly) is *that* about?" is a question asked by a lover. The idea that my songs are only and ever about exact events and individuals is kind of insulting to me. *What sort of writer do you think I am? A court stenographer?* I feel as though I've discerned a difference between writing from life and autobiography. I've even experienced the space between autobiographical and literal. Songwriting is just storytelling, so yes, of course, I use what my imagination is made of, but the "me" or "you" of a song could be a composite character or just a representation of something. "Ignore the facts and tell the truth," that's what Sekou always used to say. I couldn't have said it better if I tried. And I guess maybe I just tried. In songwriting, I try to ignore the facts and tell the truth. Yes, that's what I meant.

My songs are never really about this or that, anyway, they're really about the hidden dynamic *between* this and that. At least, that's the sincere conclusion I reach every time I search around in my head to try to answer the question, "What is this song about?" In my mind, I am pointing at the spaces in between the things, saying, "It's about the invisible part in there," but I resign myself to talking about the things themselves. The "issues" that people like so much. People seem to favor concrete things and I guess it makes sense (what can we talk about except the things with names?), but the tension between them, the dominance and submission, the attraction or repelling, the dissonance or resonance . . . that is really what interests me. But I would feel like such a girl if I just answered every query with, "I just write about the relationships between things" so I try to play interview ball. I hate trying to explain my songs, though. It feels as if magic is drained out of them in the process.

I have been talking about songwriting in terms of the most potent challenge that it presents to my brain: the lyrics, because that is the thing that sticks out and pokes me, but the thing that soothes and invites me in is the music. It's more simple and fun for me to write music, less intellectual and arduous. Back before having kids, when I was just hanging out with my guitar all the time, I'd make up little tunes all day long. I'm known for being prolific but if it weren't for this word business, I would have been way *more* prolific. Words and music, such a classic marriage, made of mutual challenge and synergy. But, of course, no sooner do you start to examine the binary system of words and music than you see that there is music in words and (if you are a really good player/composer) you can even put words into music.

I remember where I was sitting the first time I learned the word "prosody," which loosely translates to: the melody of prose. Or more exactly: the natural musical cadence of speech. Ah wow, yes! That is the thing I've been pursuing all these years in my writing! There is a *word* for it.

A RECORD OF AN EVENT

Anticipating the release of *Puddle Dive* in February of '93, I panicked about having four albums to sell on the road. Four different titles to carry in from the trunk, keep track of, and remember exactly how many sold in each place. My solution, ridiculously, was to re-record half the songs on my eponymous debut and half the songs on my second record, *Not So Soft*, and turn those into a single record called *Like I Said*. I can't imagine where I was going with that one. Did I think I was just gonna stop making records? Or even slow down? Besides, my sanity didn't lie in the difference between having three albums and four, it was in the difference between taking care of absolutely everything on the road by myself and not. I was showing signs of being overwhelmed.

I also hated my first two records so naturally I was attracted to solutions that involved burying them. I didn't yet know that it would be my fate to pretty much hate all of my records within a few years of making them, sometimes a few months . . . or minutes. It is a sad and strange relationship that I have with my own recordings. The feeling of crushing failure and the desperate need for redemption have propelled me forward more than anything. That's why I came to relish working with other people on their own art. It was all the fun of making records without the dread and shame. (Of course, then you always have to worry if you've done the other person's art justice. You have to fear that you've just spread your own suck around.) *Like I Said*, for its part, served only to confuse matters and solved nothing. People wanted my first two records anyway, so I still had to carry them.

A year after *Puddle Dive* came *Out of Range* in July of '94 and sometime around then I started to form my first opinions about this whole recording thing. Until then, I had been totally rapt with this new environment called the recording studio and just did whatever the studio guy told me to do. But each time, I watched what the engineers were doing and I learned something. I asked questions. It was antithetical to my nature to be dependent on anyone so I was subliminally striving to learn how to do it myself. While making *Out of Range*, I started piping up with production ideas and *"Can it be more like this?"* I was blessed to be working with this cool engineer, Ed Stone, and he was being really easygoing and candid with the technical process. He was inviting me in.

I went from recording in Buffalo to recording in and around Ontario, including at the producer Dan Lanois's first studio in Hamilton. They had a proto-digital reverb unit there that was actually cool sounding. All spacey and futuristic. It was three feet high and had big, colorful robot levers on top, looking like something from George Jetson's spaceship. Digital gear was all downhill from that big funky thing for a while.

These were basically the recording studios of the eighties that I walked into in 1990 and beyond. The recording culture was defined by all the infantile digital machines that were suddenly everywhere and by the lingering trance of an eighties aesthetic. Recording techniques focused on the hyper-isolation of sounds for maximum control and manipulability. There was little appreciation for the organic-ness of musicians playing together in a room and little tolerance for sonic bleed between microphones. There was no love at all for all the old analogue gear that was beginning to collect dust in the corners of control rooms, the tube preamps and tape machines, finicky from years of being poorly maintained.

Does anyone remember how many technology-driven disaster-preparedness products were marketed and sold to us around the turning of the last century? There we were, the age of computers upon us, and we were still falling for snake oils. We all had to buy our Y2K power adaptors and go stand on the street corner and wait for the grid to go down and the world to go dark at midnight on "The Millenniuuuuuum" (said with a ghostly warble). Like teenagers, we were all spooked and confused, our transition to modernity an awkward one. We didn't know what computers could do but we knew they were powerful and we were right to be scared. We had only just begun, grudgingly, to let computers worm their way into every aspect of our lives. We were still in the process of putting down our trusted twentieth-century tools and reinventing what we do, every last one of us, with the proto-machines of the digital age.

Soon enough, recording would be done totally "in the box" without any tape machines or mixing boards at all. Sometime after that, computer technology would actually be developed that could rival the sonic beauty of its analogue predecessors. Eventually, the reasons to cling to the old machines, even for the sonic supertasters, evaporated. The most significant advancements came in the area of converters. How do you turn an organic sound into ones and zeros (and sometimes back again) without degrading it? Massive amounts of bits. For my part, I just used whatever gear was available to me and I learned the hard way (in retrospect) what gear was cool and what wasn't. Not all decades for music recording can be the seventies. The seventies were right!

The nineties aesthetic of recording that took over from the eighties synthesizers involved adding compression and distortion to each one of these pristine, isolated tracks. The mastering goal then became to make every single thing as loud as it can be all the time. Compression was a game that everybody fell into "to compete." And no sooner did every sound have to be as loud as possible all the time, it had to be perfected, too. As computers advanced, they made an endless minutiae of manipulation possible and producers all went the way of musical plastic surgeons, constructing one perfect cyborg after another with every feature maximized.

The nineties were the era when everything from country to punk began getting rolled up into pop until all recorded music came out the other side with the same high-gloss sheen. Auto-Tune, one of the many computer programs designed to make people who can't sing or play perfectly sound as if they can, was employed more and more heavily until its candid presence became the very sound of modern vocals: part human, part robot.

For my part, as soon as I began to discern what was happening around me, I rebelled wildly against it. I rebelled for no other reason than my spleen told me to. As the nineties wore on, I leaned in to an uncompressed, unpolished, whisper-to-a-scream, warts-and-all aesthetic for my own records and I even developed a private snobbery to justify my choices. It's not that I can't make slick, high-impact records that sound like they could be on the radio. I just choose not to! Secretly, I hated all my raggedy, untamed records but I ennobled myself in my own narrative to beat back my crippling regret. *Fuck slick and commercial*, I told myself. *Fuck pretty and perfect.*

Making records is a uniquely different art form from song-making or performing. In retrospect, I might have done well to humble myself and seek more help but I was DIY to the core so I didn't. In the end, it would take me a lot longer to learn how to make records than to learn how to make songs or shows, for the obvious reason that those other things were things I practiced every day. Recordings, even at the pace of a couple a year in the early days, have taken me the better part of twenty years to get right. With every single choice, from the gear and the space you're in, to the minutiae of tones and tempo and key, to the musical arrangements of songs, to the monumental importance of performance choices and delivery, there are so many ways to thwart the documenting of a song. Any one of these factors can magnify and become the tragic flaw that sabotages the whole thing.

I have struggled my entire life with the task of recording a dynamic singing voice and a dynamic acoustic guitar happening right next to each other. Because my voice always goes into the guitar mic and vice versa, I was often advised to record the two things separately in the early days. Guitar first. It seems unfortunate, in retrospect, to have forgone capturing the organic interplay of the two for the purposes of having discrete sounds. Maybe just one mic for both is better? But then . . . that sounds even less like a modern recording. We are used to having singers sing right into our ears. Maybe a horizontal surface could be inserted to shield my face from my hands so the microphones could capture each thing separately? It sounds kind of ridiculous, but I've tried it. There's simply no substitute for having good microphones, choosing them carefully, and then taking your time massaging their placement until you achieve a decent, not-too-phase-y sound on both things at once.

There is a particular queasy sensation that one feels when one is experiencing sonic phase cancellation. "Out of phase" means that a sound is coming at you twice, at slightly different times, and the two like-sound waves are crashing into each other before your very ears. When they collide, some frequencies in the sound can get canceled out and others can become exaggerated. The sound can be made ugly. On rare occasions, phase tricks can make something sound as if it's coming from beside or even behind you in a cool way, but mostly, it just results in an unpleasant sensation in the listener's stomach and some degree of tonal narrowing or filtering. I would need to become acutely aware of this queasy sensation of phase cancellation before I would learn to detect when it is happening, even in small degrees, and try to deal with it.

After the recording and mixing of *Out of Range*, I worked with Ed Stone again to record *Not a Pretty Girl* and that's when I started to really put my own hands on the gear. It was now, officially, a collaboration. You can hear then my rebellion against the years of cheesy digital reverbs as my voice becomes suddenly very bald and unadorned. The records that follow, *Dilate, Living in Clip*, and *Little Plastic Castle*, I think of as all being in this particular flow. I was empowered and excited and coming into my own in the recording studio. Plus, I had good engineers and production collaborators, first in Ed Stone and later in Andrew Gilchrist.

With *Not a Pretty Girl*, I decided I wanted to capture the duo thing that Andy and I were doing live so I decreed that the two of us should play live in the studio. I wanted to keep it simple and straight up, no hiring of strangers to overdub stuff, never to be seen again. Of course, then I decided I wanted a bass to fill out the bottom so Andy suggested that I just play the bass parts myself. The fact that it was his suggestion was all the license I needed to go for it. I went and bought a Fender P bass on consignment at Top Shelf and made up some parts. Then it was on to the mix phase of the record and Andy and Ed dropped out of the picture while I went to put in time in a strip mall in Mississauga.

Mississauga, Ontario, is a windswept suburban wasteland. Or at least that's the way it felt to me in the dead of winter, driving between my motel and the strip mall which was home to the Canadian band Triumph's studio. They had a Neve console there which Ed had wisely advised me was the best sounding board around to mix on. The house engineer that was assigned to my session for the week was younger than I was, and I was twenty-four. He was a metalhead kid with long hair, just out of high school and still living with his parents. Every morning, I chipped the ice off my rent-a-car windshield and drove the cold mile to eighties-hair-band-world to collaborate with my young accomplice. We mixed *Not a Pretty Girl* in six days, just him and me.

In retrospect, I think I showed up to that strip mall in Mississauga ovulating as I remember inviting said metalhead boy to take the night off from his parents' house and come back to my motel with me. A body-driven, desperate move. Luckily, the kid didn't bite. He was still together with his high school girlfriend. By the end of the week, I hit an almighty PMS and almost lost my mind in that shitty little motel alone. I actually contemplated suicide for the first time in earnest. I felt so messed up inside, like a devastating sadness had wormed its way deep into me and made itself a permanent worm-home. I was too young then to know that nothing is really permanent.

The picture on the cover of the record shows the pale expanse of my exposed solar plexus, but in the time between the cover photo session and the album's release, I had tattooed across that skin to commemorate another one of life's little survivals. A tattoo is like a mile marker. It was prophetic that I decided to ink that inescapable squiggle smack across my chest in that particular moment because *Not a Pretty Girl* became something of a rite of passage for me when it came out. It was like the pivot point between one kind of life and a hyper-compressed, turned-up version of that life. National press got wind of my insurgency and soon media begat more media and I was the next big thing. Behind the scenes, though, we didn't have enough money to make payroll at Righteous Babe when *Not a Pretty Girl* was released. Checks bounced. We were operating close to the bone.

THE BOOB TUBE

Scot, having officially taken over my management operation, put aside his law degree and moved into a small two-room office on the third floor of the Sidway Building in downtown Buffalo. The office looked like it belonged to a private detective, with a frosted glass front door and an interior straight out of the thirties. The effect was amplified by Scot's big, lumbering, garbage-picked desk and his collection of antique filing cabinets. We stenciled "Righteous Babe Records" on the door, so people would know we were not actually private detectives. The name made our neighbors' eyebrows rise. It seems funny now, but the world seemed to react to my company's name in the early days as if it were aggressive or edgy. Like it was a tattoo on my face.

Scot never stopped driving a pickup truck (once a construction guy, always a construction guy) and big-garbage picking was one of his specialties. All the furniture at Righteous Babe was Buffalo's garbage-picked finest and his junk-man tendencies were also turning his personal abode into something of a museum of antique audio devices. He was the proud owner of a gramophone and an ancient wire recorder, among other things. The wire recorder actually worked, insomuch as it played the spools of wire that happened to come in the case with it. Somebody had recorded radio broadcasts of baseball games onto them in the thirties and we passed a whole evening once, drinking beers and listening to the bygone transmissions. After a while, we were transported back, as if we were sitting around the radio itself. RBR did knuckle down and purchase a few state-of-the-art gizmos, though, to break our old-timey trance. State of the art being: two plastic phones, a fax machine, and a photocopier. Suzi started working for me then, too, answering the second phone.

If you took the stairs all the way up, there was a door out onto the roof of the Sidway Building that was always unlocked. We went up there to enjoy the view, to catch a breeze in the summertime, or to watch fireworks. I was traveling a lot but I was also frequently hanging around Buffalo. There was always something to do at the RBR office, like working out some graphic design thing with Suzi or going down to city hall to file some papers. One day, Scot said we needed to make some photographs of me because my booking agency was asking for a new promo shot. Scot promised to make it quick and painless so he grabbed his old Nikon and we headed up to the roof.

My previous promo shot had exposed the fact that I did not shave my underarm hair, which (it also seems funny to think now) was apparently considered a bold statement of some kind. Some hardcore dyke shit or something. In any case, Jim Fleming considered it an impediment to getting me gigs so they had cropped the photo somewhere just below my neck. It was the strangest-looking thing you've ever seen, giving a whole new meaning to the term "headshot."

Being in front of cameras is my least favorite part of my job. You'll rarely find me happy or relaxed in front of a lens so I often would get goofy as a way of coping. To be funny, I struck a muscleman pose that day on the roof, not knowing that it would be a moment that would follow me around for the rest of my life, dripping with an irony known only to me. (Coping with a lack of confidence and self-possession in front of a camera is reborn in the world as confidence and self-possession! Good trick, huh?) Anyway, we got our new headshot and, now that RBR was a real record company with a tax ID number and a fax machine, we also needed a logo. After sending Jim whatever menacing, angry, puppy-eating, hairy bull dyke image (picture of my face) we deemed best, I went and traced the muscleman shot with a magic marker and made it into a line drawing. I handed the line drawing to Suzi, and Righteous Babe Records had a logo.

Before you knew it, we were moving up to the fourth floor of the Sidway Building and into a bigger office. I hired another friend, Mary Begley, who would anchor RBR's staff for the next twenty-two years. Mary is a painter who, at the time, also had a punk-rock alter ego by the name of Mimi Bourgeois making appearances around town hammering out songs on her Flying V guitar. The staff and the space that RBR occupied would expand exponentially throughout the nineties, but not many of the people who became part of the team had any experience in the "music biz" per se. I mean, we did eventually, as our associations became greater and more varied, but we were really just kids whacking our way through the weeds of an unknown terrain. At least Scot knew how to keep us all legal and businesslike. His father's experience running a law office had rubbed off on him. It was easy enough to just keep answering the phone. That is, until our 800 number appeared on MTV.

In lieu of any comprehensive distribution in record stores, we had established a direct line to fans: 1-800-ON-HER-OWN. The internet was not quite a going concern yet so our 800 number just appeared printed on my cassette and CD jackets and maybe in a magazine ad or folk festival program now and then. The number, like all things Righteous Babe, got passed around by word of mouth. It was a number that people could call to order music but also to ask questions or voice opinions, or just to talk to somebody who might understand. When Scot was working late in the evening, he would make a habit of picking up the 800 line and having heart-to-hearts with the people on the other end of the line. The 800 number, in the beginning, was part mail-order store, part youth crisis hotline, and part activist networking switchboard.

The first time I was slated to appear on MTV, we were all very excited but we had no idea just how exciting it would become. Unbeknownst to us, MTV flashed the 800 number at the bottom of the screen during my interview and we got our first lesson in the economy of scale between our little operation and the monolith that was MTV. The story aired over the weekend and when Scot and the other Babes showed up to the office on Monday, the phone was ringing. You could hear it down the hall when you got off the elevator. The phone continued to ring for days and days, like a hot potato, it rang instantly every time it was returned to its cradle. We eventually had to unplug it.

The next thing that happened was a phone bill got delivered to our doorstep that was hundreds of pages thick, looking like the phone book itself, and costing thousands of dollars. None of the calls had been orders for records, really, but were just from kids who saw a number on their TV screen and dialed it. Meanwhile, we were charged a fee for every call, even the ones the machine picked up, because that's how 800 numbers work. We ended up with a phone bill we couldn't pay. After some long negotiations with the phone company and a reduced payment plan, we chalked it all up to a lesson in the power of television.

I guess I am grateful for the handful of times that I've been invited onto the boob tube but also I kind of wish I could take them all back and opt out of the whole thing. It's a bummer to be totally uncomfortable and outside of my own skin when the most people are watching. By the time I get out of the makeup and hair curler room, I'm toast. Of course, TV feels minuscule now compared to the internet, and no one can apparently opt out there. So I guess it's officially time for me to get over myself. Every living moment can and will be held up to an eternity of scrutiny online.

If I could, I swear I would trade places with Buddy Bolden, the great jazz pioneer who was never even photographed (one shadowy image), let alone recorded. *A stunning effect on the world around you and then a magical vanishing act, now that is a cool trick, Mr. Bolden.* Maybe as *my* final trick, in the moment I leave this earthly plane I will blink my eyes and make his cornet live forever and me just disappear.

A MOTHER'S WORK

My mom was still living in Connecticut, and New York was just a short train ride away, so I visited her now and then when I was back in the city. She would always reimburse me for the train ticket and she would usually lay a hundred bucks on me before I walked out her door. A mother's work is never done. A hundred bucks had changed in size for her because, after a couple of years at the firm in Old Lyme, she'd quit the architecture racket altogether.

Being a perfectionist, she could not bring herself to delegate to junior draftsmen or she had to correct their work so much that it was a zero-sum proposition, either way, she'd fallen into the same pattern of overworking and stressing out that she'd been in in Buffalo. Once again, she would stay very late at the office, even sleeping there, to get up in the morning and resume working before anyone else came in. Her linen suit full of wrinkles. I guess that was her pattern: push herself beyond the breaking point and then break. This time, as it turns out, she'd not only quit the firm but she'd quit architecture for good. In her sixties now, on her own and having no nest egg, she fell back on the only other skill she had in spades: she became a housecleaner.

Her savings had gone to my father. He had slowly drained the money out of their joint bank account to support himself back in Buffalo when his Social Security payments began falling short. The two of them never got legally divorced and remained connected financially until his death. Luckily, my income would rise to a level where I could support them both just in the nick of time. My mother had to sell off some of the land in Quebec in the meantime . . . but not all of it. Then the sale of the donut house carried them just long enough for my career to take off. That and a lot of scrubbing and mopping, sweeping and vacuuming on my mother's part. I know exactly how seriously she took her work, no matter what it was, and I bet those rich people's houses in southern Connecticut had never been so clean. Her arms were more cut than mine and I was already developing guitar slinger muscles. For a while there, she looked like some kind of old lady bodybuilder.

I was subsisting on coffee and three-dollar mystery meat dumplings in New York and whenever I visited my mother, for some reason, I would try to detox from caffeine. The result was, I would show up at her apartment, lie down, and proceed to nurse a migraine for days, getting up only to eat some beautifully presented salad that she had prepared for us with nasturtiums picked from a neighboring garden. She didn't seem to mind that I was so strung out and exhausted whenever I turned up. I was one of the few people in the world who understood her and she was happy to have me near. I was still her biggest fan. She apologized a lot, in those days, for the misery that had been our family life back in Buffalo but I always shrugged it off. It doesn't matter, I would say. It was fine. I was actually a long way off from understanding that it did matter and that I wasn't exactly fine. But, ironically, by the time I was ready to talk about it, she was beyond talking at all.

At some point, I realized that paying New York rents had become impractical for me. I was leading the gypsy life, traveling constantly, and a New York apartment is a damn expensive storage facility for one's possessions. I was sharing an apartment with Boopha on Avenue D when I finally said uncle and moved out of New York for good. Not only was it illogical for me to be floating big-city rent for an apartment I was hardly ever at, Boopha was going off the deep end and our apartment had become something of a hostile environment. She was using hard drugs and had graduated from working at strip joints to bringing the sex work home and selling drugs herself. I never knew, when I walked into that apartment, who or what I would find. My few family photos might have been mysteriously burnt up. The arm of my grandfather's chair might be broken off. There might be a man handcuffed to the couch.

I spent the next handful of years with no official home at all. It wasn't until I had made enough money to buy my own house, back in Buffalo, that I landed again. By that time, my mother's personality had started to change. Her years of being a housekeeper in a wealthy area had turned her into something of a servant. It was a palpable change of vibe and it disturbed me so I made the executive decision that she should move back to Buffalo and live with me. Scot drove with me to Connecticut and we piled the truck up with her stuff. I set her up in her own little vector in my house. She had her own side entrance and her own kitchen. She was free. The only thing was, she never unpacked.

My mom lived in my house for years without unpacking a box. For an aesthetic soul such as hers, this was incomprehensible. She was the kind of person who needed everything to be just so. At first, I kept offering to help her, then I would gently try to inquire if there was something wrong with her space, if there was something she'd like to change, but she would never give me an answer. She would respond only with the sharp chirping sounds that were becoming her trademark. It was some sort of silent protest that I couldn't figure out. On one level, she seemed much happier in Buffalo, she was near all her old friends, she even got a job at the Albright Knox Art Gallery that she enjoyed. She seemed to move back into her own skin but she wouldn't move into my house. She had never really been able to process conflict within herself and this inability seemed to be growing starker with age. Eventually, I just gave up trying to talk to her at all.

Moving my mother in with me as an adult was one of the worst decisions I ever made. I did it to help, I thought I was helping, but that gesture ushered in the end of our sincere bond. Her silences became directed my way and eventually proved impenetrable, even to me. I was becoming more like my father as each day passed and it seemed as though I was now walking in his shoes, or rather I was tiptoeing in them, around her.

IT'S NOT AN ADVENTURE, IT'S A JOB

I was still the main driver of the minivan, I was the scheduler and the navigator, I dealt with the college students who called the soundboard a "keyboard" and the folk promoters who gasped at the sight of a drum kit. I dealt with the sound guys for those gigs that were legit enough to warrant a "professional sound engineer" and I dealt with the folksy, speakers-on-sticks venue owners who did everything themselves. I was CD seller, accountant, and roadie. I think Andy felt I wasn't paying him enough for him to bust his balls much outside of his job description (hitting things with sticks) and I suppose he was right. This was clearly my thing. Meanwhile, I had set a course on the road to exhaustion and felt many days like, with Andy around, I had another person to take care of and more gear to load in and out, but still no help.

My audiences were growing and the venues along with them, but our mode of touring remained the same. We were beginning to recreate this humorous scene where we'd pull up to a thousand-plus capacity venue, just Andy and me in a minivan, and watch the local crew's heads cock to the side like gramophone dogs. They were used to seeing buses and trucks brimming with people and gear. "This is it?" they would ask, thrilled. We arrived at the Beacon Theatre in Boston that way and the Irving Plaza in New York. I had one guitar and a box of CDs. Andy had his homemade cases.

Navigating and procuring directions in a pre-cellphone world was hard to do while driving. Often, I would just follow highway signs to a city and then roll down the window and start asking people the way to the University of Whatever. Then, when I found the University of Whatever, I would roll down the window again and start asking students if they knew where there might be a folk show that night. I was like the opposite of the classic male driver who won't ask for directions. I would sooner talk to five different people than read a piece of paper. Anyway, I was never late and I never missed a gig. Fleming didn't seem too hung up on streamlining my routing or worrying about travel loads or sleep windows, either. I was expected to pay my dues in the building of an actual career in music, which is as it should be, I suppose. I was young and lucky to be going somewhere.

Exhaustion, I discovered, is not the worst thing to walk out on stage with. Exhaustion is like a drug that serves to cancel the usual routines of stage fright and self-consciousness. Like grief or depression, it cuts right through everything and changes your overarching perspective on the world, rendering things that used to matter, meaningless. I found I could sink into the altered state of channeling music quicker when my own body's energy was not buzzing like a magnetic field of resistance between myself and the great beyond. Together, Andy and I would take even greater musical risks on nights when we were both delirious. My mic banter would veer into the surreal and I would have people rolling in the aisles between songs. Eventually, though, I felt myself start to get ground down. No amount of youthful vim and vigor could sustain me. I needed help.

The straw that broke the camel's brain was, once again, the psychologically exhausting interface with the sound guy du jour. After all the traveling and making myself available to so many people, to find myself in a needless power struggle every time I walked into a place just broke me down. They just couldn't accept my ideas about the acoustic guitar. It made them mad. Or maybe I was just the kind of person they wanted to fight with? I could never quite figure it out. And though my gigs were starting to be in places with actual sound systems, the dudes in charge of running those sound systems were not necessarily top of their field. The daily blasts of brain-splitting feedback alone were enough to make a girl question her very existence. And you'd better not react negatively to a blast of feedback or you've just sealed your fate. The gatekeeper between you and the audience is your enemy.

I started carrying a rack with a graphic EQ and a subharmonic synthesizer that I would insert on my guitar channel and tweak from stage in an effort to bypass the wall of resistance each sound guy presented. United Airlines made mincemeat of that rack in no time, though, and I learned the number one rule of gear: The more you have, the more you have to repair. There is just no good solution to being alone and defenseless on the road except . . . to not be alone and defenseless. I was standing at an increasing number of pay phones, crying over the line to Scot, saying, "I can't do this anymore."

MERCH

I f you want your own sound guy, you're going to have to sell T-shirts. That's all there is to it," he said, chewing his food. We were sitting at Santasiero's over on the west side of Buffalo, drinking wine out of little juice cups. Scot had been talking to people and doing his research and he was convinced that this was the way that I could afford to pay another person on the road. But I couldn't help it, I was dead set against it. People had actually been requesting T-shirts from me for a while though and Scot entreated me again to reconsider. I watched him eating his spaghetti. The idea of selling T-shirts was embarrassing to me, it was cheesy and capitalistic, but now I was weighing it against quitting music altogether. I was that exhausted. I knew he just wanted to see me happy. I really was contemplating quitting.

I was not so far from my former dancing and painting selves that I couldn't envision shifting gears again. I actually missed dancing a lot. My body preferred the ache of long days of rehearsals to the ache of long days of sitting behind the wheel. But then . . . who was I kidding? I knew dancing was never going to be the lover to me that music was and whiling away my life in some garret painting was not exactly going to heal my soul, either. I couldn't deny that I had been captured by the wide-open road and by the act of showing up in a community and making of myself connective tissue between the people who lived there. The inherent activism of it all.

My old pal Tanya was selling T-shirts, Scot reminded me. Tanya and Joe were hand–silk screening American-made, 100 percent cotton T-shirts with all-natural dyes, in prints of Tanya's artwork. They had started a little textiles operation called Planet Love and they were driving around to music and craft festivals plying their wares. "Think of them like you do Tanya's shirts," Scot said, "like wearable art. People have to wear clothes, y'know." "Okay," I relented, "we'll sell T-shirts but

I don't want my name or my face on them." Scot shook his head at me, "You're such a weirdo."

Over time, those rules got broken, too. I started by accepting the printing of my first name after some song lyrics (but not my last name because that would be advertisement!). Printing only the first name was like a secret message to those already in the know. It took years, but the shirts slowly went from saying Ani, to Ani D., to my full name. A few years after that, my face appeared. It is funny the things we cling to as symbols of our own integrity. Planet Love became the producers of all my T-shirts and still are to this day. It feels good, at least, to have offered some gainful employment to dear friends along the way. But, twenty years later, walking past my own merch booth still makes me feel like a jerk.

In any case, Scot was right. Once I started selling T-shirts, they started floating my whole operation. It is truly sad to me that the label "entrepreneur" has followed me around for so many years, often coming right behind "singer-songwriter." "Entrepreneur" usually comes before or even displaces the word "activist." It finally got better when I decided to stop caring about what the media say at all. Go ahead and call me Annie the entrepreneur. Call me whatever you want. I know who I am.

GOAT

The one that I hired to help drive, run sound, and be all-around crew guy was a friend of Andy's from Toronto whose mother had also named him Andrew. Since the name rationing was a little steep in our three-person operation, I dubbed Andrew "Goat." To me he looked more like a goat than a person named Andrew and I couldn't understand why nobody else had seen this. The three of us would engage in lavish discussions about music and art while cruising along and then as soon as we'd arrive at a venue, Goat would leap out and run off. Andy and I would sit there in the van watching him race around the building, trying to find the way in. He would run out of one door and into another. "Like a little goat frolicking on a knoll," we would joke as he ran by again. Goat never just walked. I loved that about him.

From my pinky toes to my aching brain, everything about my everyday life improved when Goat came along. I finally had a willing partner in "my sound" and Andy and I had a guy whose idea of soundcheck didn't involve administering blasts of literally deafening feedback. We had somebody to run interference between us and the promoter, us and the fans, us and each other. I had somebody to do the settlement and advance work and, of course, to help figure out where the hell we were going.

Goat carried with him an indestructible metal briefcase which he called his "brain" and also a red metal toolbox dubbed "Push to Flush." Push to Flush got its name from the little plaque stuck above its front latch, which he'd lifted from an Air India jetliner. Under the English was the same instruction in Hindi. Goat had been to India and all kinds of other cool places. His parents were English before they settled in Canada and with them he had traveled the world in his jaunty humor, pilfering souvenirs. The amazing thing was, between his "brain" and Push to Flush, he always seemed to have whatever random small item or tool was needed. Whatever it was, Goat had one.

My overwhelmed state subsided. Goat could fix shit, speak several languages, and run sound like aces. He had worked for years at The Music Gallery in Toronto before I came along and he introduced me to the cosmos of "new music" including all kinds of composers whose names I've since forgotten. Goat and Andy knew a heck of a lot about music in general and turned me on to all kinds of people from Brian Eno to Terry Riley to Jon Hassell. From Bill Laswell to Bill Frisell. They turned me on to records like the Talking Heads' *Life in the Bush of Ghosts* and Talk Talk's *Spirit of Eden*. The three of us might be spinning Nusrat Fateh Ali Khan and Michael Brook or we might be spinning Lee Scratch

Perry and the Mad Professor as we clocked in our miles. Every time we got in the van, we brought musical offerings to each other. It was a time of great discovery.

It was fun to tour and play again now that the painful nightly power struggle was over. Not only was our basic sound finally happening, Goat started bringing along extra effects like a delay and a JamMan sampler/looper. When Andy and I would start improvising, Goat would make loops on the fly and throw them back into the mix so we could stretch out even more and jam with loops of ourselves. I would hear my vocal phrases coming back at me through the PA and I would be freed to depart further and invent a countermelody. Goat became our Mad Professor.

His wardrobe was always perfectly outlandish and I watched his eye discover the perfection of outlandishness in thrift stores across North America and Europe. He was so much fun to walk around with. The landscape of our adventures seemed to become bigger and more vivid. With Goat as backup, I could even go into music stores everywhere, too. I was the guitar player and he was the gear guy who could tell a cool amp or pedal from a turd. As a team, we were able to go searching for musical tools on the streets of everytown in a way that neither of us could have done on our own. Goat was helping me to improve my own toolbox so that, someday, I, too, might always have what's needed.

We didn't know it, or maybe we did, but we were falling in love. Our dreams hopelessly aligned, Goat and I were doomed to fall for each other. He had an unrelenting positivity which matched my own and in our synergy, was an unstoppable joy. Despite myself, I began to look forward to getting back in the van after our short breaks off tour simply to hear what new music he would play or what crazy thing he would say. The road was becoming my home instead of home. A reversal that would remain true for a long time.

The problem with falling in love with Goat was that he already had a lady, not to mention the fact that I had this ongoing, free-floating thing with Scot. I wrote a lot of songs about the impending doom of our attraction (like "Shameless" and "Untouchable Face") and then I played them in Toronto, with Goat's lady in the audience, in order that everybody be able to enjoy the benefits of honesty by default. Our process of collective soul-searching was duly propelled by my performance. After staying up into the wee hours, paying the piper, Goat quit my gig that night and got on his motorcycle to ride alone across America and "find himself."

Shortly thereafter, I was down in Austin, at the Congress House Studio, mixing my album *Dilate*. We had recorded *Dilate* in Toronto, Andy, Goat, and I, in a rustic little one-room urban studio down an unassuming alley that had only a wood stove for warmth. It was the winter of 1995 and my illicit love for Goat was painted across my heart and across all my songs. The explosion that happened next meant that, when it was time to mix the record, I was on my own again. I went down to Austin to get as far from the scene of the crime as possible and my mixing process became an exercise in pummeling myself with low-end as sonic penance for my sins.

I was sleeping there at the Congress House, on the futon next to the pump organ, thanks to the studio's kind owner, Mark Hallman, who agreed to let me inhabit the place while I was working. Mark would come in in the morning, make me coffee, and help guide me around his patch bay and his unfamiliar gear until I became self-sufficient. I probably should have utilized Mark as a voice of reason in the mixing process but, as usual, I just wanted to do my thing. Mark and Marty Lester, the other engineer there who helped me, listened to me cry in my whiskey at night and tried to help me find distraction and levity during the creative exorcism that I was performing.

I was pretty much finished with the record when Goat pulled up on his motorcycle and I knew instantly whose wheels those were on the gravel driveway. Apparently, his journey of self-discovery had led him right to where I was. I went out on the porch and watched him dismount, my heart swelling. I tried to play it cool, we were not going to be together, he had made his choice, it had all been a mistake . . . but it was no use. He'd come back for me and I surrendered.

I had an appointment to master *Dilate* out in L.A. and he said he would take me there. Within a few days, I was on the back of his bike and we were riding out west together, staying in divey motels and drinking a lot of canned beer to quench our thirst. My hands turned eight shades darker stationed there on his thighs as the West enveloped us for thirteen hundred miles. The songs that resulted from that time—"Gravel," "Swan Dive," "Independence Day"—would anchor the record that followed, *Little Plastic Castle*, which we made back at the Congress House again, this time, working together.

My moment of reckoning with Scot had arrived. I told him I'd fallen in love with Goat. Scot said, "Well . . . you sure have been a lot happier since he came along." He said the last thing he wanted was to stand in the way of my happiness. He showed his love for me in a profound way then and took it like a man. Scot released me from my conflicted state and Goat's lady released him. Untethered, Goat and I floated like helium balloons into the air. "Let's get married," I said one bleary morning in an airport waiting room. I was watching an elderly couple sitting near us, the old lady with her head resting on her husband's shoulder. And so, we did.

HEIDI HO

No sooner had I hired Goat than I promptly hired a girl to sell merch. This business of drumming up a volunteer every night to help me sell my records was getting old and now we had T-shirts, too. The girl I hired was a meek, baseball-capped little baby dyke named Rebecca Rebecca (her mother had given her just the one Rebecca as a name but we opted, unanimously, to double it) and we commenced to upgrade from a minivan to an RV as our touring vehicle. At least we thought of it as an upgrade but, let's just say, there are reasons why bands don't tour in RVs and we spent the better part of a year learning them.

Rebecca Rebecca was out there on the front lines, rubbing elbows with the audience and making friends despite her shyness. Like with this girl who was following my whole tour, coast to coast, alone in her car. Well, not alone, exactly, but with her cat. This girl and her cat literally trailed us down the road and then there she was in the front row at every show. She even started helping behind the merch table. I couldn't help but be aware that Rebecca Rebecca's accounting became suddenly airtight. No more accidental money or merch shortages. Cat Girl had it goin' on.

Amazingly, Cat Girl managed to become a de facto part of our operation without ever once approaching me or bothering me in any way. Her charm built as I became increasingly impressed by her level of restraint until one night, at some bar, it was I who finally approached her. I was something like a cat myself, which is to say, if you pulled me onto your lap, I would most likely squirm and jump down, but if you sat there long enough with the right energy, I would eventually jump into your lap and then it was on. Cat girl, indeed. This girl understood me! By the time we met, I was already in the palm of her hand.

"So, who the hell are you?" I said, to break the ice. She smiled back at me with a face full of piercings that twinkled in the dim bar light and a shaved head that was a mirror of my former self. Her name, she said, was Heidi and, it turns out, she is one of my best friends in this world. She would soon take over my merch operation and, as I type, she has been my traveling companion for twenty-two years. I don't really know what I'd do without my Ho.

One fun fact about Heidi Ho: She has been to more Ani DiFranco shows than any person other than Ani DiFranco. Like, by far. She also used to have something of a photographic memory and could tell me the date and city I last played a certain song in (also what she was wearing and who, if anyone, turned up that night). I used her brain as my database until eventually, even she fell victim to the blur of life on the road. It was terrifying and at the same time reassuring to see her start to slip. My Heidi database eventually crashed but at least then I felt better about my own brain's abiding fog.

Heidi became my official song titler, or at least my official song title consultant. I never liked making titles. More nailing things down. But Heidi always had her ears on and when a new song started making appearances she was right there with suggestions. As the venues got bigger, though, she was rarely stationed in the room with the show anymore. She would be off in some distant lobby, unable to hear a lick of it. New songs would come out and mutate and refine themselves on stage without her ever having heard them. She would try to steal away from her table and sneak into the venue to catch the new ones but that's right when fans would want to sneak out and satisfy their merch needs. I had to learn how to title the damn things myself.

How can I even describe the kind of friend that is Heidi Ho? If we were sitting in a field right now, she would be wordlessly picking four-leaf clovers as if they were calling to her, possessed as she is of some bizarre skill to recognize and spot four-leaf clovers instantly, out of the corner of her eye. If you are walking on a beach with Ho she will see a tiny bubble in the sand and bend down to swiftly dig up a little crab. Then she will hold it out to your face and say, "crab." She is possessed of a keen curiosity and an unusual scale to her awareness. She will miss (enviably) a macro mood shift but she will be dialed in to the tiny little details of the universe that most people overlook. She always has a new subject she is studying or skill that she is learning. She is never idle.

After our first trip to Italy, we were both totally enamored and came home determined to learn Italian. She actually did it.

At some point, Heidi's outfits took a turn for the extraordinary. She graduated from a goth-y girl with a purple streak in her hair to a full-on glam punk goddess with vinyl and rubber clothing that made everyone everywhere's head turn. Her hairstyles became more fantastical and intricate and her piercings multiplied weekly. At the maximum, she had no less than twenty-two piercings and her tattoos were adding up just as fast. Her own body had become one of her ongoing projects. Occasionally, she would work a show wearing only latex body paint. When we showed up at airports with all our music gear, people would eye up Heidi and then come over to me and whisper, "Who is *that*?"

I have searched high and low for women to tour with in every single job position. I love the company of men but there is something important missing when I'm the only woman around day in and day out. I thank Goddess that my Heidi Ho has been out there with me all this time. Despite my efforts, the other women have been few and far between. There are simply way too few women in the music biz in general, at least on the touring side. Not just female musicians playing instruments, but also sound engineers and techs and roadies of all stripes. On the tech and roadie side, there are also way too few people of color.

When I grow up, I am going to start a school for sound engineers, lighting designers, production managers, stage managers, and all other crew-related jobs, aimed at the diversification of the means of music production from the ground up. All love and respect for my white boys, but this shit's gotta change! I can't help but wonder if the ability to feel and support others wouldn't predispose women to be excellent sound engineers, not to mention musicians. So much untapped potential.

CHICK SINGERS

It's no wonder that, in the music world, women have often and sometimes exclusively entered the picture as singers. Children must receive a lot of support (or at least a lot of leeway) to transform a tool into
an extension of their own body, the way musicians do their instruments.
I got my combination of support and leeway and I'm grateful for it but
girls, traditionally, aren't handed the tools of music or shown how to use
them with the frequency of boys. Our mothers and our mothers' mothers
were not handed these tools either so, long ago, it was written: Instrument playing is a man's game. In this atmosphere, a woman driven to
make or interpret music can easily find herself with only her own body
to use as a tool. Enter the chick singer. The chick dancer.

The female musician, where she is found, can be like that proverbial
ship on the horizon, invisible to the natives who have never seen a ship
before and have no frame of reference for "ship." Have you heard this
supposed story? I don't know about the story but I do know the phenomenon to be true. We can only really see what we already know to exist.
In this way, badass female musicianship can often go unnoticed, like
Karen Carpenter's drumming or Aretha Franklin's piano playing. Society
only had the capacity to witness those people sing.

All judgment of patriarchy aside, I bet it is a most natural thing for a
woman to make of her own body the tool. Even longer ago, that one was
written. A woman can use her body as currency or leverage in the world
of men. She can also use her body to build a whole other human being.
After a woman makes a new human being, her body becomes the machine that feeds it.

Yes, the chick-singer phenomenon is probably not as simple as: Patriarchy relegates women to singing by denying them access to the tools of
music. It is likely an even more complicated story including: Singing is a
feminine art. Singing being even less about the proverbial ten thousand

hours of nerding-out practicing and more about the ability to be totally emotionally present in a moment; tuned in. The ability to make of your own body and breath, the medium of art. The singer serves as the emotional bridge between band and audience, making or breaking the band's ability to go over. The human voice, with no levels of convolution, is emotionally exposed and through it, listeners can also become exposed. Singing, in this way, is simultaneously the easiest and the hardest instrument to master. ("Master" not "mistress"? Dammit, Ani! When will you ever stop using that male-centric language?)

But seriously, the instrument of the voice is a moving target like no other instrument I know. My guitar might shift slightly in its tone after bouncing from one climate to another, but the change will be unnoticeable to anyone but me. My voice is infinitely less predictable, it changes daily and even within the course of a day. It changes with every minute fluctuation of my physical and mental state, including moods so deep I don't even know I'm having them. I've learned to just stand there, somewhat helplessly, and listen to what comes out of my face on any given night. I can choose the note I sing, but I can't really choose the tone of it. That is decided for me. There's nothing for me to achieve in the area of tone but acceptance. In that way, it's true, the term "mastery" really doesn't apply to singing, as far as I'm concerned. My interactions with my voice are less about "mastery" in terms of control, and more about the ability to open up to, make room for, and be responsive to messages received.

Have you ever looked up what the most-spoken words in the English language are? You get differing accounts, but one thing remains fairly consistent across the varying lists: "He" is always way higher on the list than "she." When I first noticed that fact myself, I was struck. I sat and thought about it for a long time. *Right, of course. There it is. Where is she? At home raising children. (What is there to talk about?) And, where is he? Out there doing stuff!* Of all the speech that one can survey (the speech of public life) "he" has been empirically proven to be the going concern.

"He" is the active agent in society. Whatever women have been able to accomplish in the public sphere, they basically had to accomplish before or instead of motherhood. This has made women-as-doers a global rarity.

To say that men are the doers and women are the bearers might be a bummer sometimes, but it would not be historically untrue. Homo sapiens are born into this world in something of a larval state so being bearers hasn't proved to be something women can just do on the side. Human children must be literally carried around for years after they are born. Men, biologically endowed with more free agency, have used that to their advantage. And, why wouldn't they? They have been able to do great things.

"She" has been climbing the most-spoken lists, however, ever since I first checked. Countless shes have been pushing their way into society for a long time. I imagine 2017 alone represented a huge spike in the saying of the words "she" and "her" in the American discourse. The year that started with a massive global women's march and then evolved into the #MeToo levee breach certainly served to feminize the narrative. What happens when society experiences hearing the words "she" and "her" that many times? Do our subliminal notions shift to women as doers? Maybe it is not even the minutiae of the feminist ideas that we express so much as the repeated sounds that we utter that prick up the evolutionary ear? The primal music beneath all the words . . . delivering its own message.

For women to begin to really start picking up all these tools (trumpets, tractors, telescopes) and making stuff, however (let alone designing the tools), men are going to need to step into the void created in the home and become bearers. The good news is this: Men can absolutely be bearers because the monumental undertakings of pregnancy and birthing are only the beginning of the bearing forth of healthy, whole human beings. The even better news is this: The process of men picking up women's slack in the domestic sphere seems to have finally, actually begun. In more and more American families, men are working as caregivers and women are working outside the home. You can see this palpable shift reflected in everything from TV commercials to song.

The challenge for men will be to embrace the role of nurturer and to not succumb to anger and resentment over what is lost. It is not easy for anyone to be a bearer, and it is especially not easy when you are swimming up the big cultural stream. Patriarchy, like racism, is embedded so unfathomably deep in all of us that it is sure to claim many more victims on its way out of style.

For this new breed of full-time fathers, their ideas around "taking care of" and "providing for" will need to strike out and claim new territory. It is not just breadwinning but housekeeping and nourishing and emotional engagement that constitute work. These male nurturers will either carve space for themselves to feel proud of their work and satisfied with their own prowess and personal evolution or they will succumb to feeling threatened and thwarted by the female social agent. They will sabotage her from underneath. A readily affirmed belief that a feminist endeavor such as father-bearing is for the absolute betterment of humankind might help us each to stay the course, but that social reinforcement is hard to come by.

Still, the degree to which we continue with the paradigm of men as doers and women as bearers is really up to us. After many generations of women pushing their way into society, something has given way and we have the choice now to either participate in this cultural shift or resist it. Let's lift these father-bearers high and support them. A sustainable gender balance will be struck everywhere or nowhere at once, and father-bearers, should they rise to this challenge, shall be feminism's foot soldiers in the twenty-first century.

HITCHFEST

G oat and I got married up at the lake. We put up fifty or so of our nearest and dearest in my cousins' cabins all around and we spent the weekend celebrating together. We stocked each house with peanut butter and jelly, bread and eggs and then, for the suppers, on the day of and the day before, we cooked up a storm. I was in the kitchen at the Mott main house skewering shish kebabs on Friday night when everybody started arriving. I had no idea, until it actually happened to me, the amount of joy I would experience to have most of the people I care about walk through one door. What a rare pleasure, in this modern age, to have your love all gathered up in one place. I felt so blessed. Utah and his wife, Joanna, had taken the train across the whole continent, from California to Quebec, just to be there.

Utah had agreed to officiate the ceremony and a month or two earlier he'd mailed both me and Goat letters. "Do not share these letters with each other!" he instructed us over the phone. "Answer your questions independently, without consulting each other, and send the answers back to me." He said he was going to build the ceremony around our own words. It was a good trick. Goat and I went off in our separate rooms with Utah's letters and worked alone in secret. Of course then we saw each other's return envelopes, before mailing them, and we couldn't help but notice that Goat's seemed way more full than mine. It made us both nervous when we broke with Utah's rules enough to reveal to each other that he'd written six pages to my page and a half.

I had a dress made in all my favorite colors by this clothing artist in Buffalo, a friend of Tanya's. The sleeves were lifted from an orange thrift-store sweater, the bodice was bright orange satin, and flowing down from there, a foofy chiffon skirt of smoky greys and greens and browns. My black platform boots got me up just high enough that I didn't trip on all that chiffon. Goat rented some crazy knight-in-shining-armor suit at a costume shop and we made the scene in wacky style. Everyone was instructed to come as they wanted to and I loved that our guests were wearing everything from shorts and T-shirts to suits to costumes.

Turns out, Utah had asked Goat and me the same three questions. 1. What brought you together? 2. What has kept you together? And 3. Why do you want to get married? He read our answers aloud during the ceremony and we laughed and cried with surprise. Later, we danced and took turns playing all the instruments in the tent. Our jam into the wee hours could probably be heard clear across the lake. The loons were surely annoyed. Goat and I paddled back to our island refuge just before dawn, with slits for eyes.

Of course, it is also not an easy thing, necessarily, to gather all your love in one place. Love is complicated and carries a lot of baggage with it. Scot was there and so was Goat's ex. Andy was there but he and I were growing apart and were about to go our separate musical ways. My mom spoke, Goat's mom spoke, Scot spoke, Andy spoke, everybody said their piece. I was impressed with how real Scot was when it was his turn, impressed that he let himself cry. After I was done being uncomfortable, I felt he had honored us with his honesty.

ARBITRATION

S cot's and my stories are inexorably entwined as though the two of us had some kind of unfinished business from a past life. You can probably read it all in our palms. When he was a twenty-one-year-old student at the University of Buffalo, Scot helped organize the "Save the Whales and Dolphins" benefit concert that I played on my eleventh birthday. We wouldn't actually come to know each other until seven years later when we became housemates, but the more we compared notes, the more I realized he'd been there all along.

He came into a store where I worked at sixteen and bought a card from me which is not extraordinary for any reason other than we both remember it. I saw him and he saw me. Then I started seeing him at house parties. He was a friend of a friend, then a friend, then a housemate, then a boyfriend, and then my co-conspirator in RBR. No matter how many times we would come apart and come back together again, our connection refused to be severed.

Scot was the one who stopped the water from pouring in and destroying my family's cabin at the lake. He was the one who stood on the train platform at 4:00 a.m. and waved goodbye to me when I made my move to New York. He was the one I directed all my tearful collect calls to, for years to come, as I traveled out further and further into the world. It was Scot who wired a quarter-inch jack into an old avocado green telephone handset (as per my request) so that I could plug it into an amplifier and sing into it. The ubiquitous telephone vocal that's been on every one of my records since. It was even Scot who shot me at close range with that pen gun in Leila and Marybelle's dusty study in Ohio. Our fates were being juggled by the same set of hands.

It's no wonder that Scot was the one to receive the subpoena that got delivered to Righteous Babe Records one blustery New Year's Eve. He had gone in to the office for just a few hours and there was a knock on the door. It turned out to be the day before the legal statute of limitations would have made it impossible for him to do so but, surprise! Dale was suing me. Dale had apparently seen the door closing and went for it, thrusting in his foot. Had Scot not been so diligent and shown up at the office that day, we might have been spared the whole thing, or so we fantasized later.

I didn't have a dollar to my name all those years earlier when I was associating with Dale, but now that I did, he was back, claiming my success was all because of him. I was eighteen when I signed the one-year contract with him and now I was twenty-five and he was coming out of the woodwork with some cockamamie justification for a lawsuit. With Scot as my partner in RBR, Dale was not just suing me, he was suing us.

I recall reading about how many lawsuits were filed against Nirvana during the years of their reign and how many people they'd had to pay off along the way. When Kurt Cobain killed himself, I remember thinking, *Yeah . . . that kind of meteoric success is nothing if not a double-edged sword.* If you are cynical to begin with, a glimpse at the latent ickyness of mankind sure doesn't help. You find out things about the world in general, but you also find out things about your family, friends, and acquaintances that you wish you didn't know. It can be hard to stay in love with such a world and not to assume a defensive stance. "Well, it's all there in black and white," I said to Scot. "He doesn't own me." But I suddenly felt unsure. Had Dale purposely made our contract ambiguous? I actually had no idea.

It was shocking to me that Dale, so meek and bumbling, had made this cunning move. That was before I understood how cluelessness stands in for malice in this world, before I understood how pain is really passed around. "I'm sure he just wants to feel appreciated," Scot said. "Let me call him up and offer him a settlement." We devised a 20 percent management commission for the time that Dale and I had worked together as though my salary was then what it was now and then we went up a bit from there. It sounded fair to us, but Dale wouldn't even talk to Scot. He and his lawyer had grander visions. They wanted 20 percent of everything I'd ever made and ever would make. Album sales, concerts, publishing rights, everything. He wanted a 20 percent ownership stake in Righteous Babe. In perpetuity.

It turned out that Dale had copied our "year-long" agreement from the back of a book and printed it out on *The Buffalo News* teletype, but apparently, the paper had cut off before the sunset clause at the end of the boilerplate management contract. That was what his lawyer had seized on and what Dale, after listening to people talk in his ear for seven years, had seen as his opportunity to petition for what he saw as his just due. What followed was an extremely expensive and stressful year, defending my record company's autonomy. We were hemorrhaging legal fees and losing sleep on top of the normal white-knuckle ride that was business as usual at RBR.

My lawyers instructed me pointedly and repeatedly to not say a thing during the proceedings, so I sat there day after day, watching the circus show mutely with daggers coming out of my eyes and steam coming out of my ears. Dale had only three witnesses that he called upon. There were his wife and Richard, his pal who'd first booked me at the Mariposa Folk Festival. Richard's testimony was at least honest and, in the end, felt more like testimony for our side. His third and last witness was Silvia from Austin who said a bunch of crazy shit that made my mouth drop open. Scot and I were standing on the street outside, at the end of the grueling day of Silvia's testimony, when she and Dale and his lawyer walked out of the building. Silvia spat at me as they walked by. My mouth fell open again as I looked down at the spit on the pavement next to me. *Is this really happening?*

Dale's lawyer was another spectacle to behold, the classic ambulance chaser who was like a caricature of the shyster, complete with slicked-back hair and disheveled suit. He was solicitous and nervous with a toothy smile. The whole thing seemed like a joke but, knowing all too well that crazy things can happen in courts of law, I was terrified. This was not even a real courtroom, this was a closed arbitration session where the rules of evidence don't apply. Anybody can say anything and there is no mechanism for objection. Another way that it's different from court is that the process is not funded by tax dollars. The opposing parties are each required to pay a fee. The fee was something like three thousand dollars.

At the end of four intense days of arbitration, Dale's lawyer started immediately clamoring for a mistrial. He said the arbitrator was biased, he said there had been collusion, he declared they were appealing their case. We hadn't even seen a verdict. The reason we had not seen a verdict yet was because they had also refused to pay the nominal fee. Because of their nonpayment, the case was eventually closed and dismissed forever. They were unable to mount their appeal. All of our expense and pain and suffering was for nothing. In the end, Dale had lost by simply doing things the Dale way: fumbling.

We were happy enough to have won the case, but the strain of the process took its toll.

six

ITALIA

My musical passport was taking me to more and more exotic places. I began exploring Europe, I saw Prague and Portugal, I rode on ships across the Baltic Sea. Then I made it to Australia and then to Japan. The first time I walked on stage in Tokyo, somebody proclaimed something and the whole audience broke into spontaneous laughter. I was thrown. My insides shriveled up to about a third their size and rattled around in me for the next hour and a half. I was told afterwards that the laughter had been in response to the exclamation, "She's so cute!" (probably meaning in a Muppet kind of way) but it was too late. Refer to Performer Handbook Rule 67-C: Whatever you do, don't shrivel up! Always imagine the best scenario, not the worst, and keep going! But Japan was a whole new level of strange for me. All my gauges were off. "Fans" stood waiting to meet me at every train station, with every one of my albums in hand. They each had a fancy calligraphy pen and a white autograph placard, too, each with the same thin gold border. *How do they know my travel schedule? Who am I here? . . . What is this place?*

Italy was the place I fell in love with most instantly and thoroughly, like the way I love my dad. My dad was everywhere in that country. As with Japan, the people in Italy were all conveniently down at eye level, even the men, who were now suddenly all so hot I couldn't stand it. They looked at me and I looked back. Dropping out of America and re-surfacing in Italy became my go-to escape fantasy and stayed there in that number-one slot for years. "If George W. gets elected, that's it," I proclaimed in 2000. "I'm moving to Rome." Four years later I said, "If that guy gets elected again, I'm definitely moving to Rome." But Italy would remain a dream and anyway, nothing could top my introduction to the place.

Before Goat, before so many things, Andy and I were slated to go to Europe and we were excited when a few Italian dates got added to the tour. As soon as we crossed the Alps on the train, we were met by the eccentric character known as my first Italian promoter, and everything after that was a blur. He took us out immediately to a delectable meal with multiple plates of anchovies and multiple bottles of wine. When we were all good and drunk, he started laying some heavy card tricks on us. He was disconcertingly good at magic. On our way out of the place, he took a bottle of Limoncello off the table and shoved it down his pants. I looked at Andy. *Did you just see what I just saw?!*

We walked down into town and came upon a strange, antiquated car-nival, complete with warpy swooning carousel music and sequined women with their boobs pushed out. The whole trip had turned into a Fellini film and we hadn't been in the country twenty-four hours. We drank Limoncello and rode the carousel. Andy was already in love with the promoter's daughter, who had been pouting along with us the whole time.

We were staying at a little inn that locked not just its doors but also its front gate at 11:00 p.m. We discovered this, of course, by returning home well after eleven and finding ourselves screwed. We had ended the night down in the town's cobblestone square, one side of which faced a river. The promoter and his daughter had evaporated and, in the piazza, we'd stumbled upon a couple of old men in tweed. They were out there in the middle of the night with golf clubs and balls, attempting to hit the balls across the river to the opposite bank. Needless to say, they were drunk, too. The other side of the river was invisible in the darkness so after one of them swung his club (Whack!) and hit a ball, we all had to be very quiet to hear if it hit the water or the ground on the other side. If there was a faint *Thunk*, our quartet would erupt into mighty cheers but if there was the unambiguous *Blooop* of defeat, cries of anguish arose. Andy was allowed to take one shot but when the ball went in the river his nocturnal golfing privileges were revoked. Eventually someone came and told us all to shut up and Andy and I took that as our cue to retire.

We walked along the river, past soulful wooden rowboats to our locked gate. The whole place was surrounded by a high wall but Andy was just barely able to scale it after being hoisted up by my clasped hands. Thankfully he was then able to unlock the driveway gate from the inside. The next challenge became to scale the side of the house, up onto the balcony, in order to sneak into his room through the French doors. I bent over and Andy stood on my back this time. Against all odds and with a lot of stifled giggles, we managed to make it all the way to our beds.

Our first gig in Italy was supposed to be somewhere but then it suddenly got moved somewhere else. We found ourselves setting up and playing in the back of a restaurant, the owner of which, I got the feeling, had some connection to our magician/promoter. We played out in an open piazza one evening to children and their grandmas and to the men smoking cigars on their evening strolls. It was all so messed up and yet so perfect. It was the summer of 1996 and things would never be quite so haphazard again. My international audience would grow and my promoters would become more legitimate, my tours ever more professional . . . less memorable.

SPEWING CHUNKS

Soon enough, I found myself embarking on a five-week tour of Europe which somehow included Alaska and the Pacific Northwest. That was the kind of itinerary my agents began handing to me without blinking. The European run was especially grueling with literally no time to sleep in between some of the shows. Play a midnight show in Dublin, catch the 6:00 a.m. ferry to London, then a 10:00 a.m. flight from Heathrow to play the next night in blah blah blah . . . It was insane. At some of the rock festivals we played along the way Heidi, my female road manager, and I felt like the last three women on earth. It was our summer of dudes in leather pants.

We concluded that Euro leg at the Cactus Festival in Brugge, Belgium, where I happily intersected with Branford Marsalis and Buckshot LeFonque and also Soul Coughing and my old acquaintance Mike Doughty from my past life in New York. I was dead asleep in my bunk on the bus when it was time for my set in the afternoon and had to be roused to play. I walked on stage in a delirium and proceeded to rock out in a way that my body deemed entirely inappropriate, complete with head banging and athletic leaps of abandon. The result was that I threw my back out and could no longer move. That night, I started to run a fever.

The next morning, I shuffled painfully onto the flight from Brugge to Chicago, from which we would be transferring on to Anchorage. It took a lot of medicine to get me across the Atlantic but by the time we got through customs in Chicago, I could feel the medicine failing and disaster about to strike. Miraculously, I broke into a run in that tunnel of neon lights between terminals at O'Hare with Gershwin's *Rhapsody in Blue* mocking me from above. I just dropped my backpack, grabbed my mouth with both hands, and took off, ducking and swerving like a running back between unsuspecting travelers. I bounded up the long flight of stairs on the other side of the tunnel, knowing I had no time for the escalator, but by the time I got to the top, I was holding puke in my mouth. I saw the women's room directly across the hall and made a bee-line but I didn't make it. Goat, who was running after me with my backpack, found me stooped in the middle of the upper hallway, surrounded by a spectacular Jackson Pollack–style public vomit-art installation. An extremely uncool situation for everyone involved.

Somehow, I made it to Anchorage and, somehow, I played the show the next night, but in the meantime I had courteously gifted Goat with whatever bug had overtaken my weakened body. It struck him in the middle of the Anchorage show and he had to leave the monitor board to throw up into a garbage can backstage and then again, incongruously, he threw up into the stairwell that led to the dressing rooms. When my band and I got off stage, a catastrophically horrible smell hit us in the wings and then, when we opened up the door to the stairwell, everyone yelled and jumped back. Poor Goat. When the work lights came up on stage and the wings lifted, little vomit footprints were traceable from the monitor board to here and there and back again. I had no idea that it was happening to him during the show. He had returned each time, hero-ically, to his post.

I'd only just recently released my double live album called *Living in Clip.* Goat and I wrangled that one together back at the Congress House, from ADAT tapes that we'd been running off the live soundboard. It would become my only album ever to go gold, but that is really only because of the fact that a double album counts as two albums in sales statistics. My gold record plaque hangs over my toilet as I type. Branford told me in Belgium that they had been rocking out to *Living in Clip* on their tour bus which gave me a real goose. There was something about that record that seemed to translate my songs and the intention behind them better than any of my studio recordings. It was as though, when *Living in Clip* dropped, people suddenly got it.

"Clipping" is the term used in sound engineering when you are overloading a machine with audio that is too hot for it to handle and distortion is being created in the gain structure. That's what my life had become: constant overload.

MUSCLE CARS

Goat was the kind of guy who saw cars. We'd be cruising down the road and he'd be calling them out, if only to himself, under his breath. "Mmmmm, Mercedes-Benz 220SE . . . nice." Or, "1980 AMC Pacer! Ha! Awesome!" He had learned to work on cars from his dad and he owned an old Austin Mini and, of course, the stripped-down Honda Goldwing motorcycle that was his pride and joy. I was amazed at this ability to instantly identify makes and models and marveled at the automotive encyclopedia that he seemed to carry around in his head. I do not see cars. I see flowers, I see trees, I'll even see the tent caterpillars accosting a tree before I'll see the car parked underneath. No, cars held no interest for me at all until I met Goat but, after a while, he did manage to suck me in. I started to form my own opinions and the ones I thought were the coolest were the American muscle cars, the Chargers, the Barracudas, the GTOs. Maybe it was because of my childhood love of *The Dukes of Hazzard*, I don't know, but Goat agreed, they were badass.

It was the last day of a tour and we were ending at a little rock club in West Palm Beach. Goat, Heidi, and I had decided that at the end of this run we were going to take a few days to go down and explore Key West. We joked that it was going to be our romantic vacation for three. We hadn't made any specific arrangements or reservations or anything, we were just going to head south and play it by ear. We were exhausted from the long run and excited to go have some fun in the sun. Goat was also excited because he'd seen a fabulous-looking vintage car showroom just a few blocks from the club so, after soundcheck, I headed down there with him to check it out.

We walked into what had to be one of the most extravagant automobile store/museums in the world and we were blown away. The owner of the place came right over to us with a very friendly manner and proceeded to spend an hour showing us all the unique machines he had on his vast property. He seemed to have one of every notable car throughout history including some crazy thing designed to go in water and turn into a boat or something. We had an awesome time talking to Mr. Owner Guy and I couldn't believe how nice he was to us. Goat and I were both pierced and punked-out looking, not to mention probably not particularly well washed after many weeks on the road. We certainly did not fit the profile of legitimate paying customers and we were used to being scowled at and shooed away from lesser places, so it was surprising to be treated with such kindness and respect.

At one point, we rounded a corner and there before me was the most beautiful, sexy muscle car I'd ever seen. It was a 1969 Mustang Cobra Turbo Jet with a 428 V8 engine bursting through its hood. It was a smoky, greenish grey, like the color of an alligator lit on fire and burned to ash, and it was in mint condition. I was in love. I looked at the price tag: $16,000. Whew. Now *that* is a stunning machine.

We went back to the bar and rocked the show that night until my shirt looked like I'd gone swimming in it and then afterwards, wheels still turning around in my head, I asked Heidi, "How much money is in that fanny pack of yours?" Heidi, who was the youngest and most ridiculous looking of us all, had become adept at accumulating a tour's worth of merch money on her person and then miraculously making it back to the mothership with it all intact. It was but one renegade aspect of our scruffy little operation. You would think that cash is cash but banks didn't trust Heidi so she had a hard time making deposits out on the road. It would just pile up in her fanny pack and briefcase and somehow she became accustomed to having thousands of dollars on her person at all times.

With the poise of a drug tsar, she walked through the world holding a life-changing, and potentially life-threatening amount of cash. My way of avoiding incessant anxiety was just to never ask.

Turns out, she was carrying just over $16,000. It was a sign from the universe. What would happen if I embezzled that much money from myself?! Would the home office slip into the sea? Would the world end? I decided to find out. *So, sue me!* I said to myself. I walked back into the mega car museum store the next morning and the friendly owner guy was surprised to see me again with Goat and Heidi in tow. You can imagine how surprised he was at what happened next. *This is what happens when you're nice to people you have no reason to be nice to*, my smile said. His smile said, *Fuckin' A!*

Goat and Ho and I cruised down to the Keys in high style, checked into a shitty little motel, and proceeded to have the time of our lives. There was a little kitchenette in our room so we bought a brownie mix and some eggs and baked ourselves some pot brownies. We then had the pleasure of making snow angels, naked or nearly so, in the St. Augustine grass outside our room. What an otherworldly type of grass St. Augustine is! Especially if you happen to be naked and stoned. Some fans at the show the night before had passed back a sweet note inviting me to come to their place in Key West and, sure enough, we blew their minds and called them up. Turns out, their place was walking distance from our motel. They gave us instructions over the phone and we walked there.

Coming home late that night from our new friends' house, we passed through a cemetery. We had gone around it on our way there but now we decided to jump the fence and go through. We were still nicely stoned, mind you, and it was very late at night and right in the middle of the place we suddenly saw two men lurking behind a tomb. We were all deeply spooked and instantly, Goat took off running. Heidi and I ran after him and managed to scale the fence on the other side of the cemetery with some effort (we had helped each other over the first time) but when we reunited with Goat we gave him a good tongue lashing. "You fucking ditched us!" we yelled at him. "I can't believe you ditched us!!" We never let him live that one down.

That Mustang was tricky to start, you had to finesse it just so. Or more accurately, you had to believe in your soul that you were man enough to turn it over and then it would start for you. I eventually got the hang of it. It also had no power steering and was incredibly hard to turn unless it was going fast and momentum was assisting you. I basically had to hang my whole scrawny body off the steering wheel just to crank it around, my full weight being just barely enough to make a left from a stopped position. Driving it was an athletic activity. It was not at all like a modern car that just drives itself while you sit there. It was more like a stallion that is way stronger and more powerful than you are and may or may not choose to obey. If you were hesitant or squeamish at all, that car would laugh at you.

I loved it, though, and I soon came to learn that that car had even more dedicated fans than I do. Grown men would come up all fluttery like moths to a flame when I rolled up in my Mustang. They would stand around and tell me their stories, wanting just to touch it, to look inside. They wanted me to know what it meant to them. They told me about the Mustang they'd once had, or their father had . . . or dreamed of having. They brought themselves to tears. I have returned to my true nature now, I don't really care much for machines, especially those that run on the blood of the earth, but for a while . . . I moved in the land of people who do.

EXCUSE ME, MS.?

In 1998, I wrote an open letter to *Ms.* magazine. At the time, I was summiting the apex of my notoriety and in the media, I had graduated from an angry bisexual to a savvy entrepreneur. No sooner had the media finally embraced me than I was having trouble with the *way* that they embraced me. I quickly began missing my days of being scowled at from a great distance. If I was touted one more time for my supposed business acumen I was gonna scream. It was like a bad running joke. *I am an artist, dammit! I just also happen to be a critic of capitalism.* When even *Ms.* magazine put me in the same capitalist frame, I felt compelled to speak up.

Writing the open letter was just about the last thing I did before instituting my life-saving policy of *don't-ever-read-anything-about-yourself-ever-again.* Around the time I released *Little Plastic Castle*, that's exactly what I did: I stopped reading any press about me and I have never resumed. If I see a picture of myself in a magazine or newspaper, I turn the page quickly. Hell, even a picture can ruin my day. Tuning out my own press in this way has been essential to my emotional survival and my continued dedication to music for the last twenty years. *Little Plastic Castle*, the song itself and, in fact, the whole album, was largely a response to having become media fodder. I realized after that that it was an inward spiral to keep reacting to the reactions to me . . . so I bailed on the whole thing.

I will share with you now the letter I wrote to *Ms.* because I think it paints a better portrait of my head at the time than anything I could sketch for you now.

An Open Letter to Ms. Magazine from Ani Di Franco

So, I'm poring through the 25th anniversary issue of Ms. (on some airplane going somewhere in the amorphous blur that amounts to my life) and I'm finding it endlessly enlightening and stimulating as always, when, whaddaya know, I come across a little picture of little me. I was flattered to be included in that issue's "21 feminists for the 21st century" thingybob. I think ya'll are runnin' the most-bold and babeolishious magazine around, after all.

Problem is, I couldn't help but be a little weirded out by the paragraph next to my head that summed up her me-ness and my relationship to the feminist continuum. What got me was that it largely detailed my financial successes and sales statistics. My achievements were represented by the fact that I "make more money per album sold than Hootie and the Blowfish," and that my catalogue sales exceed 3/4 of a million. It was specified that I don't just have my own record company but my own "profitable" record company. Still, the ironic conclusion of the aforementioned blurb is a quote from me insisting "it's not about the money." Why then, I ask myself, must "the money" be the focus of so much of the media that surrounds me? Why can't I escape it, even in the hallowed pages of Ms.?

Firstly, this "Hootie and the Blowfish" business was not my doing. The L.A. Times financial section wrote an article about my record label, Righteous Babe Records, in which they raved about the business savvy of a singer (me) who thwarted the corporate overhead by choosing to remain independent, thereby pocketing $4.25 per unit, as opposed to the $1.25 made by Hootie or the $2 made by Michael Jackson. This story was then picked up and reprinted by The New York Times, Forbes, the Financial News Network and (lo and behold) Ms.

So, here I am, publicly morphing into some kinda Fortune 500-young-entrepreneur-from-hell, and all along I thought I was just a folksinger!

Okay it's true. I do make a much larger profit (percentage-wise) than the Hootster. What's even more astounding is that there are thousands of musicians out there who make an even higher profit percentage than me! How many local musicians are there in your community who play gigs in bars and coffee shops about town? I bet lots of them have made cassettes or CDs that they'll happily sell to you with a personal smile from the edge of the stage or back at the bar after their set. Would you believe these shrewd, profit-minded wheeler-dealers are pocketing a whopping 100% of the profits on the sales of those puppies?! Wait 'till the Financial News Network gets a whiff of them!

I sell approximately 2.5% of the albums that a Joan Jewelanis Morrisette [sic] sells and get about .05% of the airplay royalties, so obviously if it all comes down to dollars and cents, I've led a wholly unremarkable life. Yet I choose relative statistical mediocrity over fame and fortune because I have a bigger purpose in mind. Imagine how strange it must be for a girl who has spent 10 years fighting as hard as she could against the lure of the corporate carrot and the almighty forces of capital, only to be eventually recognized by the power structure as a business pioneer.

I have indeed sold enough records to open a small office on the half-abandoned main street in the dilapidated urban center of my hometown, Buffalo (N.Y.). I am able to hire 15 or so folks to run and constantly reinvent the place while I drive around and play music for people. I am able to give stimulating business to local printers and manufacturers and to employ the services of independent distributors, promoters, booking agents and publicists. I was able to quit my day job and devote myself to what I love. And yes, we are enjoying modest profits these days, affording us the opportunity to reinvest in innumerable political and artistic endeavors. RBR is no Warner Bros. But it is a going concern, and for me, it is a vehicle for redefining the relationship between art and commerce in my own life. It is a record company that is the product not just of my own imagination, but that of my friend and manager Scot Fisher and of all the people who work there. People who incorporate and coordinate politics, art and media every day into a people-friendly, sub-corporate, woman-informed, queer-happy small business that puts music before rock stardom and ideology before profit.

And me, I'm just a folksinger, not an entrepreneur. My hope is that my music and poetry will be enjoyable and/or meaningful to someone, somewhere, not that I maximize my profit margins. It was 15 years

*and 11 albums getting to this place of notoriety and, if anything, I
think I was happier way back when. Not that I regret any of my
decisions, mind you. I'm glad I didn't sign on to the corporate army.
I mourn the commodification and homogenization of music by
the music industry, and I fear the manufacture of consent by the
corporately controlled media. Last thing I want to do is feed the
machine.*

*I was recently mortified while waiting in the dressing room before
one of my own shows. Some putz suddenly takes the stage to announce
me and exclaim excitedly that this was my "largest sold-out crowd to
date!" "Oh, really?" I'm thinking to myself, "that's interesting . . . too
bad it's not the point." All of my achievements are artistic, as are all of
my failures. That's just the way I see it. Statistical plateau or no. I'll
bust ass for 60 people, or 6,000, watch me.*

*I have so much respect for Ms. magazine. If I couldn't pick it up at
newsstands my brain probably would've atrophied by now on some
trans-Atlantic flight and I would be lying limp and twitchy in a bed of
constant travel, staring blankly into the abyss of the gossip magazines.
Ms. is a structure of media wherein women are able to define
themselves, and articulate for themselves those definitions. We wouldn't
point to 21 of the feminists moving into the 21st century and define them
in terms of "Here's Becky Ballbuster from Iowa City, she's got a great
ass and a cute little button nose . . ." No ma'am. We've gone beyond
the limited perceptions of sexism and so we should move beyond the
language and perspective of the corporate patriarchy. The Financial
News Network may be ultimately impressed with me now that I've
proven to them that there's a life beyond the auspices of papa Sony, but
do I really have to prove this to you?*

*We have the ability and the opportunity to recognize women not just
for the financial successes of their work but for the work itself. We have
the facility to judge each other by entirely different criteria than those
imposed upon us by the superstructure of society. We have a view*

*that reaches beyond profit margins into poetry, and a vocabulary to
articulate the difference.*

*Thanks for including me, Ms., really. But just promise me one
thing; if I drop dead tomorrow, tell me my grave stone won't read:
"ani d., CEO."*

Please let it read: songwriter, musicmaker, storyteller, freak.

REBIRTH

I invited the Rebirth Brass Band from New Orleans to go on tour with
me in the summer of '98. I was on top of the world and what could be
more fun than that? Nothing I can think of. Their music is made of
you're-dead-right-now-if-you-don't-wanna-dance. We went coast to coast
together and by the end of the run, we were all friends. Especially me
and Derrick Tabb, their fluid, sultry snare drummer and also the sweetest man on the planet.

When Rebirth set out from New Orleans to join me at the beginning
of my tour, they went to the rental car counter to get a van but, having
made no reservations, they were told there were no more vans available.
They proceeded to rent two Lincoln Town Cars and hit the road with
two drivers at all times, a hilarious and somewhat questionable solution.
Not surprisingly, to anyone who knows what America is really like, they
got pulled over several times and had to talk their way out of trouble.
Eight black men caravanning in a pair of Lincoln Town Cars stand out in
Missouri and Idaho and they had some explaining to do for likely no
other reason than that. They said they dropped my name both times,
explaining that they were on tour with me, and we all had a good laugh
at that scenario. You know when you're using my name to ingratiate your-
selves to the boys in blue, you're officially in a desperate situation.

After a few weeks, Derrick was fed up traveling with his crew and moved into the back lounge of the bus. He would play video games on the TV there and then just fall asleep on the couch. It was more comfortable than sleeping with his drum on his lap in the rear seat of a car. He reported back to his band that we were just like them: constantly taking the piss out of each other and pulling pranks. Hijinks is a way of making the time pass on the road and, boy, let me tell you, there is a lot of time to pass on the road.

Midway through the tour, we had worked up some encores that the two bands could play together and we developed a habit of parading off stage at the end of the shows, out through the audience, with Rebirth doing their thing and me clanging along. At one show in particular, we didn't stop playing even after the audience was well out of earshot. We jumped and played all the way around the backstage to the building where the dressing rooms were, and up to the second floor. We all crammed into the elevator, drums a-booming and horns blazing and we played and jumped as long as we felt like it after the elevator spewed us back out again. Just because music is the best stuff in the world and when you are young and in love with your life, it can be hard to think of a reason to stop.

Ten years later, Derrick went on to found The Roots of Music, a free afterschool music program for underprivileged kids in New Orleans. The program teaches music through the lens of the New Orleans marching band tradition and also offers academic tutoring support and a hot meal to the students five days a week. The Roots of Music Marching Crusaders have had life-changing experiences like appearing at festivals in Europe or traveling out to California to play in the Rose Bowl parade. They even played for President Barack Obama when he visited New Orleans. Some have gone on to scholarships at Berklee College of Music.

At Roots, kids gain a creative outlet and a life skill (playing music) which, with a lot of hard work, can become a passport to the world, but also they gain a sense of connectedness with one another and with the rich culture that is their inheritance. It's amazing to see how plugging into something bigger than oneself can allow an individual to really blossom. Evolving the tradition (as many brass bands are these days), Roots includes girls not just as dancing majorettes but also as players of instruments, bringing the genre smartly into the twenty-first century.

One of the shows Derrick and I played that summer of our meeting was in Battery Park in Lower Manhattan. There was a colossal thunderstorm that day which seemed as though it might cancel the whole affair but, just in time, the skies cleared and the show went on. For years afterwards, an unprecedented number of people would come up to me on the street and tell me they were at that show that night and how awesome it was. *Really?* I would think each time. *I remember that show as a struggle.* We were not able to do any soundchecking that day because of the weather so we hit the stage unprepared and I was agonized by the terrible results. I was flailing through my whole set. It took me years before I realized that the reason why I'd heard so much feedback about that particular show was simply that there were ten thousand people there. That is ten or twenty times as many people as I typically play to now. The feedback was a matter of simple math.

The image that stands out for me from that day is how the low-hanging storm clouds were completely obliterating the upper half of the Twin Towers. Erasing them. We stood around in the afternoon watching the lightning splintering down from the angry seam where the towers vanished into dark oblivion. We watched and wondered together what it must be like to be up there in that storm, lightning bolts colliding into the side of your office.

Grand Canyon

i love my country
by which i mean

i am indebted joyfully
to all the people throughout its history
who have fought the government to make right
where so many cunning sons and daughters
our foremothers and forefathers
came singing through slaughter
came through hell and high water
so that we could stand here
and behold breathlessly the sight
how a raging river of tears
cut a grand canyon of light

i've been a few places now
flown through vast empty spaces
with stewardesses whose hands
look much older than their faces
and i've tossed so many napkins
into that big hole in the sky
i've been at the bottom of the atlantic
seething in a two ply
looking up through all that water
and the fishes swimming by
and i don't always feel lucky
but i'm smart enough to try
cuz humility has buoyancy
and above us only sky

so i lean in
breathe deeper
that brutal burning smell
that surrounds the smoldering wreckage
that i've come to love so well

yes, color me stunned and dazzled
by all the red, white, and blue flashing lights
in the american intersection
where black crashed
head on
with white

comes a melody
comes a rhythm
a particular resonance
that is us
and only us
comes a screaming ambulance
and a hand that you can trust
laid steady on your chest
working for the better good
(which is good at its best)
and too, bearing witness
like a woman bears a child
with all her might
born of the greatest pain
into a grand canyon of light

and because no song has gone unsung here
and this joint is strung crazy tight
and people have been raising up their voices
since it just ain't bin right
with all the righteous rage
and all the bitter spite
that will accompany us out
of this long night

that will grab us by the hand
when we are ready to take flight
seat back and tray table in the upright and locked position
shocked to tears by each new vision
of all that my ancestors have done
for instance
the women who gave their lives
so that i could have one
yes, i'm standing at ground zero
of the feminist revolution
it was an inside job
stoic and sly
one we're supposed to forget and downplay and deny
but i think the time is nothing
if not nigh
to let the truth out
coolest f-word ever
deserves a fuckin shout!
i mean
why don't all decent men and women call themselves feminists?
if only out of respect
for those who fought for this
i mean
look around
we have this

yes
i love my country
by which i mean
i am indebted joyfully
to all the people throughout its history

who have fought the government to make right
where so many cunning sons and daughters
our foremothers and forefathers
came singing through slaughter
came through hell and high water
so that we could stand here
and behold breathlessly the sight
how a raging river of tears
is cutting a grand canyon
of light

THE GUTHRIE ARCHIVES

The Woody Guthrie Archives (all of Woody's artwork, letters, original manuscripts, published and unpublished songs . . . chaotic journals overflowing with ideas) used to be housed in the other half of Harold Leventhal's office in Manhattan. Harold was once Woody's manager, and Pete's, and the Weavers'. He was old and shuffle-y and snuffle-y, with a light dusting of dandruff on his lapels, but quite gracious when I first met him there in their crowded, combined space.

I was visiting at the invitation of Nora Guthrie, Woody's daughter and caretaker of the Guthrie Archive and Foundation. Hanging on a pillar, right when you walked in the door, was Woody's original penning of "This Land Is Your Land" in a simple frame and just below it, at eye level, a telegram from Dr. Martin Luther King Jr. to Pete Seeger, inviting him to join the march in Selma on March 21, 1965. These were just two of the treasures to be found in this unassuming space. So many scraps of paper imbued with the spirits of extraordinary people.

Pete did show up in Selma with his banjo and his version of "We Shall

Overcome" to march with King and company across that bridge in Selma. They walked for days, all the way to the state capitol in Montgomery, to protest the lack of real voting rights for African Americans in Alabama. Pete and others were there as a Caucasian shield, as that particular march resulted in a bloodbath of police brutality the first time it was attempted, only weeks earlier. During the first event, the marchers, highly trained and studied in the art of nonviolent civil disobedience, did not return the police aggression and put another stunning notch on the global belt of collective nonviolent resistance. They let the white supremacist power structure in Alabama shame itself by showing its violence and insanity against a stunning backdrop of strength and higher consciousness.

The march, successfully completed, became the tipping point that secured the Voting Rights Act, a monumental accomplishment of sustained and uncompromising activism, organizing, and agitation on the part of so many. Gazing upon that yellowed telegram from Dr. King to Pete brought tears to my eyes. Hope is like a teacup held aloft while swimming across an ocean of trouble. Who amongst us can possibly make it shore to shore? Swimming with just one arm? None of us. That's why it's a relay. Think of it! Some swim through storms.

Of course, the Voting Rights Act has since been gutted and voting has been made increasingly difficult once again for African Americans and others in the big blue stream. Hope is back in dangerously short supply. It only takes a generation to go slack, to turn away from even the most basic work of voting, let alone the more sophisticated work of organizing, for hard-won democratic gains to be squandered and subject to wanton erasure. Our democracy can be slipped right out from underneath us, quickly and quietly, like a magician holding a tablecloth. *Whoooop! On the table, a teacup teeters. Wait, what just happened?*

Hello to the gerrymandered Republican strangleholds of state houses and of Capitol Hill. Goodbye Voting Rights Act. Hello to the epic lie of "voter fraud" and the judicial folly of *Citizens United*. Hello to the euphemisms of racial oppression such as "tough on crime" and "make America great again." Hello to the modern-day bondage of systematically entrenched poverty and mass incarceration. Hello to the deepening trance of misogyny with deceiving new slogans such as "pro life." Hello to America's workers (natural allies) being convinced to make enemies of each other over things that are not even really problems while quietly, in the background, the deregulation of every single industry slowly kills us all. Hello to obesity and cancer and melting ice caps and micro plastics and regularly scheduled gun massacres. Hello to right-wing extremism and the Gingrich-ification of our national discourse, wherein meaning, substance, honor, purpose, and morality . . . are all replaced by a single thing: bloodsport. The dirty game of "winning" at all costs.

Yes, we would like to imagine that socio-political evolution is a checklist—that we can check things off and then go sit back down—but social justice is an uphill climb. If we drop the ball, even for a moment, it rolls backwards. The forces of greed are there to pull us right back down.

Who among us will dare now to dream? Dream not just of a modicum of safety and a living wage but . . . the really big dreams. For me: The Reproductive Freedom Amendment. The abolition of the Electoral College. The revamp of the electoral system, the criminal justice system, the health care and education systems. The dawning of sustainability through conservation and biomimicry. Prioritizing and incentivizing the greening of industry through regulation. Regulation of the financial sector. Closing the loopholes and bringing the tax structure back into the realm of reason.

Children of the twenty-first century, born with your eyes open, can you fulfill the potential of our country? Can you help us concoct a more unified and organic whole? A resonant balance? The antidote to our disillusionment? I have but one bit of advice for you, do not skip over the patriarchy on your way to change the world.

NORA

From the instant I met Nora Guthrie at Clearwater she became my champion. Her support of my work since my first appearances on the folk scene have affirmed both my atmospheric connection to her father and my place in the tribe. At a time when many were recoiling from me with charges of "manhater!" and worse, Nora drew a straight line from Woody to me and said, no, see, here is another child of my father.

It was not just me, either. Nora has always supported socially conscious musicians like a one-woman National Endowment for the Politically Radical Arts. She doesn't preserve her father's work so much as continue to do it, commissioning radical new collaborations and reinventions of Woody's writings . . . teasing them back into the world and inviting people in. She digs through her father's stuff, dusts things off, and disseminates them. "Here!" she will say. "What can you do with this?" Woody's life was taken from him too soon by Huntington's disease but he is blessed to live on in this way. Nora and her daughter Anna embody the old man's same bold recipe of two parts curiosity and one part irreverence.

It was Nora who invited me to stand on stage at the Rock & Roll Hall of Fame in Cleveland when they inaugurated the newly expanded and official Guthrie Archives, now in permanent residence at the Woody Guthrie Center in Tulsa, Oklahoma. She invited her brother Arlo, and her father's compadre Ramblin' Jack Elliot, too. She invited Pete and Woody's most celebrated disciple, Bob Dylan, but Bob didn't show. She invited successive generations of Woody's children, including Bruce Springsteen, Billy Bragg, and the Indigo Girls, and she threw it to me to release a recording of the evening on Righteous Babe. That album we called *'Til We Outnumber 'Em.* I love Springsteen's version of "Riding in My Car" on that record and Ramblin Jack's version of "1913 Massacre."

Those were some choice moments by some true American originals. I bet Woody would have been pleased.

Springsteen was by far the biggest star on the bill that evening, and it is a testament to his respect for Nora and her father that he even allowed himself to be included on that live album released on my little label. I remember there were nowhere near enough dressing rooms that night for all the people involved in the show and Bruce immediately opened his door and offered to share his space with anyone who wanted it. He's that kind of guy. That event was also the dawning of my friendship with Amy Ray of the Indigo Girls. Our lives had been pushing us in closer and closer circles until the universe left Amy and me no choice but to become friends.

Woody himself was an original, to say the least. His work was so many things, took so many forms, went so many places. He was expansive and exploratory, fearless and restless and rambling. Woody could write a song as airtight and finely hewn as any Hank Williams number or he could write a chatty talking blues or a whimsical nursery rhyme. Or he could set a newspaper article to song and deliver the news further than any paper route. In his work and his journey lies something of a template for the American folksinger. He could be timeless or immediate, or both at once. He also could draw beautifully. His sketches and renderings bubbled over with a lust for life. His creativity, like water, flowed and shapeshifted.

Woody may have come into this world the proverbial Okie from Muskogee, provincial and somewhat narrow-minded, but he grew into a great artist, a citizen of the world and a man of the people. His story, like all of the most inspiring stories, is one of transformation. As Joseph Campbell would say, his path was the mythical hero's journey. The ball rolls into the woods and the child follows it. One curiosity leads to another and the child becomes lost. The child is gone a long time. She almost doesn't make it back. But eventually, the child emerges from the woods, wiser and stronger, with a story to tell. She is a child no more. The point of the story, if any, is not to come through the victor but to come through changed.

CULTURAL EQUITY

I did a few stints opening for Bob Dylan on the road and the highlight for me was the night I got to meet one of my heroes backstage: Alan Lomax. Without Alan Lomax, much of what we know and have access to, in terms of the many-splendored riches of our American music and folklore, would have simply been lost to us. The bedrock of our culture would have eroded away beneath us and we would be on flimsy footing not knowing where the hell we came from. But no, there was Alan fucking Lomax traveling to every last corner of America in the thirties, forties . . . the sixties, recording every person with something to offer, from the architects of our musical traditions to Jane Doe on the street.

Before *This American Life*, before a commercial recording industry with a dime to make, before an establishment that recognized anything but "high art" as legitimate or worthy in any way, Alan Lomax was on a mission. A mission not just to preserve but to exalt the art and the spiritual existence of the nonwhite male elite. Out of a great and abiding love for America and its people, he wanted us to know and respect our own particular genius: the genius of our diversity.

Magnetic tape didn't even exist yet and Alan was going into fields and down back alleys with his father, John, recording people on a wire recorder. (I happen to know what those are like!) He recorded work songs and bluesmen, Appalachian music and bluegrass, he recorded gospel music and the sermons themselves, he recorded calypso and jazz, stories and poetry. Alan would end up recording over ten thousand songs. He interviewed everyone, too, from the greats to the average joe, to the prisoner, he documented voices, stories, and lives.

It's hard to say what would have happened to Woody, Leadbelly, Muddy Waters, Burl Ives, Robert Johnson, or Pete Seeger for that matter, if Alan hadn't come along. He propelled all of them, not with profit-mindedness but with a benevolence and a deep respect. He stumped for artists tirelessly, creating venues and contexts for their work. He stumped for what he called "cultural equity," and tried to enlighten America to the reality of its economic and racial bias. He tried to shine a light on the many-splendored genius out there not getting its just due. It broke his heart to watch the very people struggle who made our culture great, to watch them go hungry right here in the breadbasket of the world. He was palling around with Zora Neale Hurston in the forties, after taking over the documenting game from his father. I mean, what could be cooler than that? Zora and Alan went around Florida and the Caribbean, and then Alan, being blacklisted, went off to Europe.

Without Alan, there would be no treasure trove of American roots music at the Library of Congress to inspire a young Bob Dylan and a lot of other people. In fact, there wouldn't have been the whole folk music revival of the fifties and sixties. There wouldn't even really be Miles Davis's *Sketches of Spain* (one of the most stunning American recordings!) because it was partially inspired by Alan's haunting field recordings in Seville. The effect on American culture of Lomax's work is so far-reaching as to be hard to quantify. His mission was clear to him, and he seemed to succeed in it. He gave America herself.

I should write a whole chapter on Abraham Lincoln. I should write a chapter on Muhammad Ali. But I never met those unfathomable creatures and anyway, I guess this book is supposed to be about me. I did meet Alan Lomax, however, and though he was old and had been recently debilitated by a stroke, I felt honored and humbled. His grandson said that he'd perked up when I hit the stage that night and that I'd really held his attention, which thrilled me. I knelt down by his wheelchair and the functioning half of his face greeted me with a big smile. "I really enjoyed your music," he said in a slurred whisper. "I hope you make a lot of money."

FELLOW WORKERS

Some Mardi Gras Indian Chief had just died and we decided to take the afternoon off of rehearsal to attend a second line parade in his honor. Utah had never been to New Orleans before and he certainly had never seen Mardi Gras Indians or been to a second line. This would be a royal funeral procession with brass band, parasols, tambourines, and the whole tribe in full feather. It would also be a much-needed opportunity to dance and walk and blow off some steam. Goat and I looked at each other in silent assessment of all the pre-production work still left to do on this record. We were just getting to square one. "Fuck it," I said. "Let's go."

I had lured Utah down to New Orleans to make an album at a big haunted mansion of a recording studio located in the French Quarter, on Esplanade. I wanted him to do his storytelling thing on tape but I figured, to get his juices flowing, he would need an audience to play to. We invited twenty or thirty people to come into the studio for several nights and the plan was to perform the whole record for them, start to finish, in the high-ceilinged front parlor. We had three rehearsal days to prepare and two nights to get it right. I brought my touring band with me to help execute the soundtrack part while Utah was busy spinning his yarn. It had all the makings of a fun creative adventure but alas, Utah, unaccustomed to this kind of wacky collaboration, was showing the strain.

Morning one, we were all sitting in a circle, me with a clipboard on my lap, ready to start forming a plan. I'd been asking Utah for months for demos of the stories that he thought he might want to do, or even just a list of the subjects of the stories, but he'd sent me nothing. "So, Utah," I began, "can you give us an idea of the stories you'd like to tell?" "Well . . . I dunno," he replied all cagey. "I guess I'd like to talk about Ammon Hennacy." "Ammon Hennacy," I wrote on my paper. Then he crossed his arms in front of his chest, lifted his chin, and looked at me. "Well . . . okay," I said, "can you tell us the story of Ammon Hennacy?" "Right now?" he balked, as if the idea was insulting. "Yes. I'm sorry," I told him. "That's why we're here. We can't just make up all the music on the spot. We're gonna need some idea of the framework we're working with."

I understand not wanting to dispel the magic of storytelling by repeating stories in front of people. The effect you are trying to achieve is that you're just hanging out, recalling things extemporaneously, and that effect is undermined (if only in your own confidence) when there are people in the room who saw the sausage getting made. I empathized with all the reasons why Utah was curling up. The solitary life of the folksinger had not prepared him for this.

Poetically speaking, Utah, who prided himself on being an encyclopedia of American folklore, had suddenly found himself in a corner of America way out of his jurisdiction. I heard him on the phone after that funeral parade, relaying the things he'd learned that day to Joanna back home, but all the information was coming out a little skewey. *Well . . . that's kind of it*, I thought as I inadvertently listened from my station at the kitchen table to his conversation in the office. I knew just enough about the Mardi Gras Indian culture to be able to marvel at the way the truth gets spun by even the most keen of ear and mind, the most pure of intention. Is this the accuracy level of all of Utah's spiels? I wondered. Does it even matter?

I thought about the accuracy level of anyone's fuckin' spiel. I thought about how much misinformation had already come out about me in the press. I am the one thing that I can absolutely verify in this world and I can tell you, there is a lot of BS that passes for news! I'm not even talking about the overt fact-jacking of Fox News, either, I'm talking about sincere "objective" reporting. So many flubbed facts and so many writers all writing about themselves. I thought about my first day in the fine arts department at Buff State when I was sixteen, how the teacher had asked us to take out our big newsprint pads and draw a pencil portrait of the person standing directly across from us in the circle. Then he asked us all to turn our drawings around and show them to the class. We looked around the circle and, without exception, each picture looked not like the subject but the drawer.

That lesson has stuck with me and has confirmed itself over and over again in my life. Us humans are all furiously projecting ourselves onto the world, creating reality as much or more than observing it. At least in the age of the internet, we are now being forced into reluctant acknowledgment that objective facts are hard to come by and that "truth" is a thing invented in one laboratory or another. I almost find it reassuring to think that this has always been so.

Somehow, we rehearsed just enough that we pulled off the recording of those sessions. On the evening of the third day, we filled the parlor with candles, set out wine and hors d'oeuvres, shined up, and treated an intimate audience to an evening with "the golden voice of the great southwest" in something like a taped live broadcast. (*Where was that old wire recorder when I needed it? It would've sounded cooler than those damn ADATs we were recording onto.*) Then, we made a few adjustments and did it all over again on a second night. With a little more wine this time.

I have a special fondness for *The Past Didn't Go Anywhere* and *Fellow Workers* because, well, because I love my friend Utah, but also because they provide direct links in the world between my more modern brand of folksinger and Utah's more traditional brand. I've loved all the comments and stories that have come back to me over the years about them. Old lefties and their daughters and granddaughters have found opportunities to bond over those records. Through the partnership of Utah and me, generations of political radicals crossed over and greeted each other.

A MATTER OF LIFE AND DEATH

After spending a few years in Roxbury, Palmer moved to Atlanta and set up shop at The Southern Center for Human Rights. Through him, Righteous Babe became involved with the center and eventually our yearly contribution amounted to a sponsorship of one of the lawyers on staff there. I loved the idea that one of RBR's employees was actually working in Georgia on the front lines of criminal justice reform. The Righteous Babe Foundation was unofficially born.

The Southern Center is a place where everyone makes the same salary, from the senior lawyers down to the kid straight out of law school. It is a not-for-profit organization in the most genuine sense of the term. Its mission is to end capital punishment, mass incarceration, and the civil and human rights abuses in the criminal justice systems of the South. It covers all the bases from educational efforts, to fighting for better laws, to defending people in all stages of litigation including defending abused or neglected prisoners who have nowhere else to turn. The stories that Stephen Bright (then the head of the organization) would tell me, in a matter-of-fact voice, about the reality inside prisons in Alabama and Mississippi would make my stomach turn.

I can picture Sarah Totonchi (who directs the center now) and me having lunch with Palmer at one of his Atlanta neighborhood joints, watching his ridiculous interface with people unfold before us. We would cast our eyes at each other and giggle as Palmer badgered everyone in the place incessantly until they, too, were laughing. Connector people can work in strange ways. Sarah was bouncing her new baby on her knee and I looked at her life in amazement, hardly able to fathom how she was doing all she was doing. What was it that I was complaining about again?

Because of Righteous Babe's involvement with the center, our stance against the death penalty became known in public defender circles and individual lawyers working on death penalty cases started contacting us, asking for assistance. It is a queasy feeling to write a random check to a pro-bono lawyer just to enable them to effectively perform their duties in defending or appealing a capital case. To think that my thousand-dollar contribution might be the difference between life and death for some poor individual whom I don't even know just seems like a terrifying and inappropriate equation. What kind of country is this that a private citizen should be in the position of having to pay money in order that a fellow citizen not be murdered by our mutual government?

Of course, there is no experience akin to getting distance from your own country, to put it more deeply into perspective. Malcolm X's trip to Mecca changed his whole outlook on . . . well, everything. Conversely, George W. Bush had never set foot outside of America when he became president of it, a fact that was skywritten across the globe for the next eight years. His ignorance and lack of curiosity became a force that guided the fate of our country despite the fact that he was a mere figurehead in his own administration. Another charismatic actor for the cameras. Traveling is still the oldest and most poetic form of higher education there is. Not traveling in some elite, upper-class bubble, mind you, but really traveling. If you want to see what it means to be a really well-educated man, take a look at the life of Barack Obama.

Places like the Southern Center are full of well-educated people. People who could be making a lot of money right now but aren't. These people are not only well educated, they are very, very smart. Smart enough to question the very idea that the boy with the most toys in the end, wins. Smart enough to know that no one's life should be thrown away in a moment, with the trigger of a gun *or* the sweep of a pen. There are many ways to be asleep and many ways to be awake in this world. These were people smart enought to know that we must always make space for awakening.

MACEO

Life on Planet Groove, Maceo Parker, Pee Wee Ellis, and Fred Wesley's live album, was one of our favorite records to spin in the van. Me, Goat, and Andy spun that thing silly. It's the kind of live album that transports you right to where the party's at, which for long drives is quite a blessing. When we moved up to a tour bus, that record went with us and kept right on spinning. My whole life had come down to Curtis Mayfield and James Brown. The Staples Singers, Stevie Wonder, and the Meters. Miles Davis and Alice Coltrane (John's equally celestial other half). Betty Carter and Ray Charles. Monk. The list went on and on. I was finally getting a childhood and I was stuck back in the seventies again, only this time I was absorbed in everything I'd missed the first time. That relentlessly funky and soulful musical geyser just the other side of the tracks.

At the beginning of every tour, I hung twinkling Christmas lights in the front lounge of the bus and we almost couldn't wait for each gig to be over so we could jump back on it and resume our listening parties. I was in that time of life that you know is special and still you don't really know how special it is: to be young and free and dancing with your friends. To be stoned and enraptured by the best music you ever heard. To be goin' and goin' at seventy-five miles an hour headlong into life's adventure, even while you're sleeping. To show up in every town and think, *I could live here.* It was the best of times but then, in the best of times is always the seed of one's undoing so, it was that, too, but first . . . since I was getting a second chance at an adolescence, it was time to go back to school.

After touring for a stint with Fred and Pee Wee as the JB's (James Brown's former horn section), Maceo had struck out on his own. My touring sphere and his began to overlap and I found myself able to catch a few of his shows. He seemed to be always out there and I was always out there, too, so opportunities arose. I immediately fell in love with the spirit that he called forth when he played and the funky, badass band that he traveled with. Maceo was the consummate front man, in the James Brown model, with foot cues and quick handoffs that necessitated an eagle eye from all assembled. His precision and authority translated through his horn, too, and when he was blowing, there were just no two ways about it. I imagine Maceo is a man incapable of being wishy-washy even in a bathtub. I watched the way he conducted his show and drove his band and I was inspired.

I proposed to Maceo that he share the stage with me for a whole tour and he said yes, so we orchestrated a coast-to-coast month-long run and dubbed it "The F-word Tour." "A funky-fresh feeling shall be felt by all," declared the Hatch Show Print poster. The world had constructed very different categories and labels for me and Maceo but I felt increasingly connected to him as we went, and he to me. "I always forget how I feel about you," he says to me now, whenever we see each other. I wait for it to all come back to him . . . our summer of familial love. "I never forget how I feel about you," I tell him.

Our bands played outside, in the company of the moon the whole summer, sharing music on stage and off. My favorite was the night when there was a Steinway in my dressing room and Mace held court there until late in the evening, singing his old church songs and Ray Charles. Whenever there is a piano around, Maceo is drawn to it and as soon as he touches it, gems fall out. I could sit and listen to Maceo sing for hours and on this particular evening, I was lucky enough to be able to. I doubt that even in his youth, Mace was much of a hangin'-out kind of guy so it felt like a rare blessing to have him there like that, letting his hair down.

I can boast now that I have spent about thirty years on the road, but Mace had spent thirty years on the road with James Brown before even embarking on his solo career in the nineties. By the time I met him, he'd already seen it all. It is no wonder that he clung to things like the old dress code. You could feel coming off him what it had meant to be a black man touring around America in the sixties and seventies. Looking sharp was first and foremost a means of self-preservation. It was at least a way to not get hassled every time you walked into your hotel. Even in the late nineties, I'm sure it was still true enough. Maceo looked sharp on his way to the dry cleaners on a day off to get his suits pressed. He looked sharp in a hotel parking lot after being evacuated in the middle of the night for a fire alarm. At 4:00 a.m., there he'd be amongst the bleary-eyed and bathrobed citizenry, in a starched shirt with his horn hanging around his neck, looking like a genius who'd just dozed off in a chair.

Me and my gang had this running joke all summer about the relative appearances of our two bands: the slacker white kids, likely not worth their weight in catering food, and the dapper African-American professors, who made it all (from the groove to the spit shine) look easy. With much premeditation and effort, my operation tried to match Maceo's operation suit for suit in Las Vegas but Mace retaliated then by busting out *the* suit. It was a finely tailored sharkskin number, which promptly put us all to shame once again. He laughed all the way through his set, taunting, "Go, suit, go!" But the best was the night in Omaha when he came out on stage and sat in with my band in his boxer shorts, just to prove that he, too, was capable of dressing down.

Mace and I are like cousins in the interlocking tribes of the touring musician, which include roadies and crew and venue staff and managers and promoters. By extension, there are studios, labels, gear companies, radio stations and TV shows, festivals and stores that become a part of this fluctuating community of "music people." The world happily gets smaller and smaller and one's extended family gets bigger with each decade out there. As in any family, we watch each other grow and flounder, we see each other on the way up and on the way down. We see who falls off and who remains. Eventually, it seems as if everyone is two degrees separated from everyone else. Waves of shock and sadness pass through when somebody dies. Enough of us die and the landscape shifts. Old doors shut for good.

One thing that I believe remains consistent across time is this: The heart of the "music people" tribe beats in all the venues where live music goes down, music being fundamentally a social act driven by the human need to get together and rejoice in time and space. From hubs like the First Avenue in Minneapolis, the Fillmore in San Francisco, the 930 Club in D.C., to soulful outposts like Tipitinas or Antoines. From the pristine clubs of Shibuya, in Tokyo, where everything miraculously works, to every other corner of the touring world (the ski bars of Colorado, the opera houses of Italy . . .) where nothing ever has. The pulse is made stronger every time people unite in the shared experience of music, the shared experience of being alive.

If you're on the folky side of life (like me) you also pass through the Ryman in Nashville and the Old Town School in Chicago. The Stone Mountain Arts Center up in Maine and the heart of Humboldt County in Northern Cali, where at least one member of the audience is usually fully naked. You have Lyons and Kate Wolf and Hardly Strictly Bluegrass and all the great festivals . . . there's WOMAD and Lollapalooza and Bonnaroo and Bumbershoot. There's Jazz Fest in New Orleans and Glastonbury in England (both of which are especially memorable on rainy years). My music has brought me into many soulful spaces, from CBGB's to the Apollo to the El Mocambo, and I've loved the whole journey of becoming distant kin with every other working musician out there. Our names on the same calendars, our posters in the same windows, our ongoing conversations scrawled in graffiti on dressing room walls.

"Do you listen to Betty Carter?" Bruno, Maceo's guitar player, asked me one day. "Yes, I sure do," I replied, "but you might be the first person to ever notice." There are the places where music critics can perceive musical influence crossing over and then there are all the many places where music actually does cross over. Music is passed back and forth, back and forth, round and round until it would be too complicated for anyone to really discern its path if they tried. I've read all kinds of critical dissections of who supposedly influenced me and sometimes, critics cite people I've never even heard of. I'm sure they also write about how I've influenced other people (white chicks) whom I haven't, just because they are following influence paths that seem probable or obvious. But music itself travels around even more fluidly than the musicians themselves and influences don't necessarily work in probable or obvious ways.

I loved the way Bruno's hands floated around his guitar and I watched him in awe every night when he played. His approach was so fluid and effortless compared with my sweaty, grunting labors. Bruno actually played with Betty Carter for years, which gave me a thrill. One degree of separation and there she was. No wonder he knew all those colorful jazz voicings. No wonder his pocket was so nimble and quick. I looked up to Bruno as a guitar master and when he gave me his fretboard necktie at the end of that tour, I felt my service to the guitar affirmed. I treasure that tie.

MAKING SONGS 4

Okay. Can we come up with a different term for PMS? After forty-seven years of living in this little body, I can say without a doubt that my reproductive cycles are deeply connected with my creative cycles. It actually feels as if it's one and the same thing, as in: the force of creation moving through me. I just think the physical and spiritual conversation with mortality that we call "premenstrual syndrome" should have a more meaningful term attached to it. To me PMS feels like a window. Yes. Grief is a window and through it you see things. I will hereby refer to this time of my cycle when I can't sleep for days on end and I'm full of turmoil and darkness (but also great vision) as: The Window.

I wonder, what is it like for other women artists? Are their artistic cycles related to their body cycles as with me? And what is it like for men, when the creative force moves through them? Do they experience a bodily connectedness to their visions? Artists, please write to me and tell me! I want to know! Women, I find it hard to believe that this is just me. It simply became unavoidable for me to notice, over time, that it is through The Window that most of my songs fly in.

When menstruation comes, I am mercifully released back into sleep and stasis. The Window closes and I shed . . . a lot. I shed my anger and my pain, the lining of my womb . . . even my hair. I've been cutting my own hair for decades now and it always seems to happen at the same time of month: right after The Window closes. This is the time when I remake myself anew. It's the hair cutting that first tipped me off to all the rest of it, actually. I began to notice, as I would drop clumps of my hair into my wastebasket, that they would always fall onto rolled-up, used maxi pads. Then I started looking up and realizing that the girl in the mirror with the new haircut also has a few new songs under her belt. Songs that immediately preceded all the stuff in the garbage. Songs that she now feels excited to go back out into the world and play. Creation is no joke.

A PRINCE AMONG MEN

We made a stop in Minneapolis on the F-word tour to play a show in some ballpark. I remember Bill Murray showed up that day and was a fine and nice fellow (I think he may have been the park's owner) and then I remember a white limousine pulling up backstage, in the mid-afternoon, and time coming to a halt. Everyone went into a tizzy and people swarmed over to me to beckon me forth. Ani, Ani, come quick! Prince is here!

Prince and I had developed our one degree of separation through journalists, having passed a joke back and forth in the media about him coming over to Righteous Babe. This was during the period when he was desperate to get out of his deal with Warner Brothers and writing "slave" across his cheek for public appearances. He had just changed his name to an unpronounceable symbol and I felt like he was making himself clear: *Prince is a free man, if you cannot acknowledge my freedom, you cannot say my name.*

I also felt like I understood his outrage at being told that, at this stage in the game, he was somehow in debt to Warner Brothers, instead of the other way around. That company had been more than paid back for their investment in Prince. I did not think he was wrong to believe that he had earned the right to conduct his art and his career as he wished. The times they were a-changing in the music biz and people like me were calling into question the indentured servitude of artists in the label system. Spurred on by my example, Prince was insistent that Warner release him to explore his own independent path. Ever a man of symbolism, he moved to literally reduce himself to a symbol rather than be the most tragic sort of human: a prince in bondage.

I also really loved that, when he became a symbol, the thing that he became a symbol of was a hybrid of masculine and feminine. Strike "hybrid" and write "unity" into that last sentence. The high-voltage gender circuitry that buzzed inside him was arresting by any measure. His energy was like that of both sexes resonating at hummingbird speed. Both passions at a fevered pitch. Of all the gender-queer revolutionary stances ever struck, Prince's was the hottest and the coolest at the same time. Utterly fearless and unapologetic . . . but vulnerable and sexy and shy. In addition to his obstinate independence, I could relate to his way of being heterosexual but queer as the day is long.

In this world now of rampant gender switching, will there ever be another to hold the middle ground as deftly as he? Hold it so fiercely and true as to prove, beyond a doubt, its potential for transcendence? It isn't easy carrying the mantle of the two-spirited in the gender theater but Prince never cowered. In fact, he went one step further: Like David Bowie, he made it look enviable. His brilliance carried his bravery and vice versa, and his holding of queerness had a powerfully liberating effect on society just like his music did. Not only that but, if you ask me, Prince's version of radical feminism was also the hottest . . . and the coolest.

Being tiny of stature and "effeminate" made his energy and countenance somewhat awkward around full-sized, manly men. I saw this energy dissonance in action. He could be subliminally demeaned against a backdrop of patriarchy's traditional mold for masculinity. Against a backdrop of femininity, however, he stood out in vivid counterpoint. Like any jewel, his luster shone best in the right setting. He played music, therefore, with women as much as or more than men. It just worked. In this way, his feminism, like the rest of him, spoke on a primal level below language. He communicated more clearly than a lot of people who use a lot of fancy words: Women are just as good. Musically, he was the ultimate badass, he could play with anyone he chose and, time and time again, he chose women.

And when it came to the realm of words, there was feminism there, too. You could hear in Prince's songs a man who had abandoned the patriarchal will of dominance over women. As a woman, you could hear the voice of a man who actually looked you in the eye and spoke to you as an equal. There was something undeniably renegade and progressive about his tone. His approach to race was just as transcendent. He was neither self-hating nor stymied by racism, he was, once again, magically and defiantly above it all. His attitude and presence made space for racial equality and harmony to exist around him. He modeled the power of possibility. The possibility of rewriting all the rules for yourself.

It wasn't exactly a surprise that he was at the ballpark that day, his people had phoned my people ahead of time to alert us of his plan to come meet me. This gave me a chance to inquire about what I was supposed to call him now that he was no longer Prince. They said he should just be called "The Artist." I wasn't quite sure how that was supposed to be done ("Hey, The Artist, come look at this"?), so I decided in a pinch I would just call him Artie. Luckily for both of us, it never came to that.

I stood in front of the limo's mirrored glass, watching my own reflection disappear and be replaced in slow motion by his face, as the electric window rolled down. There he was, lounging on the white shag-carpeted floor of the car in the most vivid purple silk chemise, looking up at me with eyelashes flapping like butterfly wings. Larry Graham (iconic bass player with Sly and the Family Stone, etc.) and his wife, Tina, were in there with him, sitting on the seats. My face was bare, but Prince was sporting full base and powder. I immediately dug this flip of the script. There we were, both inhabiting our own brand of androgyny, smiling at each other.

He hung out a little with Maceo and me and later, while Mace was playing, I got to watch him from side stage with Prince. Then I had to go and play in front of Prince myself. Unnerving stuff, playing for one of your all-time musical heroes. I heard later that Larry and Tina were out in the crowd all evening, distributing Jehovah's Witness pamphlets to my audience. That must have been a strange and delightful interface. I wonder if anyone in the audience knew that this friendly man flyering for Jehovah had invented slap bass playing?

Prince invited me and Mace to Paisley Park the next day and we happened to have a day off, so while the rest of the tour rolled on after the show, we stayed behind. The invitation was to come over and record on the new album Prince was working on, so both Maceo and I brought our axes with us to the Paisley Park mothership. Maceo showed up early in the day and blew some ridiculously funky lines over a jam that sounded awesome to me but ended up being relegated to a hidden track on the record. I showed up in the afternoon and was asked to please take a seat in the waiting room while Prince finished up something.

When I finally sat down in the control room, he hit "Play" and over the larger-than-life speakers came a solo piano ballad called "Eye Love U, But Eye Don't Trust U Anymore." It was like I was living in a dream, sitting next to the man himself, being the first to hear this beautiful, intimate recording he'd just made. "It's in G," he turned to me and said. I watched then as my dream turned into a nightmare before my eyes. You have to understand, I am not the kind of guitar player who knows what the notes in the key of G are or where the hell they might be found on my guitar neck. I have spent years cranking my instrument around from one open tuning to another, so the notes on my guitar have never stayed put long enough for me to place them. What I need is a day (or at least an hour!) alone with a track in order to teach myself what I want to play on it. In one gulp, I realized I was not going to have that time, or any time at all. I was on the hot seat. *Fuck me! This is the part where Prince finds out I can't play!*

I walked into the tracking room, discreetly trying to find notes on my guitar that matched the song I'd just heard. In the middle of the empty room was a pool of light and in the middle of the pool of light was a microphone on a stand and a chair with a pair of headphones sitting on it. I sat down and looked at Prince looking back at me through the glass. The urge to run or cry or run away crying was raging inside me. I resorted to secretly wiping away tears while putting on the headphones. He hit "Play" for a few seconds and then suddenly he hit "Stop" again. "Where were you?" he asked over the talkback, and I jumped. He laughed at his own joke. He knew I was in a mortal panic and he was messing with me. He was finding out what I was made of. I managed to play a very basic lunk-headed fingerpicked accompaniment to his song and, at the end of the take, he rolled quickly back to the bridge. The whole thing was over in five minutes.

It was early evening then and it also happened to be the Fourth of July so, next thing I knew, we were up on the roof watching fireworks together. Then Larry, Maceo, Prince, a few of his local musician posse, and I were coalescing on the soundstage for a jam session. Again, I was in a dream, looking around at my present company and thinking, *How the hell did I get here?* I watched Prince flit around from instrument to instrument, not just playing each one but slaying them, even the drums. Every instrument became another extension of his body. His body, having no clear borders, seemed to leak its spirit everywhere. He was feeling out his new material, listening for ideas in our jam session to employ on his upcoming tour. He was taking the opportunity of Maceo's and my visit to do some informal workshopping.

Maceo would end up going on that tour with him and then working for him on and off for years. I felt proud to have introduced them. It was not necessarily an easy job, working for Prince, who could be notoriously difficult, but Mace had weathered decades of James Brown, so he was adept at handling strong personalities. I always felt Prince's rough edges were just the outer expression of an epic vulnerability and an inner state of isolation. It's not like I knew his life, let alone his heart, but I instinctually felt the urge to hold and protect him. He brought out my maternal side. I wanted to shovel unconditional love and safety into him until I heard him exhale but I never did get that chance. He bid me farewell that evening with kind words, words that I carry with me, and then I only got the chance to hang out with him a few more times.

Once, when I was in L.A., I went to a party at his rented winter abode and despite the parade of famous people and fanciness, I remember being haunted by an ache in my heart after I left. He seemed even less comfortable at the party than I, and it was his party. I vowed to never want anything from him. *I love you unconditionally, Prince. I never wanted to be anything to you except a person you could trust.*

PHOTO SHOOTS

With my increasing notoriety came the interest of big pop culture magazines, signifying the advent of one of life's most excruciating experiences: the magazine photo shoot. I'd get the call that so-and-so wanted to include me in their ten-new-artists-to-watch spread and off I would go, alone and undefended, to get my picture taken and my soul along with it.

This was the late nineties and the music industry still had money splashing over its sides. There were budgets for photo shoots and lots of people standing around getting paid. There were caterers and stylists, makeup artists and photographers and photographer's assistants, and there were clothes to showcase from designers. It took a while for it to sink in but eventually I realized, of all the people assembled at a big magazine photo shoot, none of them was actually there to take a picture of "me." *These people are on a mission that has nothing to do with you. You are just a prop.* "I brought some really cool clothes for you to check out!" it would always start. "Here, try this on!"

I didn't want to be difficult. I didn't want to be rude. *Is this how it's done?* I put on the clothes and sat for the makeup and then I stood there without breathing in front of cameras, feeling like a made-up monkey in a zoo, being looked at but not seen. Then I would run home, scrub my face, and cry. I did it a few times exactly like that before I located a few of my senses and showed up with some of my own clothes. (The number one rule of the magazine photo shoot seems to be that you must change your clothes a lot.) The assembled crew would humor me for a while and then they would say, "Okay, cool. Let's try just one more shot. Maybe one kinda crazy one? Here, try this on!" Bam, they'd have their picture.

When I petitioned for no makeup, the results were about the same. "Okay, yeah, we'll do really minimal," they'd say, "just a little powder to keep the shine down." "Just a little accent on the eyes . . ." Then I would look in the mirror and quietly tear up at their idea of minimal. Suddenly it would be made very clear inside me: *You're not a poet. You're not a revolutionary. You're just another girl monkey at a monkey auction. And not even a pretty one. Look at you. You're a joke.* More running home and scrubbing myself clean. More foggy bafflement at why I felt so deeply bad. What is it about photo shoots that renders me so powerless? Where the hell were my superpowers when I needed them? Are all cameras made of kryptonite?

I don't really know the answer to my camera issue, but I think it may have something to do with the fact that my mother used to ritually cut herself out of family photographs, ruining them as any kind of memento, because she never liked the way she looked. In this way, she erased all our family memories and instead left a historical record of her own self-loathing. "Some of us are put here to make other people feel good about themselves," she used to say to me. It was her way of telling me: Don't worry, us not-pretty girls have a place in this world, too.

For a girl, the fear of not being pretty is the fear of not being a valuable object, which is the fear of not being loved. It is a conflation that is instilled so early on and runs so deep that, even when you know it's a fear perpetrated by patriarchy, goaded by fashion magazines, and used to manipulate you into buying stuff, you still can't stop the way it affects you. Being a woke feminist doesn't mean you've overcome it, it just means you've learned to live with your perpetual self-loathing and your anger around it, too.

It is the patriarchal gaze itself that contains the kryptonite, rendering who-you-thought-you-were invisible even to yourself. That gaze can disable the content of your character, the abilities you possess, the seriousness of your work, and that experience of being suddenly, radically reduced can linger inside you and imprint. Your sense of who you are can become tenuous.

You have maybe detected a little chip on the shoulder of the girl writing this book but, truth is, I have no reasonable beef with Bob Dylan. He's a great songwriter and he was only ever gracious with me the few times I was on the road with him. He knew how excited I was to meet Alan Lomax and at the end of that tour he called me onto his bus to bestow upon me the newly minted Smithsonian Folkways CD box set. He'd even signed it for me with a very kind inscription. No . . . the chip on my shoulder that I have about Bob Dylan is not his fault. It stems from growing up in a world where I inherently understood that I could never be him. And I don't even want to be him! (I wouldn't want to spend my best years afraid of being shot.) No, I simply want to know that I *could* be him, that the mere fact of my femaleness does not put me in a marginal special-interest group. I want to live in a world where the history writers and the cultural arbiters, the people who declare who "the voice of a generation" is, are not all white men. My beef is really with the overarching power structure of society and the inherent biases it still refuses to admit.

seven

LONGSTORY SHORT

S ekou and Dadedoodada made a record for a little New York label
that was jumping on the spoken-word bandwagon while it still had
wheels on it. The wheels apparently came off between the recording and
the release of his project, though, because the label opted to shelve his
finished work instead of following through with the release. Sekou found
himself in that all too common artist's position of not having the means
to buy back his own record from the company that had funded it, in
order to insure that it even see the light of day. But I had the means. I got
wind of his situation and decided to free his record from its cage and release it on Righteous Babe.

The record was called *The Blue Oneness of Dreams* and we followed it
up with another Sekou release called *Longstory Short*. Sekou and Utah
were now both officially Righteous Babes and in house we jokingly
started referring to ourselves as "Old Man Records." Arto Lindsay, the
New York nowave, noise guitar, electronica enigma, was also on RBR for

a spell and he was no spring chicken, either. As we expanded our releases, our roster was . . . not what anyone might expect. But then, essentially, neither was I.

After the release of *Longstory Short*, I embarked on a summer-long tour with Sekou and Dadedoodada as my opening act. Most of the venues we played were outdoors, from Wolf Trap near D.C. to Red Rocks in Colorado and all the way out to the Pier in Seattle. Sekou and I got to sit out on lawns in the afternoons, or gaze up at the stars together at night, exchanging thoughts as they came to us, spanning time together outside of the noisy confines of New York. It was a great blessing for me to have such time with him.

I had given Sekou a book by Lucille Clifton back at the New School years earlier. It was a collection of poems called *Blessing the Boats*. I didn't know it at the time, but that book and Lucille's voice would penetrate deeply into him. I vaguely remember his asking me at some point if it was okay with me if he used one of my songs in a show he was working on and I immediately said yes, of course. Much later, after our tenure as teacher and student had ended and our tour across America was a memory, too, I heard about a show Sekou was mounting at BAM (the Brooklyn Academy of Music). Miraculously, I found myself in New York in time to catch a performance. To my surprise, the show was entitled *Blessing the Boats*. It was a long story-poem stage play interspersed with music and, to my even greater surprise, in the middle of it a young woman launched into my song "Grey." I never felt so proud.

"Grey" was one of Sekou's favorite songs of mine and I was surprised again to hear it sung at his memorial service. He'd had many health complications over the years and eventually they caught up with him. The morning he died, I happened to be in Manhattan again, scheduled to play Central Park SummerStage that night. The skies opened up at dawn and a most spectacular raging storm unexpectedly engulfed the whole city. A few hours later, I was told that Sekou, a true force of nature, had made his exit. "See you all of a sudden," he always used to say whenever we parted company.

On the afternoon of Sekou's death, the rain stopped and the sun came out again. The city, blessed and washed clean, lifted with the steam of absolution. In a daze, I was soundchecking on the Central Park stage between the four and five o'clock hour. A majestic falcon came then and landed on the top of the bleachers out in front of me, undeterred by the racket I was making. I stopped playing. I put down my guitar and left the stage to slowly, calmly walk out and visit with the falcon. I sat down on the bleachers below it and it didn't fly away. I watched the falcon watch the world with a keen eye and then, in a moment, it lifted into the sky again and disappeared. During the show that night, I played "Grey" but I didn't say anything about Sekou to the audience. My love for him was too big and the wound too fresh.

Sekou's wife called me after his memorial service was behind us and presented me with one of the biggest gifts I've ever been given. She called to tell me what I had meant to Sekou, how he had thought of me as one of his teachers, too, and how the respect and gratitude we felt for each other had been mutual. I will always remember that phone call, the grace that Maureen showed in making it, and the honor that it bestowed upon my heart and soul. I will always be grateful to her.

WHY ARE YOU GETTING SO MAD?

The nineties were drawing to a close and there was this Q&A with me in *Rolling Stone* magazine where you could find me pontificating about things as I do, including about how, when it comes to art and writing, it's best to stick close to home, tell your own story, and not presume to speak for anyone else. Fair enough but, thing is, in the breath before that, I had been talking about my friends the Indigo Girls, who were on their Honor the Earth tour, fighting with and for Native Americans for environmental justice and the rights of indigenous peoples. Though not intentional (or at least not consciously intentional) my remarks read like a direct challenge to the validity of the Indigo Girls' work. Amy called me up.

What the Indigo Girls were doing with Honor the Earth was deeply personal and genuine and uplifting and valid, let me just say that now to be clear. Making of one's friendships and associations bridges where whole communities can cross over, become allied, and work together towards common goals: That is the Goddesses' work right there. Greater overall unity and more allegiances between people in fighting oppression and exploitation are what's needed. Even at the time, I couldn't justify how I could've been so careless with my words in the Q&A as to appear to be dissing the Indigo Girls, so when Amy confronted me, I had no explanation for her and I got defensive.

All I remember is that Amy was calm while expressing her reasonable beef with my interview but I was not. She told me she was going to write a letter to the editor in response to what I'd said and I freaked out. I remember screaming at her over the phone, defending my position, and then I remember her saying, "Why are you getting so mad?" I didn't stop at the time to acknowledge the validity of her question, but that question kept ringing in my ears after we hung up, Its saliency slowly pressing in on me. *Why are you getting so mad? What is going on with you?*

My desire to escape (everything all the time) had been building to a crescendo and I had been ignoring it. Theoretically, my life was a thing of my own design from top to bottom and yet, just like the bad old days, I wanted to run. Over the course of the whole last decade, exponential growth had been the name of the game at RBR and the pressures on me had grown along with everything else. Most of my friends, and my husband, were also my employees so no relationships in my life were uncomplicated. Even my mother was now on the payroll at RBR. There were dozens of people whose livelihoods were contingent on the health of my business and dozens of others on the periphery whose businesses were expanding because of mine. Full steam ahead for The Little Engine That Could! That was the consensus. Inside, though, I was turning into a frantic mama bird whose dreams are haunted by an endless sea of gaping hungry mouths, cheeping and chirping away.

I found myself on stage night after night trying to squeeze blood from a stone but I couldn't fathom taking the time to step away and regain my footing. How could I do that? I just couldn't do that. The subtext of my life was this: My touring income supported everything and everyone under the RBR umbrella. All our releases, other than mine, lost money and were simply labors of love. (Andrew Bird and Anaïs Mitchell would briefly break that pattern but that was not for years to come.) It had gotten so that even *my* record sales couldn't float all the RBR expenses. My touring income, plus the increased merch sales that came with it, were necessary fuel to keep the mothership running smoothly. I kept telling myself: *One day, RBR will grow beyond this phase and the financial structure will shift . . .*

Meanwhile, the story of me-the-artist had taken a backseat to me-the-girl-with-her-own-record-company and I had no choice but to resign myself to the role. It was all that people wanted to talk about. It seemed like a reflection of how keen music people everywhere were to be self-empowered and self-directed themselves. The music world had become dry and parched and the story of RBR caught on like tinder. I tried to feel whole and grateful within this amped-up media swirl but I also couldn't help but feel like this was just another clever way that "they" had of dismissing my music . . . my songs. "What is it about you?" they would literally ask me on a daily basis. "To what do you attribute your unprecedented indie success?" I would just sit there mutely with a wan smile on my face and shrug, refusing to answer this most demeaning line of questioning. *I dunno man, you figure it out. They don't come to my shows because I own my own record company, I can tell you that much.*

Yes, the specter of RBR had challenged business-as-usual in the music industry but, in some ways, what we symbolized and signaled was mightier than what we actually were. Technology was radically transforming the music industry and Scot and I were both somewhat anti-technology. This aversion made us immediately begin to lose traction in our own revolution. At the onset of the nineties, the RBR model was groundbreaking but, by decade's end, we had already become an antique. We were the last existing business on earth to get a website (in 2000) and we even took pride in that fact. We were still clinging to the idea that "the internet should be free" as in: totally free. Just fans and listeners communicating with one another unpackaged, undirected, and uncommodified. We joked about being Luddites but it was not entirely a joke. We prided ourselves on being radicals.

The internet would do nothing but speed up and speed up, with the advent of social media, but we had fallen hopelessly behind from the outset and it would take years to catch up. Scot, ten years older than me, was not inspired to immerse himself in this new world online and I was too busy traveling through the actual world and engaging actual people. The difference, in the intervening decade, was made up for in sweat equity: mostly the sweat that ran down my back and soaked my leather guitar straps as I played. I was focused on the daily task of trying to maintain square one but it was getting harder. It was only a matter of time before it would feel to me like RBR was this big, primitive, coal-burning machine and my job was shoveling coal. I had a sustainable business model only insofar as I stayed deep underground, gasping.

Not only was my life a thing that seemed to have slipped beyond my control, there were increasing numbers of others (whom I also couldn't control) whose behavior now reflected directly back upon me. For a girl who liked to make her own mistakes and have no one but herself to blame, it was a hard situation to accept. I started jokingly referring to myself in the third person as "the rock star" (i.e., the person being led around like a prize racehorse in blinders while some manager dude screams at someone in the background), but that was not really a joke, either. The culture of the RBR office was getting away from itself and its radical feminist intention. Scot's approach had become dictatorial and did not reflect, in many instances, my core ideology. Unable to deal, I turned away. I drifted further and further from Buffalo and this thing that had once been my creation. I started floating groundlessly, hotel room to hotel room, escaping, whenever possible, into music.

The truth about myself that I was avoiding lay somewhere in the fact that, behind the public façade of the self-made woman, control freak, queen-of-her-own-universe, was an unparented child perpetually searching for someone, anyone to hand over the keys to. From my early teenhood, in the shadow of The First Boyfriend, there had always been a man in the background with his fingers wrapped around my steering wheel. I had yet to admit that this was my pattern, that I secretly invited people there and handed over control because, deep inside, I craved the experience of sitting back and looking out the window, safe and strapped into my car seat. These two faces of myself (the outwardly assertive and the inwardly deeply passive), unreconciled, swung further into extremes.

It didn't help that the air supply in my personal coal mine was becoming more and more choked. The story of Ani-the-CEO was one thing, but there were other media narratives that also skewed and weighed on my daily existence. The outrage my dyke fans felt over my marriage to a man was another one that seemed to take on a life of its own. According to story after story, my marriage to Goat was seen as a betrayal by "my audience" and had resulted in a big backlash. I was asked to comment on the backlash so many times that I began to wonder if I'd missed something. I began to believe in it. There had really been no more backlash against my marriage than there had been to every other thing I'd ever done but, after a certain number of repetitions, I doubted even the weight of my own experience. All the cards and gifts and sweet messages of congratulations I'd received from listeners were eclipsed by the clamor of controversy. I no longer knew what to think. I'd gotten to the point where I could doubt anything if I thought about it long enough.

And what of my marriage? In fact, it had become the epicenter of my undoing. I could handle malicious lawsuits (there was another one after Dale's), stalkers, and hackers. (When RBR finally, grudgingly entered the world online, we got held for ransom by Russian pirates! We certainly were ahead of our time in that way!) I could handle the hate mail and the occasional moment of mortal fear. (I was outspoken about abortion rights when laser pointers first hit the market. I had experiences of looking down and seeing a little red light playing upon my chest on stage in some big, anonymous arena and my heart would leap into my throat and I'd think, *Is this it?* You gotta understand, abortion providers were being mowed down left and right in those days. In my hometown of Buffalo, Dr. Barnett Slepian was shot dead in his kitchen.) Yes, I could've possibly weathered all of what life was throwing at me but no . . . the state of my marriage was crippling me at my core.

Instead of feeling grounded by my marriage, I felt pressure there, too. I couldn't even tell you if Goat was ready to be a true partner to me because, for my part, I was too busy feeling utterly alone. My husband had become just one more person who would die without my attention, one more person to make myself totally available to, one more person to carry. He was always clawing at me, wanting to have sex. I found myself beating him back or, worse, acquiescing because it was the easiest way to get to the part where he's snoring and I am up all night gripping some deeply worrying aspect of my life between my teeth. Whatever it was I was going through, I seemed to be going through it alone and meanwhile, Goat seemed very happy. I stepped off stage every night back into the solitude of my mind and felt increasingly weighted by the question: *How come I seem to be able to make everyone happy except for me? Is this my lot in life?*

Despite all my attempts to remake the world for myself, I had actually created a reprise of my parents' marriage and found myself sinking into a remake of my mother's resentment. I was the responsible party, I was the provider of all things, I had taken over the mantle of martyr, and I was caught in the same trap. I started looking for excuses to be away from Goat and then I started cheating on him behind his back; in other words, setting landmines everywhere, hoping they would get tripped and shit would blow up. When that didn't work, I negotiated more and more open marital terms with him, but none of it felt strong or true. I recreated the blurriness of my relationship with Scot and further postponed reckoning with my own hypocrisies. In this way, I orchestrated my own undoing.

The thing that you don't realize (until you do) is that your self-respect is the foundation that allows you to weather all manner of adversity and struggle. When you lose your self-respect, everything else becomes impassible. My duplicities made me hate myself which made me crumbly and desperate at my core. There was just no one to blame but myself for this one. I was the one who'd set all these traps to begin with. I had stolen Goat away from his girlfriend, I had convinced him to marry me . . . and now I was changing my mind about the whole thing. I didn't even have the guts to tell him.

Grey

the sky is grey
and the sand is grey
and the ocean is grey

i feel right at home
in this stunning monochrome
alone in my way

i smoke and i drink
and every time i blink
i have a tiny dream

but as bad as i am
i'm proud of the fact
that i'm worse than i seem

what kind of paradise am i looking for?
i've got everything i want and still i want more
maybe some tiny shiny thing will wash up on the shore

you walk through my walls
like a ghost on t.v.
you penetrate me

and my little pink heart
is on its little brown raft
floating out to sea

what can i say
but i'm wired this way
and you're wired to me

and what can i do
but wallow in you
unintentionally

what kind of paradise am i looking for?
i've got everything i want and still i want more
maybe some tiny shiny key will wash up on the shore

regretfully
guess i got three
simple things to say:

why me?
why this now?
why this way?

with overtones ringing
and undertows
pulling away

under a sky that is grey
on sand that is grey
by an ocean that's grey

what kind of paradise am i looking for?
i've got everything i want and still i want more
maybe some tiny shiny thing will wash up on the shore

THE CRASH

It was a three-bus tour which, to this day, remains a record. The first bus we only had for a few days before it was totaled. Luckily, we all survived. The tour schedule started with a show in London and then on to a show in Stockholm two days later, so we had two bus drivers and were deadheading to Sweden when it happened. We were somewhere in the middle of the Black Forest in Germany, on the Autobahn, and the second driver had just started his shift. Everyone was asleep except for me and two of my crew.

European tour buses are all double deckers and I was hanging out, thinking my thoughts in the back downstairs lounge, while my friend Sean Giblin was awake in the upstairs lounge. Sean had taken over from Goat as my monitor engineer because Goat and I were separated. My front-of-house engineer, Steve Schrems, was up in the jump seat next to the driver. Steve saw it coming and braced himself but the rest of us were taken by surprise. Amazingly, the driver did not see it coming, this little matter of the traffic jam and the stopped truck in front of him . . . so he just plowed directly into the back of the truck.

These were the days of VHS tapes and behind me, in the lower lounge, was a double shelf of movies that spanned the whole back wall of the bus. My memory is of flying through the air in slow motion with a flock of VHS tapes flying along on either side of me. Then we all hit the wall on the other side of the lounge and fell to the floor. I was still buried under a pile of bad movies when they found me.

I was okay, a few bruises and sore muscles, but Sean had hit his head pretty hard. There was blood in his ear. He was taken to a German hospital but released with the reassurance that he did not have a concussion. The worst off seemed to be the ones who were sleeping soundly in their bunks when we crashed. They were awakened by being slammed, accordion style, into the bottom of their bunks. None of them could sleep well on tour for a long time after that. Every little braking sensation by a driver would startle them awake. The beds on tour buses run front to back and there is a rule that you always sleep with your head to the back of the bus, in case of just this kind of event. That way you don't break your neck.

We ended up getting a passenger bus and traveling for a hot minute with all the luxury of the stars of Motown, which is to say, sitting up in rows like schoolchildren. Then we got another tour bus but it was pretty raggedy and old (beggars can't be choosers) and, lo and behold, it broke down a few weeks later on the border of France and Spain. My guitar tech, who was mechanically inclined, ended up crawling underneath the bus and diagnosing the problem. "I do believe we need one of these," he said, sliding out from under with something in his hand.

In the time it took to have "one of those" delivered to where we were stranded roadside, we had plenty of time to wander the French country-side. Wine country. I guess things could always be worse. I remember walking through an orchard of cork trees. Cork, I learned, is the thick, craggly bark of twisted, gnarly little trees. Who knew? I spent a lot of time wandering alone that day. I had a lot on my mind.

LATE NIGHT

I was offered a slot on *Late Night with David Letterman* and everybody I worked with was jumping up and down. It was quite the coup that Indie Girl USA had even gained such access. My publicist, Tracy Mann, and my whole team felt rightfully proud and vindicated in their work of seeking affirmation for my significance in pop culture, despite being a total outsider. Not to mention, this appearance would represent an amazing leap in exposure for me, the power of the boob tube well proven. It was, all around, a happy day for my associates. I, personally, was not quite so thrilled. Venturing into the land of the boob tube was always scary.

I felt compelled to use my few minutes on TV to say something that needed to be said so I elected to play one of my new songs called "Subdivision." But then, the word came back that the show had rejected my song selection, saying they'd prefer something "more upbeat." Scot took a deep breath and called me up. "That's fucked up!" I bleated. "That's bullshit!" "Well . . . maybe they really do just want something more up-beat?" Scot suggested. "It's not crazy to think they might want something upbeat." "Fuck that," I said. "It's 'Subdivision' or nothing." My whole team saw their heroic win squandered then as "nothing" was indeed the result. I didn't play the show and was never invited back.

I was not about to bow to some play-it-safe, controversy-avoiding, culture-homogenizing, truth-crushing corporate network, no sir! That much was for sure! But . . . was I digging my heels in too far? It depended on who you asked.

Subdivision

white people are so scared of black people
they bulldoze out to the country
and put up houses on little loop-de-loop streets
and while america gets its heart cut right out of its chest
the berlin wall still runs down main street
separating east side from west
and nothing is stirring, not even a mouse
in the boarded-up stores and the broken-down houses
so they hang colorful banners off all the street lamps
just to prove they got no manners
no mercy
and no sense

and i'm wondering what it will take
for my city to rise
first we admit our mistakes
then we open our eyes
the ghosts of old buildings
are haunting parking lots
in the city of good neighbors
that history forgot

i remember the first time i saw someone lying on the cold street
i thought: i can't just walk past here
i thought: this can't just be true
but i learned by example
to just keep moving my feet
it's amazing the things
that we all learn to do
so we're led by denial like lambs to the slaughter
serving empires of style and carbonated sugar water
the old farm road's a four-lane that leads to the mall
and our dreams are all guillotines waiting to fall

and i'm wondering what it will take
for my country to rise
first we admit our mistakes
then we open our eyes
or nature succumbs
to one last dumb decision
and america the beautiful
is just one big
subdivision

eight

THE SHOCK WAS SUBSONIC

Touring with Maceo ruined the idea of a band without a horn section for me so I found myself with no choice but to incorporate trumpet and saxophone into my own scene. The expansion of the band pushed me further away from extemporaneous improvisation mode and into a place of more consistency. Basically, if you want a bunch of people to be able to play along with you, you've got to play it the same every time, or at least keep it in the ballpark. No more launching sideways into something else. No more stopping suddenly to tell a joke. Telling stories doesn't really work, either, when there's a bunch of musicians standing around waiting for the next song to begin, so I pushed back further from my punk-folksinger roots and I withdrew.

Coincidentally, I no longer wanted to tell stories. I was turning up lonely and miserable in bathroom mirrors all over the world when I wasn't on stage being gawked at. On the tour schedule, it was business as usual but on the inside, things that I'd been running from my whole life were catching up to me. I wanted to play music more than ever, I just didn't want to talk. I also didn't want to be seen. If I could've played shows in an invisible bodysuit and mask, under a pseudonym, I would've. But that was no way to pay the bills. Some nights, I ached to not even have to sing. I just wanted to play guitar. It was all I could do to stay put in the spotlight, naked and hemorrhaging at the heart. My shows got shorter. I could only stand there for about an hour or so before running. People complained. My response should have been to stop everything, cancel my life, and go sit down, but instead, I just started doing everything stoned.

It is unfathomable to me now that I ignored my screaming gut (or more accurately: beat my screaming gut down with clubs) and kept going. Resistance is a powerful thing. It made my labor with my first kid (a decade later, in a whole other life) go on for three days. Yes, it's true: Whatever the thing is that you are resisting the most, whatever thing will be the most painful, that is the thing you must do. That's the sick joke of being a grown-up. Your job becomes to figure out what you're avoiding.

Unlike the rest of my touring compadres, whom I traveled with for many years, the horn section in my band became a revolving door that exemplified the spinning-out-of-control vibe my life had taken on. There were now endless cycles of auditions and rehearsals to busy myself with. Musical parts that had begun as improvisations were charted out and written in stone. It was as though the machine that had built up around my thing had officially become bigger than the thing itself. I focused on the distractions of maintaining square one and I beat back the desire to set fire to my own house.

One fateful day, I was in New York City scouting for a new trumpet player. Auditions were scheduled for September 11 and 12, at a rehearsal studio in Midtown Manhattan, but the first morning, before my core band and I could assemble at ten, the Twin Towers fell. The phone woke me up in my hotel room on Forty-seventh Street and it was Scot calling from his room. "Turn on the TV," he said. And then, ". . . Look out the window."

We went over to the rehearsal space anyway because we didn't know what else to do and just in case any of the musicians did show up. Miracu-lously, some did. We met a few trumpet players under some of the strang-est circumstances there are. Cellphones stopped working, subways and buses stopped, pretty soon all vehicle traffic had vanished and the streets were empty of everything but people standing around looking south. The musicians came on bicycle or on foot if they came at all. All day we watched steady streams of stunned grey people, covered in ash, marching like zombies up the middle of the avenues towards their homes, grey briefcases in hand. We struggled as the moments unfolded to understand, like everyone else, what was going on a mere seventy blocks below us.

In a rare shift of New York culture, folks just stood out on the street and talked to each other. But also . . . not everyone. Quite a few people were just walking by looking normal. Normal things that happen on nor-mal days were also still happening. That's how vast New York is. The world as we know it could be coming to an end and still there are people buying and selling things, people just passing by. That was maybe the most surreal part. I ordered dinner at a restaurant that night. Sushi no less. I looked around at all the people going about their business and some quiet, inner feeling of isolation deepened . . . I think also, some yearning for connection with it. *Now that a huge cloud of smoke is consum-ing the bottom of the island, shouldn't we all hug one another? Shouldn't we all be hugging?*

There was a huge tropical bird in a cage in the lobby of the rehearsal space making repeated stressed-out screeching sounds and yelling cau-tions at us as we rode out that first day. A bird in a cage is a thing that sickens my heart on a good day and this one was doing the appropriate amount of screaming for the occasion. We wondered if we should try to go down there and some of us did but there were not even systems to help out with yet, just first responders and barricades and chaos.

We knew we had to get out of our hotel and off the island, out of the way. We wondered how any of us were going to get home. My drummer, Daren, lived in Colorado, Hans and Julie in Seattle. . . . The rest of the world felt suddenly inaccessible from the locked-down battleship of New York. Everyone ached to be back home holding their loved ones. Except for me. Estranged from Goat, I just ached. We wondered what was going to happen next.

What happened next was that the wind shifted north and the piercing smoke of the towers came and found us. Blue smoke, not even the smoke of burning organic matter but the smoke of burning plastic, I vote that the most evil smell there is. The official smell of Environmental Destruction and American Imperialism all rolled into one inescapable experience. We cowered indoors, ears glued to the TV and radio, only venturing out to see what foodstuffs were still finding their way onto the island as the days wore on. Shelves began to empty and the specter of war seemed suddenly real.

It has always just worked out that way: My inner life and the life of my society are mirrors of each other. It was no wonder that we hit rock bottom together. It was time for us to check ourselves. But then, of course, came the lag time. Revelations, in real life, tend to bounce as they touch down. My country and I would have some more years of flailing ahead of us. The mainstream media would be a bunch of sheep braying White House press releases into cameras until Katrina finally came to shut them up. It was all so shameful. Giuliani was a hero . . . George W. was a hero . . . *What are you avoiding, America? What is the most painful thing?*

For my part, I was right back on tour, there was never a question. I hit the road with my renewed sense of purpose just two weeks later. My band and crew once again had to kiss their loved ones goodbye and train and bus out to Missoula, Montana, where the tour was slated to begin. All airplanes were still grounded.

I tried to navigate and instigate public discourse but the obstacles of hysteria were suddenly strewn about everywhere, like the night I played the Brookdale Events Center in Asbury Park, New Jersey. We had invited The War Resisters League and Democracy Now, but when word got back to venue management that antiwar activists were slated to table in the lobby, they said they wouldn't allow it. "Can they do that?!" I asked, amazed. Apparently, they did potentially have legal standing, being a private business that had rented me their stage that night for my freedom of expression but not necessarily their lobby space. Okay, I volleyed, I will have Amy Goodman of Democracy Now speak from stage! Then they refused that, too, saying they would pull the plug on the show.

People were starting to file into the hall and big mafia-lookin' goons were puffing to my crew, trying to intimidate us into compliance. Everyone was in a tizzy at this last-minute standoff and coming into my dressing room with moment-by-moment updates as I paced the floor. *What are they gonna do?* I thought. *Pull the plug on the show? Really? With three thousand people now in their seats?* What could I do but dare them?

The goons hovered over Steve, front-of-house, at the top of the show and words were exchanged but when Amy stepped out on stage, they did nothing. We had successfully called their bluff. Amy riled up the crowd with a call to action and then I used every drop of my rented freedom of speech. The forces of fear and totalitarianism were pushing in on us and we needed to be vigilant in pushing back. The fearmongers were hard at work spinning the situation to their benefit, lying through their teeth. The Patriot Act, "weapons of mass destruction in Iraq," the Gulf War mach 2, the deluge of public money into Halliburton and the like . . . the thieves were on the march.

But of course, that was not all that was happening. There was also a feeling of American unity that made an appearance down on the street. It was like distinctions of race and class got deprioritized for a moment and, in a blinding flash, we saw each other as countrymen. Yes, after that we were led into xenophobia and war. Yes, we were encouraged to frame our newfound unity as being against a common enemy. Yes, a generic brown face with a turban was designated as that enemy and many innocent people were made to suffer. But first, before all that, we simply unified. In the opening moments of crisis, there comes a heightened consciousness and it holds inside it an unstable, tippy energy. Before the president's flight suit photo ops and incendiary chest thumping, before anyone took a side, there was just the billowing forth of compassion. I believe I was not alone in feeling its presence and then, I believe I was not alone in feeling it squandered.

I personally had never felt so included as in the aftermath of 9/11. White privilege at its finest. The image I have is of being in airports (when they finally reopened) or at American customs counters or face to face with police, feeling finally comfortable and unafraid. In this atmosphere of social insecurity and tweaking, I felt less afraid than ever because everyone, everywhere seemed to finally concur that I wasn't their problem. I was on the team. The scowl of authority was replaced by a courteous nod. If I were a Muslim or Sikh American man, things would have been very different for me but, as fate would have it, I was, once again, one of the lucky ones.

Years later, I would feel that spirit of unity during Katrina, too. I was in New Orleans when that storm hit, watching up close and personal as America confronted itself again. George W.'s government was still the biggest and most devastating part of the problem, making a bad situation epically worse by abandoning certain citizens to die and then absolving all the others who were actually responsible for the many man-made aspects of the catastrophe. Our ability to feel one another, to reach out and help one another, was officially snuffed out once again by tragic misleadership, but before that, there were many hands extended, many selfless acts. The human instinct of compassion was there, too, newborn inside people, awaiting nurturance.

CRASH NUMBER TWO

Sometimes, of course, when you think you've hit rock bottom, you find out there's still further to go. It was the middle of that same tour, that first one after 9/11, and I was soundchecking at the Backyard in

Austin when a call came. Goat had crashed his motorcycle. He was in intensive care in New Orleans. I played the show that night and the next morning I flew there. My touring companions waited together out on the road for me, with my expenses ticking up, while I went to try to help Goat.

I got there before his parents, which was a blessing. At least I didn't have to face them yet. It was Goat's broken heart that had sent him into self-destructive behavior and carelessness and now he'd almost died. He had been riding without a helmet at the time of the accident and not only had he suffered some pretty intense injuries, he'd had a girl on the back of the bike with him. She was not wearing a helmet, either.

I showed up at Charity Hospital in New Orleans and went to the ICU. "What relation are you to the patient?" the desk lady asked. "I'm . . . his wife," I heard myself say. To see him there, unconscious, with blood all over his face and blood caked into his hair, hit me like a bullet. It felt like maybe it hurt about as much. I felt responsible. I felt responsible for them both.

Over the next few days, I gingerly sponged the blood out of his hair and cleaned him up. I didn't want his parents to see him this way. The hospital itself was underfunded and understaffed and they weren't exactly attending to such details. I faced his friends one after the other as they came to visit and I prayed to the Goddesses for my beloved Goat. When he began to awaken, a steady stream of words came out of his mouth that were sent there by the deep depths of his subconscious. I don't know if it was the drugs or what, but the things he said were very revealing. It seemed unfair that he should have all the veils of decorum lifted from him by pharmaceuticals and the subliminal subtext of his whole mind flipped over and put on display. I tried to guard his intense gibberish from others. I tried to absorb it all.

After a few days, he was stable and transferred down to a wide-open floor with about thirty other men lined up along the walls of one big room. Charity Hospital was a dingy, creepy monstrosity, still using these rickety wooden wheelchairs that looked like they were straight out of the Civil War. Most of the men in the other beds had gunshot wounds. I went back and forth between Goat's bed and Monica's bed, the girl who had crashed with him. Monica was not only very young and somewhat on her own in life, she was also a single mom. My moment of reckoning was complete. I was now carrying sadness that way exceeded the bounds of my own skin.

Goat and Monica did both eventually recover, though Monica still has a metal rod under her skin and probably never again ran the way she did as a girl. The metal rod that gruesomely skewered Goat's shin, perpendicularly, was finally removed and he seems to walk again as he always did, with the same jaunty gait. I don't know if it still hurts him sometimes. We run into each other now and then but I don't ask. His big heart seems to have forgiven mine and my guilt eventually moved over to allow for some other, more useful emotions. Traces of it are still there though, in the background of my smile, when I see him. He didn't deserve the pain I visited upon him. I'm grateful for his forgiveness.

Platforms

> i got knocked off my platforms
> so i dusted off my first pair of boots
> bought on the street at astor place
> before new york was run by suits
> and i suited up for the long walk back to myself
> closer to the ground now
> with sorrow
> and stealth

PLATFORMS

I divorced Goat. I fired my band. I turned deep inside and I remained there for years. I wandered over the rocky terrain, around huge boulders of embarrassment, shame, and regret. I turned over every rock that I was strong enough to lift and looked underneath, gaining some strength as I went. I sat there alone by my campfire and tossed things in, one and then the next. I was not yet ready to live in my personal relationships with the integrity that I lived in the world but I knew I was through with the alternative. I was focused now on learning.

I went from being married and promiscuous to alone and celibate. Not that I was working this awakening thing like a monk or anything. I was meandering through it more like a drunk than a monk. For a while there, I was putting away a bottle of wine a night by myself and I'm only five foot two so that was more than enough to hit pause on the pain. In an outward statement of how hard it is to let go of things, I let the empty wine bottles pile up around me in my kitchen. They were everywhere. My fridge was empty.

One night, drunk, I ran out to the corner store in a rainstorm. Running back home, I hit the slippery brick driveway and went down. I fractured my ankle bone and the pain was so great that I couldn't stand up. I pulled myself up the driveway by my arms all the way to my kitchen door. A moment that would become the basis for a recurring nightmare that I had on and off for years. The soldier, suddenly without the use of his legs, drags himself through the mud on his belly, lightning and thunder crashing all around him. Bombs falling. All of his comrades are gone now and he faces his mortality alone.

Still, there was no recognition by my associates that I needed some time off so I was booked up. In between two legs of my endless lifelong tour, I just happened to go from dancing around on stage with a six-piece band to being alone, center stage, and stuck in a chair. I sat there in the spotlight with my swollen black and blue ankle and I shoveled coal. I was wheeled down the tunnel of lights between terminals at O'Hare, in a wheelchair, *Rhapsody in Blue* providing a little comedy once again but darker this time. I sat in dressing rooms and listened to the cheering and chanting of the crowds and I looked at my hands. On record, I went from the extravagant grappling of *Reveling/Reckoning* and *Evolve* to the solitude of *Educated Guess*. With no Goat by my side, I was recording my songs as simply as possible now, at home alone on an old eight-track reel to reel.

I played the Newport Folk Festival around this time, on a grey and dubious day featuring periods of what one couldn't not call rain. I played solo, just a girl and her sad songs, weighed down by ten pounds of dread (which had appeared in the form of dreadlocks hanging down my back, my hair having become one more thing I couldn't let go of). I was feeling weary when we pulled up to the festival grounds in the afternoon but when somebody informed me that I would be sharing a trailer with none other than Joan Armatrading, I became a starstruck teenager again. The festival also informed me that there was only one bathroom in our shared trailer and that it was on her side. "But don't worry!" they said, "She has agreed to share it with you."

Somebody may have agreed to something at some point but when I gingerly knocked to go use the can before my set, I was greeted by the fierce flash of Joan's best stink eye (an understandable reaction to someone invading your trailer). I could hear Joan and her person conferring as I used the bathroom and when I came out, she made a point of apologizing, sweetly, saying she hadn't realized who I was. And there *she* was, one of my biggest guitar heroes and deepest influences and I'm not even sure what I said. Hopefully, it was something in the vicinity of, "I have loved your music since I was fifteen. Thank you."

MAKING SONGS 5

Performing can be tricky. I have found myself on stage, searching around for the veils to lift and they just won't. Sometimes, I wrench off my clothes and underneath is a suit of armor, or a wetsuit, or a chicken costume. But in those moments, the work ethic kicks in, the discipline. I just use whatever voice I'm given and I sing with it. I try to do my job humbly as musician and power through whatever adversity the world has in store. Songwriting is just plain trickier. It seems there is nothing to be done, really, when the conduit is closed, except to stop knocking and go away. It doesn't feel like the same thing as the athletics of making music, where you can just start running and hope some endorphins kick in and a second wind comes to carry you. It's more like, without the endorphins, you forget how to run altogether.

Being a working musician my whole life has meant that there's always another gig to do and having a brand-new song when it is show time is the most exciting and refreshing thing I got. The allure of dropping a sharp new song into my set list has propelled me, in many instances, to rush the hard labor of writing. I might skimp on the brain-breaking process of elaboration and call a song finished too soon. I am impatient. I just want to get out there and *do* music. But I've gotten better, over the years, at backtracking and letting go of things that are not working when I'm writing. I guess I'm getting better at letting go in general. Plus, I'm not in as much of a hurry as I used to be. The reason (in a word): kids.

Having kids (as I would one day do) sure did change songwriting for me. My *actual* children would wrench my song-children away from me and force me (purposefully, jealously) to pour my life's blood and creative energy into them instead. Both my kids looked instantly upon my guitar as the enemy. Goddess forbid Mommy should start playing and get that faraway look in her eyes. That, my kids both insisted, was un-cool. They made it clear from the beginning that my attention was the air that they breathed. If I am in the same city with them, and they are awake, songwriting is forbidden. It would be like taking air out of their lungs.

It was excruciating, at first, to drop my most core passion (and still sometimes is) but (A) kids are awesome, and (B) the wedge my children drove between me and my writing, once I gave over to it, made just enough room for a light to shine through. Basically, my human kids forced patience into me, into my relationship with my life and, after a lot of practice, now I find I'm able to employ this newfound thing called patience in my writing. In fact, I've entered a whole new era of writing thanks to them. An era in which I'm not so quick to declare a song fin-ished. An era where I can attempt to do something crazy like writing a book (behind their backs, on tour, while they sleep). This process of: Step away and come back, step away and come back, that is how I do everything now.

Akimbo

what dreams cause me to abandon my pillow each night?
push away each of them, in fact, since there always seem to be
more than one

and then wake to aching
stiff neck twisted
legs and arms akimbo

like the high-pitched body of a jumper
waiting for her chalk outline
finally at rest

WHOLE OTHER GIRLS

I would eventually amend the entire structure and cast of my operation and I would reel it all back in. I would seek independence even from Scot and embark on a whole new era of professional relationships without slipping on any banana peels and accidentally relinquishing control. I would come to understand that the most important thing about my professional relationships is to have more than one.

Behind the scenes, I learned the art of the tantric love affair. I was relieved to realize that I didn't need to make myself stop falling in love with everyone, I just needed to learn new ways of expressing it. I learned there are lots of ways to make love with people and many of them are platonic. Music is a fine, fine one. Scot and I would settle on being only the version of us that we do best: family. He married a great gal and their kids and mine are like chosen cousins, Scot, ever and always, my chosen brother. My real brother married his high school sweetheart and they are together still. They raised three sons. His story is one of triumph, of creating happiness and stability from unlikely stuff.

My mom repatriated to Canada and lives at the lake permanently now, ever since we winterized the house. She knows which day the loons arrive in the spring and which day they choose for their exit in the fall. The adult loons are in the habit of leaving before their babies. The young ones live abandoned on the lake for weeks before they are strong enough to follow. Their pitiful cries beckon winter.

Goat started touring with Maceo as his all-around sound and crew guy, the way he used to tour with me. They travel together still.

Michael Meldrum settled down and had a family of his own. He continued promoting shows and making music happen in Buffalo until the day he died. Whether it was teaching a kid guitar or encouraging a shy adult to step up to an open mic, Michael spent his life unleashing the joy of music in people. I released his one and only album, *Open Ended*

Question, on Righteous Babe and my version of his song "Please Say Yes" on that record epitomizes, for me, that solitary era I spent at home with my eight track. Some of the sweetest moments for Michael and me would come near the end, when we were sitting around playing music together and our kids were there with us. There is nothing quite like being yourself as a child and yourself as a parent, all in one moment, in one skin. Michael had a knack for connecting me to myself.

I hope you're not sitting there right now going, Wait! This book is about to end? What about everything that happened after 2001? What about pregnancy and birthing and parenting and . . . You'll have to forgive me. I only ever intended this book to be a "making of" story. I probably should have warned you at the onset. The remake is a story that is still writing itself, right now. A story so much in motion that words couldn't even begin to nail it down. But rest assured, the greatest happiness, fulfillment, and accomplishments of the girl in this book are still ahead of her.

Truth is, this book is full of omissions and they're not exclusive to the realm of what happened next. A life, anyone's life, is vast and uncontainable and I've discovered that you can make a whole book full of people and things and still there will be that much left over. I've left so much and so many people out! I feel squeamish now, like maybe I should write this book again and tell you all different stuff . . . but it's too late for that. The court stenographer's duties are almost done and the case of the Righteous Babe is closed. Let the record show that there are, in fact, whole other girls with the same face and the same name, who lived concurrently to the one in this story, but this is the one that got written down, so this one wins. The others, momentarily forgotten by my typing fingers, will soon cease to exist. History is not only a story told but a story *chosen*. Now I see!

I just hope I left enough space for the silences. I hope I ended enough sentences with question marks.

Did I?

Imagine That

imagine that i am on stage
under a watchtower of punishing light
and in the haze is your face bathed in shadow
and what's beyond you is hidden from sight
and somebody right now is yawning
and watching me like a tv
and i have been frantically piling up sandbags
against the floodwaters of fatigue
and insecurity

and then suddenly i hear my guitar singing
and so i just start singing along
and somewhere in my chest
all the noise just gets crushed
by the song

imagine that i'm at your mercy
now imagine that you are at mine
just pretend i've been standing here
watching you
watching me
all this time
yes, imagine that you are the weather
in the tiny snow globe of this song
and i am the statue of liberty
one inch long

so here i am at my most hungry
and here i am at my most full

here i am waving a red cape
locking eyes with a bull

just imagine that i am on stage
under a watchtower of punishing light
and in the haze is your face bathed in shadow
and what's beyond you
is hidden from
sight

OTHER PEOPLE'S TRASH

One thing's for sure, making this book has given me a chance to re-remember things. It's given me the opportunity to have a happier childhood than I'd previously thought. It makes me want to keep going back and revisiting the house of memory. Ding dong! Hello? What else did I forget that I was given? What else can I notice to be grateful for? Oh! There's this: My mother was a reader and a walker. She modeled those things for me and my imitations of those behaviors have brought great joy to my life.

I remember my mom teaching me how to read in bed at night. I remember the moments of pure joy and the indelible shine of pride when she thrilled to my progress. In those few tiny, shiny moments, one intellectual made another. Then, once reading was in my bones, it quickly became a vehicle of expansion and a means of escape. From my Black Stallion novels as a girl to the more philosophical pursuits of adulthood, reading has released me many times from my earthly cage and set me loose in brave new worlds. The written word, even after coming face to face with its limitations and its downsides, remains my first great love.

But life can't be about just taking in and taking in, any more than putting out and putting out. In the middle of that binary swirl is a stasis, humming out from its axis, which also begs attending. Sometimes, just being still and idle are what's needed. Walking is my way of being still. Not only did my mom go for walks (for the sake of going for walks), she always picked up garbage along her way. Off the streets of Buffalo, off roadsides in rural areas, out of the bushes in parks, a schoolyard, our yard, someone else's yard, I watched her bend down and pick up a lot of trash. She would find the nearest garbage can or, if we were out in the woods, she would carry the shit all the way home.

It's a simple gesture, to pick up someone else's trash, but extremely rare. I've never seen anyone do it who wasn't getting paid (or being forced, as a prisoner in an orange jumpsuit) except for my mom. On the occasions when I do it now, it is her hands that I see at the ends of my arms. To try to help fix a problem you didn't create is a state of belief that is inaccessible to a lot of people but my parents handed it to me. I take my kids to vote with me. I take them to political demonstrations and benefits. We turn the water off while brushing. Sometimes, we even pick up other people's trash. I try to give them opportunities to experience the fact of their own agency. I want to make sure they understand how much power is in their own hands.

The good news is that each small accomplishment encourages the next so it becomes merely a matter of pointing yourself in the direction of self-empowerment. Accumulate enough accomplishments and you realize that the reward is not really in the outcome anyway, but in the relationships that you forged along the way.

RECURRING DREAM

I have this recurring dream where I'm pausing on an empty theater stage late at night, backpack over one shoulder, rolling suitcase in the other hand, and I'm looking out into a dark, empty house. The audience has long since gone home to bed and there is only red velvet, gold filigree, and ghosts out there now. I'm crossing the stage on my way out of the place, having ascended from my post-show ruminations in the bowels of the building to board a bus and ride out of town. The stillness is further charged by the wistfulness of my lonely exit. Such a time we had! Such an extravagance of love! *Is this a dream? Or . . . my deathbed? Or . . .* is this happening?

There is a bare lightbulb shining on a lamp stand, front and center on the stage, in the very spot where I was stationed earlier in a room teeming with life. It is the only light now in the cavernous room, save for the red exit signs. I am standing midway upstage behind it. The ghost light was put out overnight to fend off the evil spirits, as is the tradition in old theaters. They are meant as beacons to deliver us through darkness. I smile faintly in this dream now, knowing that I had the honor of standing in for the lightbulb just for a little while. I turn and continue to the stage door, out into the alleyway, and onward to the unknown.

Taking center stage is something like being on the bow of a ship, facing the mighty elements alone or with swarthy crew by your side, either way, all fists are raised. You face the shifting winds and splashing waves of the crowd and somehow you come through victorious or at least . . . changed. Yes, that was only ever the point anyway: to be affected by each other. To be summoners of some torrential moment in which all the forces of nature can meet and startle themselves. Even in the mishap and the misery is a collective search for joy. "The human spirit" people call it, though it is by no means exclusive to humans. *It is ever expanding. It is infinite*, whispers my recurring dream. *Don't worry.*

acknowledgments

thanks to Leonard Shlain for *The Alphabet Versus the Goddess*

thanks to Valarie Kaur for her vision of revolutionary love

thanks to Rebecca Solnit, my soulmate on voting

thanks to Mark Leviton for the opening shot

thanks to Anna Kapechuck for the archeological digs

thanks to Matt Mahurin for the celestial seasonings

thanks to everybody at Invasion for the ongoing support and care

thanks to Sarah Lazin and to everybody at Viking/Penguin, especially Rick Kot, my faithful ally and champion

and

many endless thanks to my first readers: Peter Casperson, Todd Sickafoose, Heidi Kunkel, Steve Dalmer, Jana Fisher, Animal Prufrock, Susan Alzner, Amy Ray, Sheba Love, Mike Napolitano, Syd Mutschier, Valarie Kaur, and especially Terri Sutton and Amanda Palmer, whose feedback and suggestions helped so immensely.